THE ART OF PEACE

Robert Moriarty

Second Edition

Typesetting and layout work by Jeremy Irwin, jc9cz@yahoo.com

Library of Congress Control Number: 2016907925
CreateSpace Independent Publishing Platform, North Charleston, SC

ISBN: 978-1-5331539-3-7

Dedication

To Barbara, my love, my inspiration and the bravest person I have ever known

And to
Staff Sergeant James F Moriarty
US Army 5th Special Forces
January 27, 1989-November 4, 2016
You left us far too soon and will be greatly missed as you were greatly loved.

"Out of every one hundred men, ten shouldn't even be there, eighty are just targets, nine are the real fighters, and we are lucky to have them, for they make the battle. Ah, but the one, one is a warrior, and he will bring the others back."
— Heraclitus

"The Way of the Warrior has been misunderstood. It is not a means to kill and destroy others. Those who seek to compete and better one another are making a terrible mistake. To smash, injure, or destroy is the worst thing a human being can do. The real Way of a Warrior is to prevent such slaughter – it is the Art of Peace, the power of love."
— Morihei Ueshiba, 1942

CONTENTS

LIST OF MILITARY TERMS

AAA   anti-aircraft artillery
AFB   Air Force Base
ALO   Air Liaison Officer
AO   area of operation
AO   Aerial Observer
AOC   Aviation Officer Cadet

BDA   Battle Damage Assessment
BOQ   Bachelor Officer Quarters
BVR   beyond visual range

CAP   Combat Air Patrol
CBU   Cluster Bomb Unit
CG   Commanding General
CO   Commanding Officer

DASC   Direct Air Support Center
DFC   Distinguished Flying Cross
DI   Drill Instructor
DMZ   Demilitarized Zone
DOR   Drop Out Request

FAC   Forward Air Controller
FCLP   Field Carrier Landing Practice
FFAR   folding fin aircraft rockets
FNG   fucking new guy

GCA   ground controlled approach

HF   high frequency
HML   Helicopter Marine Light

IFR   Instrument Flight Rules
ITR   Infantry Training Regiment

KIA   Killed In Action

LZ   landing zone

MAG   Marine Air Group
Marcad   Marine Aviation Cadet
MCAS   Marine Corps Air Station
MCRD   Marine Corps Recruit Depot
mm   millimeter
MOS   Military Occupation Specialty
MPC   Military Payment Certificate

NAS   Naval Air Station
Navcad   Naval Aviation Cadet
NCO   Non-Commissioned Officer
NCOIC   Non-Commissioned Officer In Charge
NVA   North Vietnamese Army

O-Club   Officers' Club
OCS   Officer Candidate School
OIC   Officer In Charge

PFC   Private First Class
PIC   pilot-in-command
POW   prisoner of war
PT   Patrol Torpedo
PX   Post Exchange

R&R   rest and recuperation
REMF   rear echelon motherfucker
RIO   Radar Intercept Officer

SAM   surface-to-air missile
SEA   southeast Asia
SLJO   shitty little jobs officer

LIST OF MILITARY TERMS *(continued)*

SOG   Special Operations Group

UHF   ultra high frequency
USAA   United Services Automobile Association

VC   Viet Cong
VFR   Visual Flight Rules

XO   Executive Officer

FOREWORD

"Instead of the triumph of democracy and progress, we got violence, poverty and social disaster — and nobody cares a bit about human rights, including the right to life. I cannot help asking those who have forced that situation: Do you realize what you have done?"

— Russian President Vladimir Putin in a speech to the United Nations, September 28, 2015.

Why does it take the President of the Russian Federation to ask the question all concerned Americans should be asking of their leadership? "Do you realize what you have done?"

I'm reminded of the interview conducted by Lesley Stahl of 60 Minutes with the US Secretary of State in May of 1996. Ms. Stahl was commenting on the number of children under the age of five who had died as a result of the Clinton administration's sanctions against Iraq from 1991 until the time of the interview.

Lesley Stahl: "We have heard that a half-million children have died. I mean, that's more children than died in Hiroshima. And, you know, is the price worth it?"

Secretary of State Madeleine Albright: "I think this is a very hard choice, but the price – we think the price is worth it."

That's an astonishing answer. Let me try to put that number in context; 500,000 lost children under the age of five.

If you take the high side number of total killed (of all ages) in the atom bomb dropped at Hiroshima, we have 166,000 dead. Add to it the deaths at Nagasaki, at 80,000. Include the firebombing of Tokyo in March of 1945, with 100,000 killed. Just for fun, add in the number of deaths in the incineration of Dresden, Germany in the same month at 25,000. You come up with a grand total of 371,000 deaths in Germany and Japan from the four largest bombing attacks in world history.

In less than six years of sanctions against Iraq designed to hurt Saddam Hussein and eliminate his ability to produce "weapons of mass destruction" the United States and its minions brought about the deaths of over 500,000 children. And the American Secretary of State thought the price was "worth it." You have to wonder just how many children Madeleine Albright would have to kill before her gag reflex kicked in.

Saddam Hussein was a monster but Americans neglect to remember that he was our monster. We created the prick bastard. His first ever paycheck came from the CIA for his assassination services.

When Secretary of Defense Donald Rumsfeld under President George W. Bush accused Hussein of possessing weapons of mass destruction, Rumsfeld remembered that he had turned over those chemical and biological precursors to Hussein during his visit in December of 1983. He still had the receipts.

The United States began its second war against Iraq in 2003. By then probably another 500,000 children had died due to the sanctions. But after the invasion in March of 2003 their parents got to share their fate, and the number of Iraqis killed in the last dozen years as a result of the sanctions and invasion exceeds one million dead, plus four million displaced.

Alas, there were no weapons of mass destruction and the war was fought for naught.

Do Americans realize what they have done?

All empires collapse when their leaders embark on military adventurism. It happened to the Greeks, the Persians, the Romans, the Spanish, the French, the British and the Russians and all the other fools who forgot that wars cost money as well as the blood of their young men.

If there really is a hell and Saddam Hussein resides, he is probably enjoying a hearty chuckle as the Iraq war brought the United States to the brink of financial chaos. No one is foolish enough to think of it as a military victory, unless you think of it as a Pyrrhic victory where we would have been better off if we had suffered a total defeat. We created a desert and called it victory.

I happen to be married to a Brit. College in the UK focuses on a different approach than that of the US or Canada. In a British university you are taught that the questions are more important than the answers.

In the US we do rote memorization. In Britain they ask questions until they come up with the right answer.

It's an interesting difference. After all, if you don't ask the right questions, you will never arrive at the correct answers. The question is more important than the answer, after all.

I suspect that most people asked to name the opposite of war would say, "peace." But to come to the right answer, we need to keep asking questions. If peace is the opposite of war, what is peace?

Any dictionary can help. These are some of the synonyms for peace. Accord, friendship, love, reconciliation, unanimity, union, truce, unity, amity, armistice, cessation, conciliation, concord, neutrality, order, pacification, pacifism, treaty.

Those all sound like pretty nice words. Perhaps that's where Matthew came up with the phrase, "Blessed are the peacemakers" in the New Testament.

You never hear anyone saying, "Blessed are the warmongers" and that may have to do with war being the opposite of peace. Again, any dictionary will have a list of antonyms or opposites of peace. They would include disagreement, hate, hatred, discord, agitation, disharmony, distress, fighting, frustration, upset, and worry.

All wars destroy. There are no victories in war, no one wins. Wars are destruction and mayhem. Nothing gets built, only destroyed. If you want to build and love, you must have peace. All war is evil, there are no good wars just as there are no good synonyms for war.

But the Congress of the US benefits from a perpetual state of war as big corporations buy their votes. Wall Street and the banking system benefit; you can be assured that if they didn't benefit, there would be no wars. The military command structure benefits in promotions and the opportunity to pass through the revolving door and straight into service with those same corporations providing the most expensive and useless military equipment possible.

The people lose. They lose their children, their homes. The children of their grandchildren find themselves caught in debt slavery to pay for useless wars they never voted for.

Switzerland and Costa Rica provide an interesting contrast in the approaches that other governments take towards peace. Both are richer than the countries that surround them. Costa Rica had no standing army and no interest in "Defense." They neither start nor get involved in wars.

Is that a good model for peace? Well, in contrast, Switzerland is the most heavily armed country in the world. Every fit male between the ages of 19 and 34 receives military training and remains in the militia. Swiss soldiers are issued fully automatic rifles and ammunition, which they store at home. Some militia members may serve up to the age of 52 for summer training. But the Swiss neither start nor get involved in wars. Home robberies are rare as well.

My experiences in war taught me to hate only war. I read a book by the greatest and most decorated general in Marine Corps history, Smedley Butler, entitled "War is a Racket." His experiences in the many banana wars of the early 20th century made him realize he wasn't fighting for democracy or freedom or any of the meaningless buzzwords we are fed. He was fighting for Wall Street.

With the advent of the internet and instant communication to all reaches of the world, we no longer need big government. When you no longer need big government, you also don't need war, the funding agency for big government.

Chapter 1
INTRODUCTION

How many roads must a man walk down
Before you call him a man?
How many seas must a white dove sail
Before she sleeps in the sand?
Yes, how many times must the cannon balls fly
Before they're forever banned?

The answer my friend is blowin' in the wind
The answer is blowin' in the wind.

Yes, how many years can a mountain exist
Before it's washed to the sea?
Yes, how many years can some people exist
Before they're allowed to be free?
Yes, how many times can a man turn his head
Pretending he just doesn't see?

Yes, how many times must a man look up
Before he can see the sky?
Yes, how many ears must one man have
Before he can hear people cry?
Yes, how many deaths will it take till he knows
That too many people have died?

Blowin' In The Wind
Songwriter: Bob Dylan
Copyright: Bob Dylan Music Co 1963

PRESIDENT GEORGE H. W. BUSH won his wings as a Naval Aviator just before his nineteenth birthday. He became the youngest Naval Aviator of World War II. I use the term Naval Aviator rather than Navy pilot because Marines are Naval Aviators as well, undergoing exactly the same training as their Navy pilot buddies. George Bush flew 58 missions in combat against the Japanese.

Indeed it was a Marine pilot who became the youngest Naval Aviator during the Korean War. That would be the attorney F. Lee Bailey who became a second lieutenant in the Marines and a designated Naval Aviator before his twenty-first birthday. Bailey flew 85 missions as a fighter pilot and attack pilot against the North Koreans.

The youngest Naval Aviator during the Vietnam era was another Marine pilot who had a date of rank as a second lieutenant when he was nineteen, got his wings and was flying the hottest fighter aircraft in the world, the F-4B, when he was only twenty. He became a 20-year-old first lieutenant and a 22-year-old captain in the Marines. He flew 832 missions in combat in Vietnam.

That would be me. I was a warrior.

Getting my wings at that age was an accident of timing. The legal justification for the Vietnam War was the Gulf of Tonkin Resolution, passed on August 7, 1964. My eighteenth birthday was a month later, on September 9, and I enlisted in the Marine Corps a week after my birthday. I became the youngest Naval Aviator because I started earlier.

Fifty years ago as I write, I was in primary flight training at Saufley Field in Pensacola, and a few days away from my first solo flight in the T-34B.

I've given a lot of thought over the past 45 years about writing the definitive book telling of my experiences flying the O-1 aircraft in combat as a Forward Air Controller (FAC). The O-1 Bird Dog was the smallest and oldest tactical aircraft the US used in Vietnam. I haven't read anything that did a bang up job of telling the Bird Dog story. Of all the aircraft used in Vietnam, the O-1 lost the highest percentage of planes but their pilots earned the greatest number of personal decorations.

I was awarded 42 Air Medals and three Distinguished Flying Crosses along with another dozen or so of the "I was alive in '65" medals that you get for surviving. I was put in for two Silver Stars and deserved at least one of them. I did about 700 of my combat missions in the Bird Dog with another 125 missions in the F-4B.

But I've come to realize that while I've read hundreds of tales written by those in combat of all sorts, there is little reflection after the fact. Literally it took the President of Russia to make me realize that what we really need to read is some commentary about war not as remembered but as reflected on with the test of time. What I think about Vietnam now is not even close to what I thought as I went through it.

I became a warrior. While warriors love combat, they hate war because they understand it.

Chapter 2 (Part 1)
THE DEADLIEST CRIME

Galveston, oh Galveston, I still hear your sea winds blowin'
I still see her dark eyes glowin'
She was twenty-one when I left Galveston

Galveston, oh Galveston, I still hear your sea waves crashing
While I watch the cannons flashing
I clean my gun and dream of Galveston

I still see her standing by the water
Standing there lookin' out to sea
And is she waiting there for me?
On the beach where we used to run

Galveston, oh Galveston, I am so afraid of dying
Before I dry the tears she's crying
Before I watch your sea birds flying in the sun
At Galveston, at Galveston

Galveston
Songwriter: Jimmy Webb
Copyright: Jobete Music Co. Inc. 1969

AS MARINE FORWARD AIR CONTROLLERS flying the O-1 Bird Dog in Vietnam, we considered accidentally attacking our own troops to be the worst thing that could happen. In the way of the military, accidental attacks by us on our own forces were termed "friendly fire." That was about as accurate a description as "military music" or "military justice." Friendly fire simply wasn't friendly.

As Marines we trained to be efficient killers but we didn't really think of our job as going out to kill Viet Cong or North Vietnamese Army soldiers – the VC and NVA. War isn't a football game where whoever gets the highest score wins the game. Killing people has nothing at all to do with winning wars.

Instead, most of the pilots I flew with considered their job to be saving the lives of Marines. Anyone daring to shoot at our Marines, or at us, made a most serious mistake – often a fatal mistake. We were just trying to change their attitude and on occasion we needed to kill them to get them to think differently.

In May of 1969 I discovered something worse than accidentally dropping ordnance on our own troops. Firing on Marines deliberately surely had to qualify as the worst of sins.

I was on another typical Bird Dog mission in the neighborhood of the Da Krong valley, just south of Route 9 which ran from Dong Ha to Laos. After takeoff from the Marine base at Quang Tri I checked in with the Direct Air Support Center (DASC) at Landing Zone (LZ) Vandergrift.

"Hello Vandy DASC, this is Seaworthy Mike. Do you read?" I keyed the transmitter button on the power lever and spoke into my lip mike. The temperature had soared into triple digits and I had the side windows open on the Bird Dog. I could still hear the whisper of the wind through my clammy helmet. I had a giant salt circle on the back of my Nomex flight suit from sweat.

"Seaworthy Mike, Vandergrift DASC, I read you loud and clear. Go ahead." The Marines maintained the DASC at LZ Vandergrift, just south of the Razorback west of Dong Ha on Route 9 going to Laos. They gave us our assignments when flying in their area of operation (AO).

"Vandergrift, Seaworthy Mike is on flight Seaworthy 97-2. We have six Willy Pete and 2.5 hours on station. Do you have a mission?"

The Bird Dog carried about three hours' fuel depending on how hard you pushed the airplane. The O-1G carried four of the 2.75-inch folding fin aircraft rockets (FFAR) with Willy Pete or WP (white phosphorus) heads used to mark targets. The smoke could be seen from miles away, or from 15,000 feet by the fast movers we used for air strikes.

The Bird Dog carried a crew of two. The Marines used experienced bomb droppers from A-4s or F-4s or A-6s as the pilot in the front seat as FACs and volunteer infantry or artillery officers as Aerial Observers

(AOs) in the rear seat. The theory held that experienced combat pilots understood the issues and limits of aviation, while combat-experienced ground officers understood the issues on the ground. It seemed to work for us.

The O-1C version with the constant speed prop and slightly more horsepower carried six Willy Pete smoke rockets. Often when we ran out of Willy Pete we would fall back on smoke grenades as a backup. They were handy but you had to fly low to use them and they weren't nearly as visible.

The enemy liked it when we flew low as it gave them more chances to shoot at us. We liked it when we were low and slow. We could hear them shoot at us, and when we could pinpoint their position we could nail them.

"Seaworthy Mike, Vandy. We have an emergency we need you for. Recon Team Cloudy Sky is in contact and needs an emergency extract. They have two WIA [wounded in action] and one KIA [killed] already. We have a CH-46 for an emergency extract standing by at Vandergrift and two flights of fixed wing air that should be checking in shortly that we will give you as soon as they arrive. Contact Cloudy Sky on Fox Mike [FM] 109.6. They are at about 22 nautical on Channel 109 on radial 238," Vandergrift responded.

Reconnaissance teams performed as the eyes and ears of the Marines. The 1st Marine Division surrounded the giant Da Nang airfield, in 1968 and 1969 the busiest airport in the world. Da Nang lay some 75 nautical miles to the southeast of Quang Tri. The 3rd Marine Division called Dong Ha home, just northwest of the Quang Tri airfield. Dong Ha was only a few kilometers south of the Demilitarized Zone, or DMZ.

Recon teams provided intelligence to the Division looking to determine enemy intentions and often were used to provide battle damage assessments (BDAs) after B-52 strikes.

The 3rd Marine Division landed at Da Nang in May of 1965 and departed Vietnam in November of 1969. Recon teams of either six or thirteen men would be dropped by CH-46 helicopters in remote areas of the 3rd Marine AO to sneak around and peek on the enemy. They would carry food, ammo and communications equipment enough for them to stay in the field for up to a week.

The NVA hated recon teams because they enabled our higher command to know when and where attacks were going to take place. The Marine recon units were by far the most heavily decorated troops in Vietnam. Silver Stars were as common as Purple Hearts. They were almost all warriors.

Those in the military don't refer to themselves or others in uniform as heroes. Certainly no one in the military thinks it heroic to be killed. Getting killed is getting killed, no more and no less. If there are heroes in war it would often be the wives and children, mothers and fathers of those who actually serve in combat. They are the ones who suffer the most. Those in uniform know they risk death or injury but they signed up for it. Families don't sign up. They have to suffer silently.

The real heroes in the Vietnam War were the draft dodgers and war protestors. During the war I looked down on them but in hindsight I realized that everything they said about the government lying proved correct. No one in our military leadership, on active duty or retired, ever said straight out that it was a stupid and expensive war. It was a war we didn't need to fight and the only victory was in leaving.

In hindsight, given that 58,209 young Americans died, was the price worth it? If we had won, what would victory have looked like? Since we left with our tails between our legs in 1975, are we any worse off by having lost, other than the enormous cost in the blood of our young men, the drain on our economy and the increase in national debt?

I enlisted in the Marines following graduation from high school. While I did face the prospect of the draft, I volunteered for the Marines. When you take the oath of office in the military, in theory you understand that one of the things that might happen is people trying to kill you and sometimes succeeding. Wives and children don't sign up for that and don't take any oath of office. Little children don't want to be handed a neatly folded flag, they want daddy back.

While the military is devoid of heroes, it is not devoid of men doing brave things. I worked with recon teams on hundreds of missions. They were the bravest people I ever saw and they have never been given even a token of the gratitude we owed them. They fought the enemy at close quarters with minimal equipment and often died.

I chattered with my AO in the back seat of the tiny O-1C as we headed out to the Da Krong valley. This team Cloudy Sky consisted of only six men. If they had one killed and two wounded already, they were up shit creek without the proverbial paddle. This was not going to be a piece of cake mission. One man had died and more were about to die if we didn't act.

Light observation aircraft have served with Marine divisions since the early 1920s. At the time, all combat aircraft were some variation of light observation. We did in the air what the recon guys did on the ground. We were the eyes and ears of the division and the Air Wing.

I went through Infantry Training Regiment (ITR) at Camp Pendleton as a PFC fresh out of boot camp in early 1965. I remember seeing the O-1C flitting around. A Bird Dog was the first Marine combat aircraft to land in Vietnam, in 1962. But for some reason, when the Marine observation squadrons VMO-2 and VMO-6 were sent to Vietnam, they took only their helicopters, to be used as helicopter gunships. A few Marine Bird Dogs made it to Vietnam eventually but the Marines were in a transition period moving from piston engine prop aircraft into fixed and rotary wing planes using jet engines. Literally, the Bird Dog had no mission and no glory.

As combat ramped up in 1967 it became apparent that the UH-1E "Huey" gunships didn't do all that well in their dual role of gunship and forward air control. They were ok as gunships and useless as FACs. The Marine Corps begged half a dozen O-1G Bird Dogs from the Army and brought over to Vietnam the remaining O-1Cs still in the inventory. The Bird Dog detachment that had been assigned to a maintenance unit at Phu Bai near the city of Hue joined VMO-6 in Quang Tri in July of 1968.

Both the Air Force and the Marine Corps recognized the value of having experienced bomb droppers flying the observation aircraft. The UH-1E pilots understood the concept of forward air control but had no experience of dropping ordnance and didn't understand the limits of what you could and couldn't do with fixed wing aircraft. Using former F-4B or A-4E or A-6B pilots with combat records immediately improved the quality of FAC work when the Bird Dogs arrived.

In addition to having combat qualified pilots in the front seat, the Division would send over volunteer AOs to fly in the back seat. They knew how to fire artillery and how to coordinate with ground troops. Their military occupation specialties (MOS) varied. Some were 0302 ground pounders, some were 0802 artillery officers. We did have a couple of former recon officers and they proved invaluable.

Of all the Marine combat units, those in the Bird Dogs were the most qualified to be used for a specific purpose. We were not only the eyes and ears of the ground recon teams; unlike the recon teams we were also the cutting edge of the sword. We went looking for trouble and found it daily. They didn't look for trouble but found it regularly.

On this particular day in May of 1969 we found a whole sack full of trouble.

"Cloudy Sky, Cloudy Sky. Do you read?" my AO called on the FM radio. "This is Seaworthy 97-2. We have 2.5 hours on station. Do you have us in sight?" he said as we drifted over the deep green valley.

"Seaworthy, this is Cloudy Sky 14. We are in a shit sandwich. I have one KIA, three WIA and we are completely surrounded. The fucking gooners are fifteen feet away and throwing grenades at us. If you don't fuck these guys up quick, we are all dead. I need you to have a 46 on standby and hit my position with 2.75-inch rockets. I have you in sight; you are in a slight left turn. We are at your nine o'clock. I'll pop a purple smoke. Tell me when you have me in sight."

Wow. We were barely on station and already up to our ears in trouble. I told my AO I would take over the radios.

"Cloudy Sky, this is Seaworthy Mike, I'm flying the Bird Dog. I've got two flights with nape and snake standing by. You don't really want us firing rockets, we will kill all of you," I mumbled into my mike. Nape referred to napalm. Snakes were retarded bombs with special fins that slowed them down for ultra-accurate delivery at low level.

He came back at once. "Seaworthy Mike, this is Cloudy Sky. We are totally surrounded; we can hear them on all sides. They are so close that you can't do anything with napalm or snakes. Get us those big rocket pods with nineteen rockets as soon as you can. You may kill us but if you don't kill them we are all dead anyway."

I leaned back in my seat against the parachute protecting my back and thought for a few moments. He was asking me to hit his position. On the Marine attack aircraft the 2.75-inch rockets came in 19-shot pods that you could fire all at the same time – the timing of firing could be modified. But basically you were firing nineteen rockets with 2.2-pound warheads. The rockets were fin stabilized but they were an area weapon, not a pinpoint munition. If I could get the fixed wing to fire all nineteen rounds at the same time, the explosions would cover half the area of a football field.

I had never heard of anyone using rocket pods to clear a position where they were in the center. One rocket was like a 2.2-pound grenade going off. The frag pattern would extend for thirty to forty meters. And he wanted me popping off a lot of them on his head? Was he nuts or brilliant?

"Cloudy Sky, are you certain? If I hit your position, I risk killing you. A pod of rockets will land fifty meters all around you. You are putting your life on the line. I can do it but you have to make me believe you know exactly what you are asking of me."

I released the mike button with reluctance. Hitting friendlies by accident was bad enough. If I killed these guys I would take the memory to my grave. And I could hit their position with great precision. If I told the fast movers to hit their position, they would hit their position. He was demanding something I wasn't sure I was prepared to do.

"Seaworthy Mike, I know exactly what 2.75s will do. We are dug in in deep fighting holes. Give us some warning and we will be down. But do it quick, we are running out of time and ammo. You can save our lives," he ended.

That did it for me. It was the bravest thing I had ever heard. I might kill him and his team but it was his life and in the end, his decision. If he died and his team died, it would be bravely. It doesn't get any more real than that.

I called to the DASC. My AO thought I was crazy but the team leader had a point. Either we saved their butts or the NVA would kill them. Combat doesn't get any easier to understand than the choice between life and death.

"Hello Vandy DASC, this is Seaworthy Mike with an emergency request. I'm in communication with Cloudy Sky. He is in close contact and requesting 2.75-inch rockets for machine gun suppression. This is an emergency. They are being overrun," I radioed. I wasn't about to tell the DASC that I was about to rocket our own troops. There were things they needed to know and other things better left unsaid.

The team leader had the best information and only he was qualified to make such a request. He had to have a lot of confidence in me and my ability to hit his position exactly. Rockets hitting a hundred meters away from him wouldn't help. I had to hit his position perfectly.

The DASC came back. "Seaworthy Mike, we have a flight of A-4s with two pods apiece. Will that do?"

"Vandy, Seaworthy Mike. That would be perfect. Send them to 22 miles nautical on the 240 radial of Channel 109. I'm in a left-hand orbit at 1,500 feet," I responded.

The Bird Dog had one UHF radio for communication with fixed wing aircraft and two FM radios for talking to the ground, artillery batteries, and ships when we had a naval gunfire mission. The pilot generally used the UHF while the AO in the back was communicating with the ground on the FM radios. But nothing was written in rock and we would often switch roles when an experienced backseater would control an airstrike or the pilot fire an artillery mission.

I had been grounded for six months during 1967 after an operation for ulcers. A pilot in an F-4 squadron who can't fly front seat is about as useful as teats on a boar hog, so during that time the squadron sent me to every school for which they had a quota. I ended up as a very well trained lieutenant skilled in both intelligence and forward air control. I spent four weeks that summer going through the Army Basic Intelligence school at Fort Holabird in Maryland, and another two weeks going through Air Liaison & Observation school in Norfolk, Virginia.

While the Marines trained dozens of guys as FACs using on-the-job training, I was the only FAC in VMO-6 who actually had any classroom training. Everyone else learned on the job. The Army intelligence school actually turned out to be worthwhile. The Army taught you to ignore everything you were told and pay attention only to what you can see for yourself and know to be true. People mislead or lie a lot.

I'm reminded of when Secretary of Defense Donald Rumsfeld spoke and said, "There are a lot of people who lie and get away with it, and that's just a fact." He certainly knew what he was talking about. He was intimate with lying and liars.

"Seaworthy Mike, this is Hellborne 258, a flight of two A-4s. We have two 19-shot pods of 2.75-inch rockets apiece, 20 mike-mike [20 millimeter bullets] and four napes [napalm]. We can give you thirty minutes on station and are just crossing feet dry now. We can be in your area in about five minutes," the flight leader called on UHF. "We are at 15,000 feet descending to 8,000. I'll call you when we approach you."

"Hellborne 258 lead, this is Seaworthy Mike, I have a recon team in contact. I need your rockets only. I repeat, only your rockets. I do not want you dropping nape for any reason or firing 20 mike-mike. I'm in a left-hand orbit at 1,500 feet over the Da Krong valley, about 235 radial for 22 miles off Channel 109.

"I want you using an east-to-west run in. Use a left-hand pullout. Elevation is 600 feet; you can expect small arms fire and perhaps 50-caliber fire. Nearest safe area is the South China Sea, which will be east at twenty miles. I want a 30-degree dive and it's vital that you have my clearance before you fire. Do you copy?" I transmitted to them. "The high ground will be at your nine and three o'clock, the weather is 10,000 broken and ten miles visibility. Altimeter is 29.96. Don't worry about where the friendlies are."

I wasn't about to tell these guys they would be firing at our own troops. I might spook them and get them trying to miss and in this case I needed perfect accuracy, not a near miss. I searched the sky for sight of them.

Only the Navy and Marines flew the A-4 Skyhawk. The Navy operated off carriers and used 60-degree dives because they were used to the high threat of anti-aircraft artillery and surface-to-air missiles (AAA and SAMs) in North Vietnam and Laos when bombing the Ho Chi Minh Trail. The Marines operated only off land based fixed runways. Our fixed wing aircraft south of the DMZ took a lot of 50-caliber fire and small arms, but with a 30-degree dive they would be well above the range of small arms fire when completing their passes.

"Seaworthy Mike, Hellborne 258 lead. I think I have you in sight, you are in a left-hand turn. Reverse your turn for a minute so I can identify you." I heard, "OK, we have you. Now where is our target?"

Airborne FACs controlled virtually all air strikes in South Vietnam. Accurate communication was vital; under the stress of combat, mistakes were easy to make. For example, if an FAC called for a left-hand pattern and the fixed wing flight replied, "Right," did he mean "correct" or did he mean a right-hand pattern? If the fixed wing rolled in, dropped their ordnance and pulled off to the right, they might just hit a mountain that the FAC had been guiding them away from.

The FAC had to correctly identify the flight he was trying to control. There were hundreds of flights filling the airspace over South Vietnam on any given day, and just because you thought you saw a couple of A-4s didn't mean that they were your A-4s or even A-4s at all.

The fixed wing had to identify both the FAC and the target. Under combat stress and poor weather, death was only a tiny mistake away. Some FACs were excellent at communication and some weren't. All the Marine FACs in Bird Dogs had dropped ordnance under combat conditions in fixed wing aircraft so we were forewarned as to the potential problems.

"Hellborne 258, this is a tough target. Because of where the friendlies are, it's vital that you fire perfectly. I want you to give me a long run in and a 30-degree dive so I know you have the target. I'll get the guys on the ground to pop a smoke so you know exactly where to hit. The wind is coming from the west so I want all four pods rippled right into the base of the smoke."

I got onto the FM radio to talk to the recon team leader. "Hello Cloudy Sky, I'm about to make things a lot brighter. I have a flight of two A-4s with two rocket pods apiece. Are you sure you want to do this?" I asked. I couldn't let him know just how terrified I was. At the end of my tour, I counted 832 missions between the F-4B and the Bird Dog. This mission was the very worst. And the most dangerous – not for me, but for the ground troops.

"Seaworthy, this is Cloudy Sky, that's affirm. We will pop a purple smoke right in the middle of our team. Hit the smoke. If you can, give me thirty seconds' warning. But hit the smoke and do it as fast as you can, we can hear them crawling all around us."

I got the flight set up in a racetrack pattern with the Dash-2 aircraft on the opposite side of the circle. With any flight of two aircraft, that was always the standard. The first aircraft, the section commander, was called "lead" and the second plane was called "Dash-2."

When the lead aircraft was abeam the team, I called the recon leader again. "Cloudy Sky, pop your smoke," I ordered. He did, and plumes of purple smoke started coming through the trees. I saw it clearly, but did the A-4s?

"Hellborne lead, do you see the smoke?" I asked. "If you do, I want a roll-in to the west and wait for my clearance. Make sure you have the target."

"I've got it," called the lead A-4.

"Cloudy Sky, this is Seaworthy Mike, get your heads down *now*. The first aircraft will be firing in about thirty seconds; the second will be firing about a minute later. Keep your heads down," I said on the FM radio.

The lead aircraft rolled in on a heading of east to west. He was in a 30-degree dive and clearly had the target.

"Hellborne 258 lead, you are cleared hot. Dash-2, I want you rippling both pods into the base of the smoke. Dash-2, do you have the target?"

"258 lead is in hot. I have the target. Dash-2, remember there is a slight wind from the west, make sure you hit the base of the smoke."

An eternity passed as the flight leader dropped down in his dive. At about 3,000 feet I saw smoke shoot out of the backs of the rocket pods as thirty-eight 2.75-inch rockets fired in little more than the blink of an eye. Explosions blanketed the target area as they went off, one by one. I was glad that I wasn't in the middle of that storm, no matter what color uniform I wore.

"Hellborne 258 lead is off target, pulling left. I'll circle overhead at 10,000."

"Hellborne 258 Dash-2 is in hot, are we cleared?" he asked.

I saw the target area was covered in smoke from the rockets' impact. "Dash-2, if you have the base of the smoke to the west, you are cleared hot," I radioed.

Throughout the flight joining up with us and acquiring the target and doing their roll-in, my AO and I were talking and wondering if we were the best FAC team around or simply fools. We would know in a minute or two. If we acted in error, we would enter the Marine Corps history books as the Bird Dog crew that killed an entire recon team.

Dash-2 rolled in on a heading of west and dove into the cloud of smoke before firing. Another thirty-eight rockets peppered the area. Both aircraft hit the target perfectly. But who would die as a result? He pulled off to the left and joined his flight lead as they circled over the target area.

I credited them with 15 KBA (Killed By Air) and 100/100, where

100 per cent of the ordnance covered 100 per cent of the target. We gave every fixed wing flight or artillery mission or naval gunfire mission a BDA at the end of every mission. It was all nonsense. We hoped we had killed the enemy in the immediate area but had no way of knowing how true our claim was.

Another eternity passed as we waited to hear if the recon team had survived or not.

Chapter 3
THE MAKING OF AN AVIATOR

He's five foot-two, and he's six feet-four,
He fights with missiles and with spears.
He's all of thirty-one, and he's only seventeen,
Been a soldier for a thousand years.

He's a Catholic, a Hindu, an Atheist, a Jain,
A Buddhist and a Baptist and a Jew.
And he knows he shouldn't kill,
And he knows he always will,
Kill you for me, my friend, and me for you.

And he's fighting for Canada,
He's fighting for France,
He's fighting for the USA,
And he's fighting for the Russians,
And he's fighting for Japan,
And he thinks we'll put an end to war this way.

Universal Soldier
Songwriter: Buffy Sainte-Marie
Copyright: Caleb Music Co 1964

THE GULF OF TONKIN INCIDENT took place in early August of 1964. According to US government reports at the time, the rotten North Vietnamese Navy attacked the USS *Maddox*, a destroyer, with three torpedo boats. The attack was reported to have taken place for no reason at all; they just had nothing better to do.

Only years later did Americans learn that the *Maddox* was escorting South Vietnamese PT boats as part of an attack on North Vietnamese positions. It was an act of war on our part. The North Vietnamese knew the truth of what happened, and the South Vietnamese knew what we were doing for they were part of the operation. The US government knew the facts. Only the American people were kept in the dark, ignorant of acts of aggression undertaken on their behalf. It was the first of a long line of false flag operations that would result in the deaths of 58,209 Americans and an unknown number of Vietnamese in a war fought for no reason and where it was impossible to define victory.

Few Americans have ever read the Gulf of Tonkin Resolution, passed by Congress in mid-August of 1964. It provided the legal basis for the next seven years of carnage. In hindsight, given that we now know it was the US and South Vietnam who were the aggressors, Americans should reflect on what was done in their name. While it's true that 58,209 Americans died it's also true that 1.1 million North Vietnamese died and 400,000 South Vietnamese. Eighty per cent of the American servicemen who died were 25 or younger. They were still kids, most not old enough to vote or drink a beer.

Gulf of Tonkin Resolution

Eighty-eighth Congress of the United States of America

AT THE SECOND SESSION

Begun and held at the City of Washington on Tuesday, the seventh day of January, one thousand nine hundred and sixty-four

Joint Resolution

To promote the maintenance of international peace and security in Southeast Asia.

Whereas naval units of the Communist regime in Vietnam, in violation of the principles of the Charter of the United Nations and of international law, have deliberately and repeatedly attacked United Stated naval vessels lawfully present in international waters, and have thereby created a serious threat to international peace; and

Whereas these attackers are part of deliberate and systematic campaign of aggression that the Communist regime in North Vietnam has been waging against its neighbors and the nations joined with them in the collective defense of their freedom; and

Whereas the United States is assisting the peoples of southeast Asia to protest their freedom and has no territorial, military or political ambitions in that area, but desires only that these people should be left in peace to work out their destinies in their own way: Now, therefore be it

Resolved by the Senate and House of Representatives of the United States of America in Congress assembled, That the Congress approves and supports the determination of the President, as Commander in Chief, to take all necessary measures to repel any armed attack against the forces of the United States and to prevent further aggression.

Section 2. The United States regards as vital to its national interest and to world peace the maintenance of international peace and security in Southeast Asia. Consonant with the Constitution of the United States and the Charter of the United Nations and in accordance with its obligations under the Southeast Asia Collective Defense Treaty, the United States is, therefore, prepared, as the President determines, to take all necessary steps, including the use of armed force, to assist any member or protocol state of the Southeast Asia Collective Defense Treaty requesting assistance in defense of its freedom.

Section 3. This resolution shall expire when the President shall determine that the peace and security of the area is reasonably assured by international conditions created by action of the United Nations or otherwise, except that it may be terminated

Congress based the Gulf of Tonkin Resolution on a lie. The entire war was a lie.

When I was flying combat, after every mission we sat down and had a post-flight debrief, talking about what went right and what went wrong. Each time I filled out and filed for permanent reference an After Action Report (AAR). The purpose was so we knew exactly where we stood. We could change tactics should we need to and the battle could be studied after the fact. As a nation we should have conducted a post-war debrief so we understood just what went right and what went wrong. Why did we get into the war? What did we stand to gain, and to lose? That has never been done. America, do you realize what you have done?

All healthy young and unmarried American men not attending college faced the prospect of being drafted between 1950 and 1970. It was a fact of life that you had to plan your life around. After the Korean war ended guys were by and large ok with being drafted until the possibility of dying in combat popped up again in the mid-1960s.

I turned eighteen a month after the Gulf of Tonkin incident. We knew from the newspapers and Walter Cronkite on the evening news that something was going on in southeast Asia. Frankly no one really paid any attention. There was always something going on somewhere in the world. They had to fill out the news broadcasts with something. The US had troops stationed all over the world to protect us from godless Communism. We were policemen to the world.

After graduating from high school in Fort Worth, Texas in May of 1964, I drove a 1954 Ford to California for a friend. Once there I ran a gas station in San Mateo for the summer. As fall approached, I planned on hitch hiking back to Texas to go to college. I left San Mateo and made it as far as Salt Lake City on my thumb before running out of money.

I made a decision that thousands of other young American men made during those years. I walked into the recruiting office of the Marine Corps and signed up. But while green, I wasn't that green; I hadn't fallen off a turnip truck the night before. The Marine recruiter offered me the wonderful option of going for four years instead of three. He told me of the great opportunities the Marines gave bright young lads such as myself, but the best opportunities were for the fellows signing up for a full four-year enlistment.

What he didn't bother mentioning, and I neglected to ask about, was that if you signed up in 1964 for a three-year tour, you were going to be an 0300, a Marine rifleman. Three years meant grunt. I signed up for three years.

The recruiter was kind enough to put me up in a small but dingy hotel for the night. He gave me a voucher good for dinner and breakfast at a nearby diner. He seemed like such a nice thoughtful man. The next afternoon he personally drove me to the Salt Lake City airport so I could catch a DC-6 to San Diego. I was eighteen years and one week old.

"Don't worry about a thing," he smiled, "I'll call a friend of mine in San Diego and have him meet you at the plane. He's a limo driver and will give you a ride over to MCRD San Diego. Maybe in the limo. They will check you in and get you a bunk and you can start your training in a day or two. You will cherish the memory."

That lying bastard. I spent the next three months cursing him under my breath. Every night before I passed out I swore I would find him and burn his house down and kill his dog, if I survived boot camp. He lied about everything, including the bit about cherishing the memory. "Cherish the memory." Was he fucking kidding? Nobody cherishes the memory of boot camp. They spend the rest of their life trying to figure out how they made it through.

The plane arrived in San Diego and sure enough there was a neatly dressed Marine sergeant greeting me with a smile. He seemed like a friendly fellow. In a few minutes I would realize it was the smile a vampire gives a potential donor. He took my thin Service Record Book (SRB) and asked if I needed help with my bag. I'm thinking, "All those guys who came back from boot camp with stories of how tough it was were lying. These people are really nice, friendly, and helpful. I can't wait until they issue me those neat dress blues. I wonder how soon I get a weekend off."

He forgot the limo, I supposed. We went out to the curb and there was a green bus with wire mesh over the windows with a bunch of other nervous-looking civilians already on board. It said USMC on the side so no one would mistake it for a prison bus. I couldn't figure out why the other guys were so nervous, this wasn't all that bad.

I was one of the last to arrive in San Diego and as soon as I sat down the driver closed the door and we set off for the nearby MCRD San Diego. The nice Marine sergeant who greeted us lost his smile and his charm sometime during the short trip.

We arrived at the main gate at MCRD and drove across a wide and long parade field to a low-lying building of Spanish design where we would check in. The nice, friendly smiling Marine sergeant turned from Dr. Jekyll into Mr. Hyde. "All right, you fucking maggots. Listen up. You have three seconds to get off my fucking bus. Get off, get off, get off."

He began grabbing people and literally hurling them to the front of the bus. "Get off my fucking bus and find a set of yellow footprints to plant your fucking feet on. If you fucking breathe I will cut your fucking head off and shit down your throat."

I couldn't help but wonder if his superiors knew he was talking to new Marines in this tone and with such crudity. It wouldn't take long for me to learn that it's almost impossible for a real Marine to communicate without using a variation of "fuck" at least one time per sentence, perhaps more.

Fifty or sixty civilians who had signed up to be Marines stood on the yellow footprints and quivered, fearing to take even a single breath. "How many Marines do we have here?" he asked at the top of his lungs. All of us raised our hands.

"Put those fucking hands down, you fucking scum. None of you are Marines. You have to earn the Globe and Anchor; you are nothing but a bunch of lowlife scum. You are lower than whale shit. I love my Marine Corps and none of you have a chance of surviving boot camp. Do you understand? You do not have the right to call yourself a Marine. That has to be earned."

There was a general mumbling of "Yes, sure, ok, yeah."

"What the fuck did you say? Did I hear someone say 'yeah'? Are you fucking kidding me, you maggots? From now on the first word out of your mouth is 'Sir' and the last word out of your mouth is also 'Sir'. Do you fucking hear me?"

"Sir, yes sir," we said, more or less in unison.

"Are you fucking kidding me, you fucking maggots? Did I pick up the wrong bus and I have a load of fucking doggies or squids by mistake? My fucking three-year-old is louder than that. I want to fucking hear you. Do you fucking understand?'

"Sir, yes sir," we sounded off, a little louder this time. After all, we didn't want to wake the neighborhood. Evidently he did. "I can't fucking hear you, you faggots. Sound off like you had some nuts, not a pussy. Are you a bunch of pussies?"

"Sir, no sir," we bellowed at the top of our voices. The hell with the neighbors.

Chapter 4
BOOT CAMP, MCRD SAN DIEGO

Oh my name it is nothin'
My age it means less
The country I come from
Is called the Midwest
I's taught and brought up there
The laws to abide
And the land that I live in
Has God on its side.

Oh the history books tell it
They tell it so well
The cavalries charged, the Indians fell
The cavalries charged, the Indians died
Oh the country was young
With God on its side.

The Spanish-American
War had its day
And the Civil War too
Was soon laid away
And the names of the heroes
I's made to memorize
With guns on their hands
And God on their side.

With God On Our Side
Songwriter: Bob Dylan
Copyright: Special Rider Music 1964

PLATOON 385 FORMED UP and we commenced our training a few days later. Our platoon lost a few people and gained a few people over the eleven-week period. We began with eighty-five members and ended up graduating eighty-six.

The pre-Vietnam Marine Corps was pretty much a white organization. We had six blacks in the platoon. As the war gained momentum the percentage of blacks grew higher, but in 1964 you didn't see many black Marines.

Platoon 385 contained just one college graduate, Jon Reynolds of the Reynolds tobacco fortune. He was smart enough to sign up for the Reserves. He spent six months on active duty and the remainder in monthly drills.

One or two more of the recruits had attended college. Maybe twenty per cent had graduated from high school. One fellow from Louisiana was a true redneck Cajun. He had never seen a toothbrush. The Marines removed his remaining teeth and issued him his own set of false teeth.

A few Marine recruits had been in trouble with the law for one reason or another. A kindly judge, thinking only of their best interests, would offer offenders the choice of spending ninety days in the iron bar motel or joining the Marines. We got a lot of good Marines that way but they all regretted not taking the ninety-day option. Boot camp would be a whole lot harder than the slammer.

Most recruits were eighteen or nineteen years old. Our oldest was perhaps twenty-two or twenty-three. War is a young man's game because young men can never be killed, or so they believe. The sixty or so Marines in 385 who became grunts were in the first unit ashore in Da Nang in May of 1965. During boot camp I got orders as a basic infantryman, an 0300, but at the time my friends from boot camp hit the beaches in Da Nang, I was still being held at Camp Pendleton pending my orders to flight training.

A year after joining the Corps, half my boot camp platoon had been killed or wounded in Vietnam.

The Vietnam Memorial Wall contains the names of 58,209 personnel who died in the service of the United States during the war. The first died on June 8, 1956 when most Americans couldn't have located Vietnam on a map if their lives depended on it. There are 39,996 names of kids twenty-two years old or younger; 8,283 of them were only nineteen and 3,103 were only eighteen years old.

Statistics reveal that 997 servicemen died on their first day in Vietnam. Another 1,448 lost their lives on the day they were scheduled to leave country. On January 31, 1968, at the start of what would be called the Tet Offensive, 245 young Americans were killed. In May of 1968, the worst month of the war, a total of 2,415 died.

For the Marine Corps, Vietnam was a bigger war than World War II. True, the Marines had a total of 475,604 in uniform in late 1944 compared to only 315,000 in 1969, but the Vietnam war lasted years longer than WW II and the Marines had more killed and wounded in Vietnam.

More Marines served during Vietnam than during WW II. The USMC spent only about 200 days in ground combat during World War II. Marines in Vietnam served 13-month tours, or almost twice as long as the Marines served in the Pacific during WW II.

Something between 30 and 50 per cent of Marines in Vietnam actually served in combat. Marine grunts, the 0300 MOS infantry, were shot at an average of three times during their entire tour but were hit twice.

Jon Reynolds swore to us that boot camp was easier than the physical conditioning he went through as a football player at Duke in college. I didn't believe him then. I still don't. We were pushed to our limits physically and mentally. And beyond.

The incident portrayed in the movie *Full Metal Jacket* where a recruit saves a couple of rounds at the rifle range and later uses them to kill his drill instructor (DI) and then himself actually happened in 1963 at MCRD San Diego. Recruits still talked about it a year later. We all thought about killing our DIs or swinging at them but none of us had the balls. If you hit him, you better kill him.

The first half of the movie has the most realistic portrayal in any war movie of what boot camp is like. All war movies share the same problem. Describing war is nearly impossible unless you have been there. It's like trying to describe the color purple to a man who has been blind his entire life. But its portrayal of boot camp was perfect and accurate. We felt the terror for eleven weeks. Hell, I still have a twinge of that terror now and again.

So my recruiter was partially correct. I still have the memories of boot camp. The word "cherish" does not come to mind.

Platoon 385 began boot camp at the end of September 1964. Twenty or so recruits (the DIs had made it crystal clear that we didn't have the right to call ourselves Marines just yet) lived in each of the Quonset huts neatly aligned in rows in the recruit living area.

We spent a lot of time piled up on top of each other in a sand pit just outside the entrance. The DIs loved screaming, "385, *in the pit*" whereupon we would swiftly jump onto each other in the sand pit. You didn't want to be the first in the pit but any delay was worth a smack upside the head as the DI made sure we were in the smallest pile possible. I never did figure out if there was a purpose other than to train recruits to obey every order instantly.

Our platoon reflected the youth of America. Unlike today, we were mostly skinny and underfed. If someone was ten pounds over their best weight we thought of them as fat. Boot camp is not a good place to be carrying extra weight. We lost several recruits to the Motivation Platoon where they went through hours of physical exercise every day to either get their weight down or their stamina up. One recruit was a little too interested in the other recruits for the Marine Corps and he was quietly ushered to the exit. For the most part, recruits didn't have enough experience with the subject of sex to know if they liked boys or not. For the most part, we didn't care.

One of the recruits found a piece of chalk on the first day and liberated it. A few minutes' work on the concrete fashioned it into an acceptable pair of dice. We began a nightly game of craps that continued throughout boot camp. As I would do later in flight training, I financed my way through boot camp betting against recruits not as knowledgeable about probability and permutations as was I. I understood the odds and they didn't. That can be very profitable.

San Diego qualifies as one of the most livable cities in the United States. We started boot camp after the heat of summer and finished before the worst chill of winter. It was a lovely time of year in a charming city.

I hated every minute.

MCRD San Diego lay next to Lindbergh Field. As we marched and ran the obstacle course we could see the planes taking off and landing. All I could think of was how wonderful it would have been to be on one of those planes, going anywhere.

It seemed to me the purpose of boot camp was to break the spirit of the recruit thinking of himself as an individual and to remake him as a member of an unthinking, instantly responding team. In my experience, Marines weren't big on discussions about philosophy or chess but were great at taking hills from the enemy. As an adult I resent others presuming to think for me, but in combat you need to respond instantly, without question.

Marines are big. At 5' 8" and 133 pounds soaking wet, I was the second smallest guy in our platoon. We had a lot of guys well over six feet. I had so little mass that going through the obstacle course was actually easier for me than for the big guys. DIs like guys with heart. When we went through the obstacle course we were kept going for the entire time. I would make it through and be passing guys a lot bigger and stronger than me on my second lap.

Up until the Korean War, a Marine qualifying as Expert on the rifle range was paid a monthly bonus. Accurate shooting was a Marine theme as far back as World War I.

The Marine Corps transitioned to the M-14 rifle in 1963 from the WW II era M-1. With the change, the rifle range changed from being in yards to meters. So when qualifying with the M-1, Marines would fire from 200 yards offhand and sitting to 300 yards prone and sitting and 500 yards prone. With the new M-14 rifle the range now measured 200, 300 and 500 meters.

At the conclusion of our seventh week of boot camp and major inspection we were trucked to Camp Pendleton and made a forced march to the shooting range at Camp Stuart Mesa. There we went through a grueling three-week course on marksmanship. The instructors taught us the basics of accurate shooting with both the M-14 and the Colt .45 automatic.

Growing up in Texas, I was perfectly familiar with rifles and pistols. Everyone I knew owned a gun and knew how to use them. Guns were a part of our upbringing. But in our platoon we had a lot of recruits from major eastern cities such as Chicago, with a few from Boston and New York. The young men from the big cities had never seen or used weapons, and it showed. We had one recruit named Wayne Brockman from New York City who was terrified of the Colt. We didn't have to shoot the weapon for qualification; all we had to do was fire off a magazine of seven rounds for familiarity. Our training instructor had to step in and take the weapon from Brockman, otherwise he would have fired a round through the roof, he was so terrified of it.

As a Marine you never called your weapon a "gun", or dire things would happen. The DIs acted as if they had never heard anyone ever call a weapon a gun and they would look shocked.

"A gun? Did you just call your weapon a gun? I'm shocked to my core. This shit-eating maggot just called his weapon a gun," they would respond in horror.

"A gun?" The DI would grab the recruit by the balls and squeeze as he banged the M-14 up the side of the recruit's head. "This is your gun down here. Don't you dare call your weapon a gun.

"Tell you what, why don't you carry your weapon at high port with one hand around the grinder and hold that tiny thing you play with at night with the other, and sing, 'This is my weapon and this is my gun. This one's for killing, this one's for fun' so the other recruits keep it straight?"

At moments such as that, all I could think was, "I'm sure glad I didn't make that mistake." Hauling a nine-pound rifle around with one hand for a few hundred meters wasn't any fun. The recruit usually ended up dropping the weapon and that was worth another round of cursing.

At Stuart Mesa, the rifle range part of Camp Edson, we spent a week learning the theory of marksmanship and two weeks in practice. I don't remember how many rounds we fired to train for Qualification Day but it was a lot. If you were going to shoot well, at least you had the training. The course was 10 rounds offhand at 200 meters for 50 points, 10 rounds sitting at 200 meters for 50 points, 10 rounds sitting for 50 points at 300 meters, another 10 rounds kneeling at 300 meters for 50 points and finally 10 rounds prone at 500 meters. The maximum score was 250 points.

Basic qualification for Marksman was 190 points, with 210 points for the Sharpshooter badge and 220 for Expert. Marines didn't think much of those who didn't qualify but shooting Expert brought you up in their eyes.

The three weeks at Stuart Mesa proved to be a life-changing event for me. The platoon had undergone some testing in Marine Corps history, the basics of guard duty and the General Orders. I aced all the tests, not that it mattered much to the Corps. The Marines want killers, not boffins.

At the rifle range I shot "Expert". Every member of the platoon put $1 into a pool that would go to the highest shooter. I wasn't the highest shooter in the weeks prior to Qual Day but I had shot well.

In 1964 E-1 privates going through boot camp received $78 a month. The pay automatically went up to $83.20 a month after four months. So even $1 out of your pocket was a fair bit of money. After all, you could buy four packs of cigarettes for $1. Winning the pot of $85 would be a giant windfall.

After fifty years my memories have faded a bit. I don't quite remember the circumstances but our DIs had the platoon in one room and were briefing us about something. One of the DIs began to speak.

"All right you fucking maggots, listen up. The smoking lamp is lit. Light them up if you have them," he shouted. Lighting up was always a time to relax. Probably half the recruits smoked. If we had them, we lit up and listened.

"OK maggots, listen the fuck up. My Marine Corps has a deal for you scumbags. If you qualify – and that's a big fucking if – *if* you qualify you can apply for flight training. The Corps needs pilots. As an active duty Marine *if* you qualify you can fucking become an Airedale and fly around the sky while the real Marines kill the enemy all by themselves on the ground. You will get more pussy than you ever dreamed possible." Anyone from the infantry thought little of those in the air, so "Airedale" was a slang term implying uselessness.

My ears lit up. Second lieutenants made an incredible $241.20 a month base pay and another $100 in flight pay. That was a fortune. I did some quick calculations. Did I want to stay an E-1 private at $83.20 a month with an automatic pay increase to $85.80 in six months with a promotion to E-2 Private First Class, or did I want to take home the magnificent sum of $341.20 a month? Did he mention all the pussy I dreamed possible? I was a virgin. Even one would actually be quite nice.

"Listen up, maggots. To qualify for the Marine Aviation Cadet Program you need to have 20-20 vision, pass a two-year college GED test and be in perfect health," he said. "Put your name on this list and we will get back to you."

To me this was like a dream come true. I knew there was an

aviation cadet program where you went through flight training and got your wings and commission at the end, but it had never occurred to me that if you were on active duty you could apply without any college at all.

Passing a two-year college equivalency test might be a bit of an issue, though. It might be a giant potential deal breaker. It wasn't a "score well on the test" issue; it was a "pass it or you are out" issue.

But $341.20 is a whole lot higher than $85.80 and there was all that pussy to think about. I signed the list with three or four other recruits.

Qualification Day came. I was in the first group to fire. Everything I had been taught came together and I fired a 233 out of 250. That was the highest anyone had fired during our prequalification. It was a record for recruits that stood for eighteen months. It earned me the $85 pool.

As I rested at the rear of the butts the senior DI came up to me and spoke quietly. He asked, "See recruit Smith on lane 48?"

I answered, "Sir, yes sir."

He continued, "I'm going to put you in lane 47 at the 500-meter line and give you ten rounds. I want you shooting for him. We need to get him up to 190 to qualify and that fucking maggot couldn't hit the broad side of a barn if he was sitting in it. He needs another 40 points to qualify. Don't fuck up."

My head spun. The senior DI was telling me to fire for someone else. If we got caught I was going to be in deep doo-doo.

As we moved back to the 500-meter line for the final ten rounds, the DI slipped me a loaded magazine. I stepped up to the firing line and loaded my rifle just as if it was my turn to shoot. I carefully adjusted my sling and assumed the correct prone firing position.

"All ready on the right? All ready on the left?" the range supervisor called out. "All ready on the firing line." He looked to the right and then to the left before shouting, "Commence firing."

This was going to be a little tricky. I had to time my shots after Smith so his paper target went down at the appropriate interval after he fired. I was actually worried he might hit the target and there would be two holes through it. The DI assured me that wasn't going to happen.

Smith fired and I fired just after him. The target dropped down in the butts so the man handling it could mark it. The target came back up with a white square in the center. We had our first five points.

Firing continued. Smith would blast away, I would fire, and the target would go down for scoring. I kept hitting the bull's eye. I was starting to get really pissed. I was doing a better job of shooting for Smith than I had done for myself. After eight rounds I had 40 points.

The DI came up and kicked my boot. "What the fuck are you doing, maggot? You had better miss something or I'm going to shove that rifle up your ass."

I was on a roll and now I was supposed to miss the target. Well, fuck the DI. I clipped the target for three points on each of the last two rounds. It's actually harder to clip the target than to hit the center. Smith got up with a giant grin, thinking he had shot better than he had ever shot in his life. He had also shot better than he ever would again in his life, unless I was in the next lane shooting for him. The DI grunted and in Marine-speak that means a job well done.

DIs don't think much of scoring high on tests but they love recruits who can shoot. Setting a record as a recruit advanced my position in the platoon. Soon the DIs made me the guidon bearer – the guy who carries the flag with the platoon number on it and leads the formation. I was moving up in the Marine Corps. I was so full of myself. High man on the tests, high man on the rifle range and guidon bearer. I was 133 pounds of twisted steel and sex appeal.

When we got to the pugil stick training I learned just what my size really meant. The DI called me up and called up the biggest guy in the platoon and said, "For most combat, it's not the size of the dog in the fight, it's the size of the fight in the dog. Now Moriarty here is a little fucking squirt but he's smarter than most of you and can outshoot all of you. Big guys make much better targets than little guys because there is more of them to shoot at. This little fucker..." He put his hand on my shoulder. "This little fucker can outrun all of you cocksuckers on the obstacle course. Now I want to show you just what a little fuck can do to a big fuck with a pugil stick."

I was a little nervous but after a speech like that I just knew I was going to toss my opponent like a Greek salad. We charged toward each other and I gave him my best vertical butt stroke. Lightning seemed to strike as we came together and the next thing I knew I landed in a heap fifteen feet away. When a 133-pound squirt gets into pugil stick training with a 250-pound gorilla, the squirt is going to get his ass kicked. My giant ego shrank that day.

The DI pontificated, "A big guy will always beat a small guy with a bayonet. Shoot the motherfucker first and you won't need your bayonet."

It was a lesson learned.

The DIs figured that of those few who thought they might apply for the Marcad flight training program, I was the only one faintly qualified. In hindsight, I have to give the DIs of my boot camp platoon a lot of credit for getting me into the program. I would go on to become Honor Man of the platoon and get the dress blues awarded to the top man in every platoon and a promotion to Private First Class, but my DIs were determined to get me into flight training.

One day late in the training cycle Platoon 385 was marched over to have our dog tags made. With over eighty recruits in our group, mistakes happened. The DI ordered us to inspect our dog tags carefully to make sure they were correct in every detail. When we died the Corps needed to correctly identify the remains. My serial number was wrong. I had to remain behind to have another dog tag made.

When the new dog tag was pressed and inspected carefully to make sure everything had been corrected, I made my way back to the Quonset huts that 385 called home. As I approached I saw the rest of the platoon surrounding our senior DI, who was briefing them.

"You maggots are going to be going into combat soon. You will have more senior NCOs directing you but at the top you will have officers telling them what to do. You had better hope for the sake of your young butts that you have officers with guts. Nothing will get you killed in combat faster than some gutless second lieutenant who doesn't have a clue."

He continued, "You may or may not know it but your guidon bearer has been put in for flight training. The little squirt has to run around the shower to get wet, but he's got heart. When you are in battle you want to be led by someone who has guts if you want to survive. We are going to do our best to get him into flight training and in a year or so you may well be saluting him. He's a fighter and it doesn't get any better than that."

"It's not the size of the dog in the fight. It's the size of the fight in the dog. The smoking lamp is lit. Fire them up." He ended.

I thought about it for a few moments before I realized he was speaking about me. I'd listened to the senior DI speak and thought he was talking about someone else. I thought, "Damn, I'd like to serve under that officer, he sounds like a hell of a Marine." But he was talking about me.

My decision to join the Marine Corps was the first decision in my life that I made by myself and for myself. I consulted with no one else, not brothers, not sisters, not stepmother. For better or worse I made a decision and got to live with the consequences. You may safely believe that many times during the eleven weeks of boot camp I regretted my decision, but at the end of the day it was my decision and I had to live with the consequences, good or bad.

I grew up in a dysfunctional family without encouragement to do anything or to make anything special out of myself. I was in the eighth grade before I attended one school for an entire year. I was always on the outside. Now, for the first time in my life, I was able to compete against others with a similar background and rise to the top. I literally had never had an adult praise me for anything. It was a heady feeling. I was only eighteen but had learned that success breeds success. Something as minor as being the high shooter at the rifle range in boot camp helped me get into flight training.

Boot camp teaches recruits to work together, to obey orders without question, and that you can do a lot more physically than you believed. I've always had mixed emotions about not questioning orders; I'm more than a little skeptical of taking orders without question. But when you want a hill taken you want a platoon of Marines. They aren't going to debate the wisdom of charging up the hill in the face of heavy fire, they are just going to do it.

But at the upper reaches of leadership I think we need those who question the wisdom of orders on a regular basis. The shame of Vietnam was that a lot of people died for no particular reason. If you are real cynical you can say those millions died to fill the coffers of the military-industrial complex that Eisenhower warned us about in his farewell speech, just as the Vietnam war began to kick into higher gear. There would be at least a little truth to that.

In boot camp we didn't dream of questioning orders. We did what we were told, when we were told. But at some time during the 1955 to

1975 era someone at the top should have been asking himself or herself, "Why are we doing this?"

All Marine enlisted men must successfully complete boot camp just as each Marine officer must successfully complete Officer Candidate School. Before putting on a uniform they are all required to take an oath of office. It begins, "I, *[name]*, do solemnly swear (or affirm) that I will support and defend the Constitution of the United States against all enemies, foreign and domestic." The oath comes with no expiration date. In theory everyone who has ever been in the military remains duty bound to support the Constitution of the United States without reservation.

I always wondered about "all enemies, foreign and domestic." I understood the bit about foreign enemies. Anyone who was a commie was the enemy. That was easy. The VC were foreign enemies, the NVA qualified as foreign enemies, the Pathet Lao naturally were foreign enemies. There was a whole list of foreign enemies and all you had to do to qualify was to be a commie. Even Castro made it into the ranks of foreign enemies once we realized he supported a set of different economic policies than the United States.

But how did the framers of the Constitution define a "domestic" enemy of the Constitution? In retrospect I always felt that we should have spent some time in boot camp defining just what was a domestic enemy. Luckily, under President Johnson first and then Nixon, we learned that any American opposed to our invading foreign countries and killing the locals was a domestic enemy of the Constitution. If you were pro-war, you were ok. If you were anti-war, you were a "domestic enemy" and it was ok to violate the Constitution in order to persecute you.

Today we have the US Attorney General defining domestic enemies of the Constitution as being those "right wing extremists" who are always muttering about the Constitution and "rights." In the future when young men come of age and join the service, when they take the oath of office to support the Constitution they are already on the verge of becoming "domestic enemies" of the Constitution.

In boot camp, and in OCS for officers, a few hours were spent discussing the Geneva Conventions. In Vietnam we were required to carry a Geneva Convention Card with our name, rank, branch of service, date issued and serial number on it. The card identified us as combatants protected by the rules of warfare set out in the Geneva Convention. It was a real shame that we didn't issue Geneva Convention Cards to all the civilians we attacked day and night, since the Geneva Conventions clearly protected civilians. They also prohibited torture of prisoners of war and insisted that we not execute POWs. We never tortured prisoners in Vietnam; we turned them over to the South Vietnamese so they could torture them.

I remember in boot camp listening to an instructor talk about our rights under the Geneva Convention and making it clear that our enemy, whoever qualified as the enemy of the day, didn't obey the Geneva Accords. The implication of course was that while we had rights under the Geneva Conventions, our enemies really didn't, so we didn't have to obey them either.

On December 10, 1964, Platoon 385 proudly marched onto the grinder at MCRD San Diego for its final inspection and graduation ceremony, with a young PFC and platoon Honor Man wearing a crisp new set of dress blues and soon destined for flight training as the guidon bearer. I was actually most proud of wearing a sterling silver Expert Marksmanship badge. If you are going to be a warrior you had better be able to shoot straight.

Chapter 5
ITR, SAN ONOFRE, CAMP PENDLETON

The eastern world it is exploding
Violence flarin', bullets loadin'
You're old enough to kill but not for votin'
You don't believe in war but what's that gun you're totin'?
And even the Jordan River has bodies floatin'

But you tell me
Over and over and over again my friend
Ah, you don't believe
We're on the eve of destruction

Don't you understand what I'm tryin' to say
Can't you feel the fears I'm feelin' today?
If the button is pushed, there's no runnin' away
There'll be no one to save with the world in a grave
Take a look around you boy, it's bound to scare you boy

And you tell me
Over and over and over again my friend
Ah, you don't believe
We're on the eve of destruction

Eve Of Destruction
Songwriters: Steve Barri, P. F. Sloan
Copyright: Universal Music Corp. 1965

BECAUSE OUR PLATOON GRADUATED shortly before Christmas, little training could be done until after the holidays. A graduating platoon would be given ten days' recruit leave after boot camp and prior to ITR. After graduation we had one day on which our families and friends could visit with us before we proudly marched onto green buses for the hour-long trip to Camp Pendleton.

Platoon 385 went through boot camp together but there were other platoons graduating about the same time. At Camp San Onofre on the giant Camp Pendleton Marine Base, we were assigned to various ITR companies. Training would not commence until after New Year's so this proud new PFC packed his dress blues away to become a mess man for ten days before my leave began.

While I was on mess duty someone who thought he recognized me came up to greet me.

"Hey," the fellow said, "I know you. I went through high school with you."

Sitting on a barrel, I was busy cracking eggs for morning chow. I looked up at him.

"I don't know you," I said. I had never seen him before in my life.

"Sure you do," he continued, "we went through high school in Texas together."

"I went through high school in Texas but not with you," I said.

"Yes, you did. Your name is Jim and we were in high school in Houston." He was determined to prove to me that I knew him. But I didn't.

"My name isn't Jim. It's Bob, and I didn't go through school in Houston, I graduated this year in Fort Worth."

He looked at me as if I was lying to him. He had convinced himself he knew me and nothing I said would change his mind, notwithstanding the fact I had never spent a day in Houston, much less gone to school there.

"Naw," he said in a slow drawl. "Your name is Jim Wilson and you went to school with me in Houston."

I responded, "Well, my name is Bob Moriarty. I went to high school in Fort Worth and I have never seen you before in my life." I added, "But I have an identical twin brother named Jim and his last name now might be Wilson."

My parents divorced when I was four. Not being able to agree on just who should have custody of their twin boys, they split us up. One parent raised one; the other parent raised the other. The divorce caused a lot of animosity between my parents. The last time I had seen or heard from my twin brother was when we were eight. I'd heard nothing of him until this chance meeting at Camp Pendleton. My family was a little weird and more than a little dysfunctional. I have never heard of any other parents splitting up identical twins.

Writing down the details of the high school this fellow attended, I determined that I should stop in Houston on the way home to Fort Worth on leave and see if I could locate my twin. I owed it to him to get the same opportunity the Marine Corps gave me. It never occurred to me that he might not look at it exactly the same way.

I took a bus from Camp Pendleton to San Diego to fly to Houston. My ticket was from San Diego to Houston to Fort Worth and back to LA. At the terminal at Lindbergh Field in San Diego I looked over across the runway at MCRD San Diego. I shivered at the thought of what I had been going through just two weeks before. Don't let anyone ever kid you. Marine Corps boot camp is a lot rougher than anything that ordinary people ever go through voluntarily.

Once in Houston I checked into a cheap motel near the airport. No one, much less PFCs in the Marine Corps earning $85.80 a month, used credit cards except those from gasoline companies. They didn't exist yet. Everything I spent was in cash. The motel cost a lot of money, $9 a night, so I couldn't afford to stay there for long.

My quest wasn't the easiest. I had no contact number for my brother or for my mother. There were a lot of Wilsons in Houston and at ten cents a call, I couldn't afford to call all of them to ask after my long-lost twin brother.

I knew the high school he had attended. I started my search there but of course it was closed for the holidays. I stood in front of the now closed and shuttered school wondering just what I should do then when a girl of high school age walked by. Stopping her, I asked if she went to that school. She said she did. I explained my predicament, that I was trying to locate my long missing twin brother. She reached into her purse and pulled out a directory of the students from the prior year. Sure enough there was a Jim Wilson listed.

I called the number. A woman answered. Once she thought she recognized my voice she began to chew my ass. "You were supposed to come over for dinner last Saturday. You didn't come. You didn't call. Who do you think you are?" she harped rapidly. "Why are you so thoughtless?"

"Sorry, but if you are Shirley, this is your other son. I'm not Jim, I'm Bob," I responded.

"Oh," she said, with a long pregnant pause.

I went over, we got caught up on the last ten years and eventually my twin brother came over to the house for dinner as he had been supposed to. He didn't know I was there. Watching him come into the living room was as much of a shock to me as to him, and I knew what was happening. It was like watching myself.

When Marines finished boot camp and went on their recruit leave, they were told that if they convinced someone else to enlist in the Marines they could get an extra five days' leave. So I sold my twin brother to the Marines for five days' free leave.

He's still pissed.

Upon my return to Camp Pendleton I found myself assigned to a company for ITR. Marine Corps tradition calls for every Marine to be a rifleman. Some battles such as Saipan and Okinawa found units being swarmed by the enemy, causing even the cooks and bakers to grab rifles and repel the attackers. All Marines, enlisted or officer, go through basic infantry training. Mine was done at Camp Pendleton, the west coast home of the 1st Marine Division.

In 1965 we were only twenty years beyond World War II. As far as the Marine Corps was concerned one rifle was as good as another, so we used the aged but accurate M-1 rifle firing the 30.06 cartridge as our primary weapon during ITR. All our ammo dated back to 1944. It still worked just fine. For all I know, they may still be using 1944 ammo today. They had a lot of it.

ITR taught all the enlisted Marines the basics of the entire suite of company grade weapons. We fired the Browning 30-caliber machine gun, the Browning automatic rifle firing the same 30.06 round as the machine gun, and the 3.5-inch rocket launcher. Everyone had to rig at least one demolition charge and the hand grenade range was always fun, waiting to see if someone managed to drop a grenade after pulling the pin.

We learned that pulling the pin on a grenade with your teeth was a really bad idea unless you were that Cajun I went through boot camp with that had a new set of dentures compliments of the USMC. Much of what you see in movies wouldn't work in combat. And you don't throw a grenade as much as lob it.

Men love war. For all the whining and crying about how terrible war is, men still love it. It's in our genes. For the last thirty years or so we have been taught this nonsense that men and women are the same. They are supposed to be equal in all ways. It's bullshit. When the fetus has been fertilized, at about eight weeks into development the brains of what will be male children are soaked in testosterone and the two hemispheres separate. That doesn't happen to the female fetus. It is perfectly accurate to say that males and females are wired differently and they think differently.

You run into a bit of a problem because there is a range from the most female-females to the most male-males. In the middle there is an overlap and some with female bodies think and act like males. Likewise, some with male bodies think and act like females. I don't have conclusive proof but I think homosexuality is hard wired as the fetus develops and it's not an option.

That's good in a way because while my observation is that men love war, it's also true that it's perfectly natural for women, especially mothers, to hate war. They don't want young baby Johnny coming home in a box no matter how many medals he may have won.

It seems to me that the way of nature requires men to love playing war and women to despise war because of what it does to their babies. Certainly going through ITR and getting to blow things up was about as much fun as anything you can do with your clothes on. We only got to fire one 3.5-inch rocket in training but we were firing at old tanks 250 and 350 yards away. Most of the group managed to hit the hill but other than blowing away a few bushes, didn't accomplish much. With my steady deadeye shooting I whacked a rocket round right in the side of the tank I was shooting at. That's real handy talent to have as a civilian if your neighbor ever needs to take out a tank and needs some help.

For most of the men I served with in Vietnam, the experience of combat would be the biggest thing in their lives. I often see my compatriots at reunions still wearing old parts of their uniforms. Of the women who had husbands, sons and fathers, all they cared about was that their loved one returned safely. I don't think women give a shit about war and for the most part men love playing at war. Few of the people I served with ever gave much consideration to what we were doing or why we were there.

It makes about as much sense to put women into combat as it does to have men give birth.

I suspect the lunatics who run most governments play on those tendencies. True warriors love fighting but hate war. They don't focus on playing at war, they focus on getting their men home safely. I wasn't a true warrior yet but I was learning the tools I needed to know how to use.

I've never heard a serious discussion about the fundamental difference between men and women from the point of view of how they pass on their genes. Life is about reproduction. That's why men think about bopping women and women think about bopping men. At the heart of all sex is the desire to reproduce, to pass on your genes.

But men and women are totally different on how they reproduce. If a woman produces one egg every 28 days for a reproductive life span between the ages of 15 and 45, she in theory produces only about 390 eggs or rolls of the dice. Men on the other hand can produce literally an unlimited number of offspring. A very busy woman might have ten children in her life if she hasn't learned about sleeping pills and TV.

In theory, men could emulate Chinggis Khaan who got laid more than all of the Blue Angels combined. Ten per cent of the men living today in what was the Mongol Empire at the time of his death are direct descendants. That's 16 million men in the world today, or 0.5 per cent of all men.

When a woman loses a son, that's as little as ten per cent of her genes that will not be passed on or as much as 100 per cent. Women care about their offspring. Men care about getting laid; they can always replace any they lose. That's a fact, not opinion. So if you are confused about which sex protects their offspring the most, go to a game farm in South Africa. Try petting one of the cute little lion cubs and see who takes the first bite out of your ass. Daddy lion will be sitting under a shade tree while mommy munches on your arm. Go ahead and try screwing with Mother Nature.

After graduation from ITR, everyone went to his next duty station. Those who were basic infantry, as I was supposed to be, were mostly assigned to the battalion that rotated to Okinawa and became the first battalion-size unit to land at Da Nang in May of 1965.

During my tour going through ITR, I took the two-year college equivalency test and took a flight physical. I passed both, much to my great pleasure and surprise.

My orders to a grunt unit were changed. I was put on an indefinite hold at the 2nd Infantry Training Regiment until the Marine Corps either accepted me into flight training or rejected me. I went to work for an ancient sergeant major who had fought at Guadalcanal, 23 years before. When I say ancient, I mean ancient. He must have been over forty years old.

On April 23, 1965 the sergeant major grinned as he handed me a set of orders with my name on them. That obviously had to mean something important. I'd never seen him smile before. He grinned. That was cool.

The orders read:

Subj: Application for the Marine Aviation Cadet program; approval of

I had to go over the orders for a minute or two to make sure it concerned me, but sure enough they were sent

To: PFC R. J. MORIARTY 2100885 USMC

Marine Corps serial numbers used to be a way of keeping track of seniority. The Corps issued each enlisted man or woman a serial number at the time of acceptance into the Marines. Officers got their numbers when they took their oath of office. It was a way of determining the "old salts" from the new Corps.

My serial number was in the low two millions, but there weren't really two million Marines before me. Serial numbers began in 1920 and not all were used. In 1971/1972 the Corps discontinued serial numbers for identification and replaced them with the Social Security numbers issued to every worker. Remember the little blue card saying it was illegal to use the Social Security number for identity? Serial numbers were interesting. Social Security numbers are really boring.

The orders were mine. Soon I was on my way to flight training, starting in Pensacola, Florida. While it seemed an eternity to me at the time, my application for flight training went in on March 16, 1965 and the orders to flight training came back only about five weeks later.

It was the biggest moment of my life. It thrilled me to share it with Sergeant Major Meehan of the Old Corps. At the age of eighteen I had been approved to try to become a Marine pilot. Move over John Wayne.

Chapter 6
PREFLIGHT, NAS PENSACOLA, 1965

What the world needs now is love, sweet love
It's the only thing that there's just too little of
What the world needs now is love, sweet love
No, not just for some but for everyone

Lord, we don't need another mountain
There are mountains and hillsides enough to climb
There are oceans and rivers enough to cross
Enough to last 'till the end of time

Lord, we don't need another meadow
There are cornfields and wheat fields enough to grow
There are sunbeams and moonbeams enough to shine
Oh, listen; Lord, if you want to know

What the world needs now is love, sweet love
It's the only thing that there's just too little of
What the world needs now is love, sweet love
No, not just for some, oh, but just for ever, every, everyone

What The World Needs Now Is Love
Songwriters: David Hal, Burt Bacharach
Copyright: Warner/Chappell Music, Inc, BMG Rights Management
US, LLC 1965

THINK OF BEING GIVEN THE KEYS to the biggest candy store in the known universe. To a teenage boy in the mid-1960s, that's exactly what I had been handed. If it were up to me, I would have packed my sea bag and been on a bus to Pensacola the day my approval to flight training came through. For the next two weeks I was on tenterhooks. Finally my travel orders came in, telling me to report to the Naval Air

Training Command on May 26, 1965.

Visions of John Wayne, Guadalcanal and the Cactus Air Force filled my brain. I could see myself defending Midway when the Japanese attacked or rolling in at 15,000 to put a carrier in the cross hairs of my bombsight. I awoke every morning in a daze, feeling as if some wonderful thing had just happened. As my mind cleared I realized that something wonderful did just happen. Think back to being five and being given both a pony and a Roy Rogers cowboy suit at the same time.

Eventually I packed my sea bag, I completed checking out of the casual unit at 2nd ITR and said goodbye to Sergeant Major Meehan and the other flight training hopefuls still anxiously awaiting their orders.

I spent a few days in Fort Worth with my stepmother before getting on a puddle jumper bound for Mobile, Alabama, the nearest commercial airport to Pensacola. After a hot and muggy bus trip from Mobile to Pensacola I arrived at the base and checked in with the duty officer with the Naval Air Training Command. Although born in New York State, I hadn't lived east of the Mississippi since I was a tiny tot. I had forgotten just how humid the south could be. I wore a summer khaki uniform soaked from my sweat. I arrived in the evening and it was still steaming. It was late May. Summer would be worse.

I arrived a day early in Pensacola. It was a habit I made early in the Marine Corps. It gave me a chance to look around and see what was going on. In the USMC the early bird truly gets the worm. As part of my orders came a set of general instructions for Marcads. The instructions explained that as potential aviators we needed to be in tiptop physical condition. As such, no smoking would be allowed for the first week.

When the next day broke I checked in with the Marine Detachment. Captain Steve Pless, the Officer in Charge (OIC) introduced himself to the seven Marcads who would be part of Preflight Class 18-65. Captain Pless looked young only because he was young. At twenty-five he was the youngest captain in the Marines. He was the youngest Naval Aviator in the Vietnam War until I came along. I had never even imagined someone as young as him being a captain. It seemed quite remarkable.

This was still the pre-Vietnam Marine Corps. The first battalion-sized unit of the Marine Corps just landed at Da Nang a day before. During the next two years the Marine Corps would almost double in size. The Marines even started taking draftees, something unheard of in 1964. During the war 42,000 lucky American lads would be drafted to serve in the Marines. They were almost as thrilled as the rest of us about having draftees in our Corps.

In 1964 an enlisted man with more than three years' service would typically be an E-3 Lance Corporal if he was squared away and his Service Record Book showed no disciplinary action. At the end of a four-year enlistment the chance of a promotion to E-4 Corporal would be dangled in front of him if he would sign up for another tour. A corporal with less than four years' service was unheard of. A captain under the age of thirty or a major under the age of thirty-five was also unheard of. Pless was promoted to Captain (O-3) at twenty-four and Major at twenty-nine.

Preflight Class 18-65 contained seven Marcads, thirteen Navcads and sixteen other Navy officer aviation candidates. The Navcads (Naval Aviation Cadets) were the Navy equivalent of Marcads. Cadets could either come from active duty or qualify for the pilot training program with two years of college and entry as a civilian. The other Navy officer candidates were four-year college graduates destined either for pilot training or aviation crewmember training. All the college graduates received their commission at the completion of preflight. Marcads and Navcads didn't receive a commission until they got their Naval Aviator wings 15-18 months later.

So for most of the people in Class 18-65, Preflight in Pensacola was their Boot Camp or OCS. They needed to get into top physical condition to be able to complete the rigors of flight training. The few of us just out of boot camp were already in great physical shape. So the first thing I did when we were assigned quarters was to find a place where I could hide my smokes. The rest of the class may have needed to go without smoking for a whole week but that wasn't going to happen with me. Under the sink was perfect. The cigarettes were handy but hidden from all but the most knowing of eyes.

Platoon 385 in boot camp comprised a bunch of pretty ordinary American kids from the lower and middle classes. We were a cross section of the young men of the country. In contrast, my preflight class pretty much represented the best and brightest of young Americans. We were told that there were 400 applicants for every flight training billet.

The government estimated that in 1965 dollars the total cost of pinning a set of aviator wings on a young man exceeded $1 million. We were all males; this was years before it was decided in the name of political correctness that women had balls big enough to be combat pilots.

I don't bemoan women pilots; in fact there was a higher percentage of civilian women pilots in 1939 than in 1965. At the 133 pounds that I weighed, most of what I could do, a woman could do. But never before in history have peacetime military units figured they needed women in combat. It happened in the Soviet Union during WW II but even Germany on the verge of defeat never felt it needed women combat pilots. Israel began the concept of women in uniform. All young people in Israel have to serve for two years, male or female. But even Israel doesn't use women in combat. I don't know how much of the reason is that a volunteer army needs to draw on the pool of all young people, or how much was done in the name of political correctness rather than military needs.

I'm old enough to realize there is a giant physical and mental difference between men and women. Reproduction exists as a result of that difference. Traditionally the male role was to start wars and the female role was to end wars. It worked successfully for thousands of years. The US has gone so far overboard in the name of equality that we have forgotten that gender equality is not the same as saying everyone is identical. It is our differences that make us human. Combat flying takes balls and I'm not sure cutting the balls off young men and handing them to young women make either of them better pilots. That's a lot like giving very bright people stupid pills to make everyone equal.

While the Marine Corps had a few African Americans, flight training was almost lily white. I have my 1965 preflight yearbook. Glancing through the pictures of all of the Marcads, Navcads and AOCs in the forty-six preflight classes, few black faces appear. The Tuskegee Airmen proved during World War II that color was no barrier to courage or flying ability. While Truman desegregated the Armed Forces in 1948, the word still hadn't arrived in the Naval Air Training Command seventeen years later.

When Class 18-65 was fully formed we started our training. For most of the first couple of weeks we marched and did physical exercises. This was so much easier than boot camp that I could have slept my way through it. I was again the platoon leader as a result of my boot camp background. That lasted right up until I failed to memorize the Code of a Naval Officer. Frankly, I took the marching and petty chickenshit stuff pretty lightly. I didn't really care how the Code of a Naval Officer read, I was a Marine anyway. The DIs here didn't miss a trick any more than they had in San Diego during boot camp. One of them spotted me lip-syncing the words and I was promptly demoted to squad leader and another cadet took my place.

The portion of preflight dedicated to preparing cadets to become officers and gentlemen consisted of a lot more than just aviation-related subjects. While we took map reading, Morse code, dead reckoning navigation, aerodynamics and geography, we also had classes on how to balance a checkbook, how to determine the simple interest rate on loans, the Navy even insisted we take a speed-reading course. I thought that was a great idea until our class took a speed-reading test before doing any training.

The Navy wanted to get all aviation candidates up to a speed of 600 words a minute. Tests over many years and thousands of students showed than the average reader read about 250 words a minute before taking the course. Obviously the faster you can read, the faster you can consume reading material. We finished the test. My reading speed measured at 800 words a minute. Even the instructor found himself impressed.

I loved most of the classes with the sole exception of aerodynamics. I could never get my head around the math and barely skated through during all of flight training. But speed-reading I aced right out of the box. Obviously I didn't need to attend the course.

Our instructor set me straight. A period of instruction would only make me faster, so even though I already exceeded the goal of the class, I would do the same training as everyone else. I ended up reading 2,000 words a minute. I still consume books at an absurd rate, one a day.

During boot camp, I competed with eighty or so ordinary American young men from across the lower middle class social spectrum. In preflight my competition came from the upper middle and upper classes economically, and certainly from among the best and brightest. Each class that we took was mandatory and it was also mandatory that you pass the course. There could be a makeup test but if you failed any course you were out of flight training and back to the fleet. For Marines it meant they shaved your head and sent you to Vietnam.

As the war heated up in southeast Asia, we followed the news closely. We feared peace the most. The last thing we wanted to do was to waste eighteen months spent learning to fly hot airplanes only to miss the war. Little did we realize that that wasn't about to happen.

During this time my twin finished boot camp and ITR and transferred to Memphis, Tennessee for avionics training. The Marine Corps eased into the Vietnam era Corps. Jim made lance corporal in less than six months. A year earlier that would have been impossible. Guys in the military love the first stages of wartime; promotions come fast and easy.

All of my fellow classmates were older than I was. Most of them had college degrees; the rest all had some college. To the best of my memory I was one of the very few with no college at all. These guys weren't going to give an inch.

Everything you do in the military is based on your scores. If you wanted to pilot the hot fighters rather than helicopters that served as lead magnets, you had to have the best grades in every area. If you wanted the cool duty station, you had best hit the books. At first I was very self-conscious about my seeming lack of education but I soon learned that all the books I had consumed gave me more knowledge than most of my contemporaries. I not only could compete, I could excel. And this was some tough competition.

Military schools measure everything. Everything is graded. Failure was not an option. The DIs and instructors constantly reminded us that thousands of applicants were on our heels, and if we couldn't hack the course maybe they could. Naval Air Training Command had a quaint phrase for dropping out. If you felt there was something you couldn't do or you rethought just how much you wanted those wings of gold, you could always DOR. That stood for Drop Out Request. It was a tiny slip of paper; you filled in your name and signed. When you did you were gone overnight. Anyone could DOR for any reason at any time.

Me, I figured that anyone even considering a DOR had to be certifiable. The military wanted to give us hot planes, all the fuel we could carry, 20 mm guns, the training to use it all together and paid us to do it. DOR? How about not a flipping chance?

Our instructors were motivated and excellent. I don't know how many courses I took over a six-year period in the Corps, but it had to be dozens. The military finds qualified instructors and shoves them in front of students eager to learn. This wasn't like the boredom of high school or the dumbing down of subjects for recruits in boot camp. Our courses were complex and for the most part necessary.

As my now slowing memory cells recall, we were sequestered the first couple weeks of preflight. For me that was no big deal. During the eleven weeks of boot camp we didn't crap or shave unless and until ordered. Even those first couple weeks of preflight were pretty loose in comparison. But eventually the cuffs came off and we had weekend liberty.

To visualize flight training during the mid-1960s, think of the Tom Wolfe book *The Right Stuff* and the movie of the same name. Wolfe captured the period perfectly. We all felt that we had this image to live up to. We were aviation cadets destined for combat. If you've got the name, you have to act the part.

Part of the act was driving a cool car. Face it; during the 1950s and 1960s cars were far cooler than they are today. When I was a kid, when we went out on a drive we would try to figure out what all the other cars were. You had to be up on your automobiles to know the difference between a 1963 and a 1964 'Vette. For the most part I could identify not only the model but often the year of make of the majority of cars on the road.

Today I can't even figure out what decade a particular car was made or what country made it. Automobiles today are about as interesting as a bowl of lukewarm oatmeal.

On the first weekend we were allowed to escape from NAS Pensacola everyone shot down to the section of highway with all the sports cars glistening in the summer sun. Pensacola is a Navy town, called the Cradle of Naval Aviation. A number of car dealerships specializing in hot sports cars catered to the incipient aviators.

During preflight the cadet made half a second lieutenant's pay. For those of us with less than two years' service that was $147.30 a month. That went up as soon as we began primary flight training and collected flight pay, when we would make the magnificent sum of $197.30.

One of our pet phrases ran, "It's better to be dead than look bad." While it applied to dating ugly women and pulling silly stunts in aircraft, it also applied to the cars we drove. If you were going to be an ace pilot, it was mandatory that you have a sports car. Everyone I flew with had a sports car.

But $197.30 a month for smokes, dates and wine doesn't leave much in the way of skins for a fancy sports car. So the dealers came up with a magnificent solution. They would work with Navy Federal Credit Union such that for the first eighteen months the cost of the loan and interest was capped at $50 a month. That way, a poor cadet could afford a nice Corvette or Porsche and still pay for insurance and gas. However, and this was a big *however*, when you got your wings and your pay doubled, you had to pay down the remainder of the load in the next eighteen months.

In a way, this was the first known use of derivatives in finance, and the end result was about the same. A cadet would have cool wheels all during flight training on an affordable budget, and when he got his wings, his pay went up by $197.30 a month and his loan went up by $400 monthly.

But while he went through training he was cool. One sporty but rather poor driver had crashed three brand new Corvettes by the time he got his wings. I couldn't see the math working out in my favor so I determined that I could afford $50 a month for a car, to be paid off in thirty-six months. I bought a well-used Triumph Spitfire for $1,499. I wasn't quite as cool as the other cadets but I was as cool as I could actually afford to be.

There are side benefits to flight training that those who haven't gone through it don't understand because no one ever talks about them. There are some giant fringe benefits to being an aviation cadet. The Navy Federal Credit Union was one. As a cadet, even an 18-year-old cadet, I could borrow money to buy a car. At the time you couldn't walk into a bank and get a loan at eighteen, but NFCU understood the needs of aviation cadets.

Another giant benefit was with United Services Automobile Association (USAA). At the time, only officers or potential officers could join USAA. It was and still is the highest rated insurance company in the US. Their rates were fair and the way they treated cadets was better than any company I have dealt with since. I called them and arranged for insurance on my Spitfire. First of all, how many companies would even insure an 18-year-old? The annual cost came out to $155. I agreed and promised I would send a check.

The USAA representative on the phone asked if we ever had special parties or formal dances. Intrigued, I answered that I was sure those came up now and again. She told me that if I was ever short $50 or so, I should call USAA and report a broken windshield. Since the amount was so small, they wouldn't investigate, they just mailed a check.

Could I believe my lying ears? Was this woman suggesting that I fake a broken windshield just to get them to send me $50? I thought about it and realized it was an insurance company I could work with. Fifty years later I am still with USAA insurance, and no, I have never had a broken windshield, as a cadet or since.

Times have changed in the fifty years since I went through Pensacola. We all drank, most of us smoked and we partied hard. It was an important part of the culture, that of the live-fast-die-young-leave-a-good-looking-corpse mentality. The drinking age in Florida was twenty-one. Most of us were under twenty-one and no one would refuse to serve us alcohol. I never heard of anyone getting a ticket for a DUI but I don't doubt we had a lot of drinking and driving. The police wouldn't dream of giving a hard time to student aviators. We were the ones who were going to have to fight the war. Today, not making a full stop at a stop sign is enough of an excuse for a cop to shoot you and claim that you were resisting arrest.

Pensacola in the mid-1960s seemed like heaven to student aviators. Someone would rent a room at one of the few hotels out on Pensacola Beach. The rest of us would show up and drink until we got stupid. Women came and went like the tide. We were young, healthy and full of vigor.

During the fourteen weeks of preflight we went through 353 hours of classroom instruction, many more hours of parades and drill on the drill field, and parties every weekend on Pensacola Beach.

On a regular basis we had parades and class formations wearing our dress uniforms. Summer ruled in Pensacola so we wore the lightest uniforms we owned. Seeing hundreds of marching cadets wearing eye-scorching dress white uniforms must have been a stirring sight. I remain convinced the VC and NVA had nothing to compare. Marines always had the coolest uniforms and we didn't mind showing them off.

Sundays called for church service in the giant base chapel at NAS Pensacola and we got to wear our spiffy whites again. The highlight of the service came at the conclusion, where hundreds of flight training students in their brightest and best uniforms attempted to sing The Navy Hymn in unison. We got it more or less right.

It went:

Eternal Father, strong to save,
Whose arm hath bound the restless wave,
Who bidd'st the mighty ocean deep
Its own appointed limits keep;
Oh, hear us when we cry to Thee,
For those in peril on the sea!

I never heard the song without feeling a tear drop down my cheek. I felt for those poor souls out on the water who risked everything. Not that I had any goddamned intention of floating around on a boat when there were perfectly suitable land bases to fly from.

We had an eight-hour liberty on Friday nights and usually that meant going into town for a drink or three at Trader Jon's bar. Young women from many miles around found themselves attracted to Pensacola in the hopes of snagging a potential future airline pilot.

The officers spent a lot of time chasing young women but the cadets were too busy with studies. I did manage to make it out to the dog track where they held greyhound races every Friday and Saturday night. A group of us went out one Saturday night. Naturally you had to make a bet even if you were a lowly paid Marcad. It seems to me the smallest bet you could make was $2. I studied the race sheet carefully before determining one hound had the right stuff to be a winner. The odds were 15-1 and when he won I would be in high cotton for the next week or so. I never collected my $30. As a matter of fact, I never learned if I won the bet or not. The doggie is still running as best I know.

I still carried my virginity around but I was as eager as I could be to dispose of it. I did date the stepdaughter of the Navy architect who designed the Mustin Beach Officers' Club at Mainside, NAS Pensacola. I not only never got a home run, I really never got to first. I liked her a lot but more as a sister. Unless you are from the backwoods of Georgia, that gets really weird. I liked her as a buddy but it would have been nice to feel the pangs of love.

The Navy reserved Saturday mornings for sports. It didn't matter what you did, you had to engage in some form of sport. I still couldn't get up to 140 pounds and so baseball or football or any of the strength activities were out of the question. My former Camp Pendleton friend Woodie Patton found just the sport for us to participate in. He was called Woodie for Forrest Patton. It's been fifty years since he screwed me and I have yet to forgive him. It easily could be another fifty.

We would be roommates several times in the future and he was forever getting me in trouble. We met at Camp Pendleton in early 1965 when we were both on hold for flight training. He got his orders six weeks before I got mine. Since he was so much more experienced than I was in preflight, I made the mistake of listening to him. It proved to be my downfall.

One Saturday morning we were trying to figure out what sport we should engage in. My vote was for none of the above. Woodie grinned and said to me, "Mo, I've got just the thing. Let's go over to the hanger." He wouldn't be any more forthcoming until we got to the hanger and sat down.

"I've got it, Mo. We will become boxers," he announced as he lay back against the row of aluminum seats behind him with his hands behind his head. He never lost that silly grin.

I looked at him in horror. "Woodie, have you lost your ever-loving mind? Look at this face," I demanded, and pointed at my finely chiseled visage. "Do you think for even a moment that I am going to let someone pound on this beautiful face?" I continued, "How many young stunning hot beauties are out there dreaming of latching onto a stud like me? Handsome, debonair, wise in the way of the world and, I have no doubt, the potential to be one of the finest aviators to ever draw breath."

He grinned even harder. "Chill out. We don't actually have to box. Look at those fools down there with the gloves on. They take this shit seriously. Let them pound on each other and we can sit and watch."

I'm very good at watching fools beat on each other. Every Saturday for the next few weeks Woodie and I sat in a clump of other cadets who had figured it out. We could sorta watch boxing and that was a whole lot safer than actually doing boxing.

Then some flipping brown bar ensign had the duty one Saturday morning. I hope there is a special place in hell for brown bar squids who want to mess up everyone else's plans. I saw the clown ease into the hanger. He had that look of a rattlesnake watching a mouse with his tail wagging and shaking in the wind before striking.

The brown bar wades into the small group of guys boxing and pulls them apart. He motions the rest of us down from the aluminum stands and tells us to surround him. "Now listen up," he began. That's always a bad sign, when a flipping ensign wants to emulate a Marine DI. "I see you have twenty sets of gloves and we have about twenty guys here, so everyone can box at the same time."

Sure, as if everyone wants to box. He starts pairing off guys of about the same size and weight. "You and you. You and you." He grabbed my arm and teamed me up with some guy who must have outweighed me by twenty pounds and probably had six inches in height on me. The right thing for me to have done was to begin my boxing career by punching the ensign. Let's see what he thinks about boxing then.

So there I am. Woodie was kind enough to help me put the gloves on. He was way too tall to find a sparring partner so he got to be my second as I got killed. I wanted to punch him after I got though with punching the duty officer. Asshole.

I've got my back to my opponent as Woodie laces up my gloves. I can't think about anything except how handsome I was when I shaved in the morning and how it's all going to be ruined shortly.

I hear my opponent talking to his second. "How come he's wearing red shorts? Most of the guys here are wearing blue shorts but those two are wearing red trunks. What's with that?" he asked.

Casually his second responded, "Oh, those two must have been active duty Marines. They get those red trunks in boot camp."

Then I heard my opponent gasp, "Don't tell me I have to fight some fuck who just finished boot camp? He'll kill me."

Instantly I realized he was more afraid of me than I was of him. That day I learned that battles are won before they are ever fought. One side knows he's going win and the other side knows he's going to lose.

That belief becomes self-fulfilling. I would never get into a fight without knowing in advance that I was going to win. The concept of fighting just to be fighting doesn't exist for a warrior. You fight for a reason and can define victory.

We turned to face each other and the bell rang. I cleaned his clock. He knew he was going to lose so I made it true.

That Saturday morning physical routine had some interesting effects down the road.

Captain Pless, the Marine OIC of the Marcads in my battalion, loved boxing. He wasn't playing with a full deck either. When he found out I was a boxer, all of a sudden he puts me in charge of the six or eight other fools in our battalion that boxed. It didn't mean all that much. Every afternoon we ran around for half an hour and practiced boxing while holding bricks in our hands. Boxing wasn't about physical strength nearly as much as it was endurance.

A new preflight class began almost every week. The Navy was putting through 2,500 aviators a year in 1965 and 1966. Each incoming class would be assigned to one of the three training battalions. It didn't really mean anything; the classes graduated just as fast as they came in. But there was a friendly competition between the three battalions in academics, military skills, inspections and physical activities. As it turned out, just before Class 18-65 was due to graduate, a boxing smoker came due on the schedule. That happened once every quarter; I had luckily just missed the previous one as 18-65 was forming.

After all the numbers were tallied, the three battalions were within a few points of each other in the standing. The smoker would determine the winner of the battalion competition. The eagerly awaited bout was scheduled for August 19, a Thursday night. I seem to remember we had four guys scheduled to fight. Luckily for me, I would only have to box if we had a three-way tie between battalions.

Woodie and I looked over who was going to fight and assessed how good they were. The bouts started and it pretty much ran as we thought. So I'm sitting there smoking cigarettes and drinking a beer. For me to have to fight, Battalion 3 would have to beat Battalion 1 in the last fight and that wasn't about to happen.

It happened.

Once again Woodie is lacing up my gloves and I'm cursing him to beat the band. Now don't think for a minute we were actually about to hurt each other. We were fighting with sixteen-ounce gloves. They are actually pretty hard to lift, much less swing at someone. It's like boxing with a pillow in each hand.

The bell rang and the three-minute round began. It seemed to last for an hour. I swung and swatted and punched as best I could. Again and again and again. Unfortunately Avroc T. R. Shaffer kept swinging back. He didn't give a damn if I had just finished boot camp or not. It went on for three endless rounds. He wouldn't give up. I wouldn't give up. I must have outlasted him because in a split decision I won the smoker and we received the trophy for being the outstanding battalion for the quarter.

That night Captain Pless took the entire boxing team over to his house for a celebration party. Even though it was a weeknight and we had classes the next day, we all got soused and told war stories about how tough we were and what we would do once we got into combat.

Pless thought he was a warrior. He loved boxing and fighting. He swore to the entire gaggle of drunken cadets that he was going to go to Vietnam and win the Medal of Honor. Even I wasn't that drunk.

To add injury to insult, in our last week of preflight the top cadets in our class were assigned as cadet officers over the other classes. I was assigned as the Commander of Battalion 3, the same unit I had just humiliated. It seems to me now that Navcad Tolly Swallow became Regiment Commander, the only person senior to me.

My scores in preflight were going to be of critical importance. Marine student pilots took one of two different paths through flight training. All Marines went through preflight, fourteen weeks for Marcads and five weeks for already commissioned officers. Then the cadets joined with the officers going through primary flight training in the T-34B at Saufley Field in Pensacola. Our combined scores from preflight and primary flight training determined who would go to the jet pipeline in Meridian, Mississippi and who would go to helicopter training in Pensacola. Everyone wanted jets but only one or two of every class would get their choice.

Chapter 7
PRIMARY FLIGHT TRAINING, SAUFLEY FIELD

Business goes on as usual,
The corn and the profits are high
And TVs boom in every living room,
They tell us what deodorants to buy

Business goes on as usual,
Except that my brother's dead,
He was twenty-five and very much alive,
But the dreams have all been blasted from his head

In a far off land with a gun in his hand
He died in a war he did not understand

While business goes on as usual,
There's plenty to choose from the rack
But rumor goes that the latest thing in clothes,
The latest things in clothes will be black.

But business goes on as usual, as usual, as usual.

Business Goes On As Usual
Writers: Fran Minkoff, Fred Hellerman
Copyright: Kohaw Music Inc. 1965

IN 1965 PRIMARY FLIGHT TRAINING for Navy and Marine student pilots took place at Saufley Field, about ten miles north of Pensacola. We still underwent ground training while at Saufley. That would continue throughout all of flight training. It seems to me that beyond the aircraft systems for the piston engine T-34, we studied Morse code and dead reckoning navigation.

As cadets we knew we had hit the big time. Our pay went up by $50 a month with the addition of flight pay. The chickenshit regulations and nonsense of preflight were a thing of the past. We still held inspections and marched a lot but we were getting into the real world of naval aviation.

All our primary flying was done in the T-34B Mentor. The airplane joined the Navy in 1955. All Naval Aviators went through primary flight training in the beast. It had a tandem cockpit carrying an instructor and the student and would be flown solo from the front cockpit. The plane had a 220 horsepower engine up front and was fully acrobatic.

In a masterpiece of timing, Class 18-65 graduated from preflight on September 3, 1965 just as Hurricane Betsy began to gather strength in the Gulf of Mexico. Our class made its way over to Saufley and checked in just as preparations were being made to move all the squadron aircraft up to the Naval Air Station in Meridian, Mississippi. The commander of the base wanted all the planes out of the area and as many student pilots as possible out of the path of Betsy as well.

As cadets, we thought we had died and gone to heaven. We were getting a free ride in the plane that we would be training in with no pressure at all on us to perform. I don't remember just how many aircraft we had on the field but it had to be sixty to eighty T-34s. The evacuation turned into a Chinese fire drill with aircraft after aircraft taking off and heading for Meridian. Somehow the base found rooms for all of us and we stayed drunk for two days.

As luck would have it, Betsy swung more to the west and hit Louisiana before losing energy and going right up the center of Mississippi, requiring all of us to leap into the planes and return to Pensacola as it was out of the storm zone entirely.

My good luck was to have a great instructor in primary flight training, a Marine captain named P. M. Cole. We got along well and he took me through my eleven primary flights. The twelfth flight was with another flight instructor and he graded me safe for solo. I wasn't totally sure I was ready but on November 2, 1965 I made my solo in the T-34. My instructor and I flew to one of the outlying fields and he got out saying, "Good luck. If you can find the field, come back and get me in thirty minutes." Other than my touch-and-go landings at entirely the wrong field, the flight went smoothly, considering.

Up until this time, cadets wore no insignia of rank. We were all just cadets. However once we had completed a solo, we were issued a single bar to wear over our left breast pocket indicating that we had soloed.

Until you have tried and succeeded at a task you must always ponder just how well you would do. I arrived at Saufley as an 18-year-old kid and passed my nineteenth birthday during the Betsy saga at Meridian. Once I actually got my hands on an aircraft I learned that I loved flying. While I made the same stupid mistakes all the other students made, I was turning into a pretty fair pilot.

I would make an additional fourteen flights after my first solo, consisting of both solo and dual instruction. The fifteenth flight after solo was another check ride to determine if I was safe to continue with my training. I passed with flying colors.

Our scores were tallied from preflight, primary ground school and primary flight training. I had the highest scores among all the Marines so had my choice of jets or choppers. I opted for Basic Jet Training at Meridian and soon was on my way.

Chapter 8
VT-7 BASIC JET FLIGHT TRAINING, NAS MERIDIAN, MISSISSIPPI

Lay the green sod on me
carve my name in stone
lay the green sod on me
the soldier has come home

don't mourn for me, my darling
don't cry when I am gone
don't mourn for me, my darling
the soldier will come home

my friends have gone before me
and laid their tired bodies down
my friends have gone before me
to prepare the resting ground

let me go to sleep now
to march and fight no more
let me go to sleep now
I'm tired, my body's sore

so lay the green sod on me
put the wreath upon my stone
lay the green sod on me
the soldier has come home

The Soldier Has Come Home
Songwriter and copyright: Barry Sadler, 1966

I TOOK A SHORT LEAVE between primary at Saufley and basic jet training at Meridian. I went back to Fort Worth for a week. When I drove back to Mississippi I stopped in Memphis, Tennessee to see my twin brother Jim who was going through a year-long avionics school at NAS Memphis. I picked him up from his quarters and drove over to the Officers' Club. He didn't want to go in because he feared they would card him and refuse to serve him a drink. I told him, "Not a chance, they wouldn't dream of asking for ID. Follow my lead."

In the service, by and large you can do anything if you act like you belong there. Tennessee had the same drinking age issue as Florida. The law said you were supposed to be twenty-one; we were nineteen. As an aviation cadet I had all the right in the world to use the O-Club along with any guest I wanted to take, even my enlisted twin brother. We went in, acted like we owned the place, ordered and drank a couple of drinks and never had an issue with anyone. No one questioned the fact that two teenage kids were sitting in the bar swilling drinks.

When we left the club, I told Jim about my broken starter on my Spitfire. He reluctantly agreed to push start the car. RHIP (Rank Hath Its Privileges).

Woodie Patton and I would cross paths over and over again in our careers in the Marine Corps. Woodie finished primary a month before I did but had promised to save a room for me in Meridian. Once I completed checking out of VT-1, the T-34 squadron at Saufley, I loaded all my gear in the Spitfire and headed for Meridian. Sure enough Woodie had a spare bunk and soon I was checked into the Bachelor Officer Quarters (BOQ).

In 1965 Mississippi may as well have been on a different planet than the rest of the US. As far as they were concerned, they were still fighting the Civil War. The Southern Baptists had rammed through a "no liquor by the drink" law. The law called the selling of liquor illegal. Unless, of course, you were the sheriff. If you were the sheriff, you could sell liquor. No shit. It came under the Nixon doctrine. "If the president (or sheriff) does it, it's not illegal." Then as now, if the government breaks the law, it's ok.

During 1964 the KKK and some of the local police kidnapped and murdered three civil rights workers attempting to register blacks so they could vote. It turned out later that the FBI actually infiltrated the group that committed the murders. Several of the group went to jail for minor offences but no one was convicted of murder. *Life* magazine ran a special on corruption in Mississippi in 1965. The sheriff of Harrison County was the highest paid public official in the United States. He got a cut off of every bottle of booze his officers sold. Biloxi and Gulfport, Mississippi were located in Harrison County.

If you were on the base and wanted a bottle of booze, you just called the sheriff's office, told them what you wanted, and in an hour or so they would deliver it in a silver step van. Since cadets couldn't keep liquor in their rooms we never ordered booze, but I will admit every time I saw the sheriff making a booze delivery I wondered about the sanity of voters in Mississippi.

At NAS Pensacola and Saufley Field, our quarters were wood-framed buildings constructed during World War II. We slept four to a room. Each of us had a footlocker and a small closet but not a lot of room. The quarters at Meridian were a giant step up. Our room was a lot like a hotel room with two beds and two closets, and we shared a bathroom with the twosome opposite us. The base had opened only in 1959 so everything was nearly new.

Woodie Patton and I couldn't be in the same room together for very long without one of us trying to figure out some mischief to get into. On my first weekend in Mississippi he and I were sitting in the O-Club on a Friday night drinking a beer during happy hour.

John McCain was a flight instructor in VT-9 and he would surround himself in the club with a bunch of ass-kissers who thought sucking up to him would somehow help their careers. Daddy McCain would later become CINPAC (Commander In Chief, Pacific Command) and had a lot of stroke. Every marginal Navy pilot in Meridian wanted to be drinking buddies with McCain in the hopes of being remembered.

After a couple of drinks Woodie pipes up and suggests, "Let's go into town and get a drink."

"Woodie, in case you weren't aware, Mississippi is a dry state," I responded with a sigh.

"Sure it's dry," he continued. "Unless you buy your booze from the sheriff. Let's go into town and get a drink."

"Woodie, what part of 'dry state' has you triple confused?"

"Mo, let's go into town and get a drink."

He wasn't about to give up. Obviously I had to let him drive as he was far too drunk to sing. We jumped into this tiny VW of his and drove into Meridian, some ten miles south. As we cruised down the highway Woodie pointed out a low-lying building off to the side of the road. It looked just like a bar. We pulled in, parked and went in the entrance. Sure enough it looked just like a bar from the inside, too. We sat down and a pretty young woman who resembled a waitress came prancing over.

Keep in mind I was a kid and had never set foot in a drinking establishment other than a couple of Officers' Clubs.

She chirped, "And what would you young men like to drink?" Just as if this was a real bar.

I'd never been in a bar in my life. I was underage but I was now pretty certain that this joint looked like a bar. I responded the same way every kid would. "What do you have?"

She just smiled, "Honey, for you we have anything you want, just ask." Looking back, I'm certain she was telling the truth. I didn't just have a dirty mind back then. Well, my mind wasn't that dirty. Yet.

We ordered. She served, and after a few sips I realized that we were in an illegal bar in Mississippi drinking illegal booze. If alcohol had been legal in Mississippi it wouldn't have made any difference because I would have been under the drinking age anyway.

Woodie grew mellow with the fine rum he sipped. In the past fifteen minutes he hadn't gotten us in any more mischief. Clearly the lack bothered him. "Mo, what do you say about doing a little gambling?"

By this time I was sufficiently juiced up that I would have gone along with anything, including the cute little waitress and whatever she was peddling. "Sure Woodie, I'd love to gamble."

I never set out to have a misspent youth. It didn't happen naturally or through any effort on my behalf. But it happened. In my last semester of high school I took an advanced algebra course. Our teacher had finished the required study a couple of weeks early. It was high school; they couldn't do something as absurd as let you leave early if you finished your required work. So he had to fill in the dead time teaching us something mathematics-related.

He chose to teach us probability and permutations. As in, how to figure the odds on a pair of dice for every roll. It's a mere step or two down the path to perdition to understand how you could use that knowledge to actually make money.

Woodie and I left a tip for the waitress and sauntered over to a small door in the middle of the back wall. Woodie taps the door a couple of times. After a minute or so it opened. In the back of this illegal liquor joint selling illegal booze and with no doubt other illegal activities going on, it also had a casino attached. Now, as I said before, I had never before set foot in a casino, but I did watch movies. I knew what a casino looked like.

I had to ask under my breath as we eased our way into the bustling casino in the illegal bar, "Woodie, what the fuck is this? Is this the Mob or something? We get caught in here and they are going to toss us so far in the slammer they will have to feed us with a slingshot. We are going to be doing mess duty for the VC in a week in a sultry hot jungle camp."

The fucker smiled as he looked down at me. "It's ok, Mo. The sheriff owns it."

I let out a sigh. That made it all ok. The sheriff owned it so we couldn't get in any trouble. All the laws we were violating came under the control of the sheriff. It must have been one of those "Keep Mississippi green, bring money" sort of moments.

I headed over to the nearest crap table. At least there I understand the odds. But this was an illegal crap game. I pondered if that would actually make any difference. The dice came my way. I took the slim roll of cash out of my pocket and made a $1 bet out of my entire wealth that I needed to make last for another two weeks. I shot a seven and made $1. I was on a roll, literally. I must have made six or eight points and I was up $10.

A short squat guy waddles through the door. He's easily as wide as he is high. He's got a clump of $50 and $100 bills clamped firmly in one little fist with fingers that looked like sausage. He's got his stubby arm wrapped firmly around the butt of this sweet-as-pecan-pie bottle blonde with really great boobs. She had to be on the dark side of seventeen at least. He throws down a wad of money on the table and a bunch of oddly colored chips are placed in front of him.

I start thinking deeply.

Illegal bar. Check.

Illegal booze. Check.

Prostitution. Check.

Underage girls. Check.

Gambling. Check.

I asked myself what the odds of winning were for the guy at our table about to throw the dice, and who happens to hold the biggest bankroll in his pudgy fist. Check.

I wasn't responsible for my misspent youth but I was quite willing to admit it and make the best I could of it.

I love dice.

On a crap table, you can bet the don't-come line and be betting against the shooter. There wasn't a chance in hell this guy was leaving with his wad intact. He wasn't going to make a come shot until he was in the back seat of his Caddy with the sweetie puffing on his little wienie.

For the next five months I financed my way through flight school shooting dice in an illegal crap game in an illegal bar owned by the sheriff. Warriors need to study the odds carefully in all aspects of life. Especially in illegal crap games. And screw the odds, all you have to do to win is bet against the guy at the table with the most money.

Meridian was the home to training squadrons VT-7 and VT-9. All fixed wing jet pilots went through basic flight training in Meridian. Since the Marines had a lot more helicopters than fixed wing aircraft, far more Marines went the prop pipeline. Since the Navy had more jets than helicopters, Meridian carried more students undergoing training than any other base. Our training in Meridian lasted about six months so there must have been 1,000 to 1,200 students between the two squadrons, VT-7 and VT-9.

Our basic training aircraft was the T-2A, a single engine jet trainer that entered Navy service in 1959. Variations of the T-2 continued to be used in flight training for a remarkable four decades. The T-2 carried two people, the instructor and the student, and soloed from the front seat. In a screaming dive the plane could do 400 knots. It was an agile critter, climbing at over 6,000 feet per minute in later variations.

Like we did in primary flight training, we underwent ground school on the aircraft systems before actually flying the plane. I arrived in Meridian in the middle of December of 1965. Everyone in the training command would take a week to ten days off for Christmas. I made several flights in the plane before going on leave to Texas.

The T-2 required a lot more flying than did the T-34. For a long time I felt the plane was flying me. I was just along for the ride. Clearly it was going to require more from the pilot than what I had been flying.

I went on leave, came back from leave and started the course again after not flying for about two weeks. I was a disaster.

At the time, training squadrons had both Marine pilots as instructors and Navy instructors. By and large your primary instructor would be the same service as the student. My instructor was a Marine and a screamer. Anything that I did wrong, he screamed.

I've found that in life there are two kinds of people: people who like getting screamed at and people who don't like getting screamed at. For those who like getting screamed at, it's the only way you can get them to do anything. Those who don't like getting screamed at, and that includes me, stop dead in their tracks if you yell.

My instructor gave me a down on a check flight. That was the first step in getting bounced out of flight training. I didn't take that well. Flight school was my dream and I was about to lose it. But I will give him full credit. He recognized that I had not flown for two weeks and didn't respond well to the screaming. He talked to another instructor, a Navy pilot, and asked him if he would take me over. My Marine instructor said that he saw potential but I wasn't getting with the program, and unless I did, I would be out of the program.

My new instructor and I got along well. He thought that my problems weren't with the requirements of flying; they had more to do with the way I responded to instruction. Later I would fly a four-plane formation in basic jet training with the original Marine instructor. He admitted he had been wrong about how he was instructing and commented that my four-plane formation flight was the best he had ever seen from a student.

The aviation aspects of flight training became more interesting by the day. Each student went through dozens of hours of simulator training in the Link trainer used to emulate instrument flight. The T-2 was a real jet but handled like a little old lady. The course consisted of basic flight operations in the plane followed by a check ride and then solo. Instrument flying and the all-important Instrument Card that qualified us to take off or land in instrument conditions came next. It got more interesting as the syllabus went on. All aviators needed to know how to take off and join up with other aircraft and fly in close formation to complete your mission in fair weather or foul.

We did navigation flights, both high and low. Any time students could link up with another student on a solo flight determined to get into trouble, we would come up 333.3 on our UHF radio and dogfight until fuel ran low. We called the frequency Cadet Common.

While we had a primary flight instructor, once we had completed our "safe for solo" flights we got handed around a lot. I had two dozen instructors, some Navy, some Marine. Most of them were pretty good. I found it interesting to see the variations between pilots. I began to realize I was better than some of the instructors. Not in total knowledge, for I had maybe 180 hours total, but I was a lot smoother than some.

It was rare to have an instructor from the other squadron at Meridian, VT-9. I was in VT-7, not that there was any real difference between them. One day the schedule called for me to fly with a VT-9 instructor. It was Lieutenant John McCain. And he was just as full of himself in the plane as he was in the bar. He was one of the pilots I was certainly better than.

The closest I came to getting the boot from flight training was on one of my first solo flights. I had completed the required navigation and air exercises but had both fuel and time remaining before I was due back at Meridian. Bored silly, I figured it was time for a cigarette.

Believe it or not, since most pilots and student pilots smoked, we often lit up in planes. During World War II all the airplanes had canopies that would open, so smoking wasn't difficult. Face it; given the relative risks of air-to-air combat and dying of lung cancer, there was no issue.

We wore helmets carefully adjusted and fitted to each pilot and got pressure oxygen through the mask. I unlatched one side of my O_2 mask and fired up a cigarette. Unfortunately I neglected to turn off the oxygen.

Did you realize just how flammable everything gets in the presence of oxygen, especially oxygen under positive pressure such as we flew with?

My cigarette ash touched the rubber of the mask with the oxygen blasting through and all of a sudden my mask turned into a torch. I did have the presence of mind to stuff my leather flight glove in the mask to put out the fire. And to turn off the oxygen.

My aircraft still flew; it didn't affect any of the aspects of flight so I figured I would just fly back to the base, enter the landing pattern and act as if nothing were amiss. Except for the fact that my microphone, my sole microphone, had been turned into a crispy critter.

I could navigate. I could listen to the radio; I just couldn't talk on the radio. It wasn't a major problem. We had no-radio procedures. I had them memorized and adhered to them as I returned to Meridian. I came back into the pattern with my gear down, wagged my wings, and the tower understood I couldn't communicate. They transmitted landing instructions and gave me a green light for landing. I made a nice landing. As I taxied into my parking slot I pondered just how I was going to get my microphone replaced.

The lineman who parked me put the ladder in place and climbed up to put the safety pin in the ejection seat. As he reached the cockpit he exclaimed, "Holy shit! What happened to you?" This surprised me. He couldn't see my burned up mask, since I had already thought to safely park it in my brain bag that we kept our helmet and flight gear in.

As casually as I could, I asked in innocence, "What do you mean, what happened?" just as if I had no idea what he was talking about.

He pointed to the top of the canopy, covered with carbon black from the burning rubber. It was a mess. I mumbled pretty much to myself and as fast as I could talk, "Ilitacigaretteandsetmymaskonfire."

"What the fuck did you just say?" he asked.

I mumbled a little louder in the way you do when you are in Mexico and they don't understand your English, just say it louder and they will get it.

"ILITACIGARETTEANDSETMYMASKONFIRE."

"You mean you burned up your mask? Are you shitting me? You are pretty fucked now."

I just hate it when people come up with the obvious. I was trying to figure out how to get my mask fixed while I was taxiing in with a canopy that looked like a pair of skivvies with a giant skidmark in the bottom. And it's not like I really wanted to advertise just how stupid I had been.

Like a real champ, the lineman grabbed a buffing rag and bottle of Plexiglas cleaner and promptly cleaned up the carbon black from the canopy. Alas, there wasn't anything he could do about my fried mask. "Sir, you had better get with the flight equipment guys and get that fixed right away."

Right. Except everything the Navy issued us was in our names and any replacements had to be justified. If you wanted a new flight suit, just show up with one with a hole in the knee. No problem. If you needed new sunglasses, take your broken pair in and exchange them for new. But if you have a burned-up mask because you had a brain fart, basically you are pretty screwed.

I went to the Non-Commissioned Officer In Charge (NCOIC) of the flight equipment shop and explained my problem. While he felt bad for me, for him to change it I would need to come up with a new mask assembly and new microphone. The only place to get that was from supply.

Depending on how high a cadet ranked during flight training and how well he was liked, there were a lot of things one cadet could get away with that another couldn't.

During preflight we had the son of a Marine Corps two-star general in Class 18-65, named George Bowman. Everyone figured that the oak couldn't fall far from the acorn but in his case it did. Plump and clueless described Bowman. The issue wasn't if he was going to get bounced from flight training but when, and who would have the balls to ground him permanently and send him back to the fleet. Finally some brave squid instructor stepped up to the plate and gave him a down and a recommendation to be released from flight training. It stuck and there was no feedback.

I had friends and pull, but not that much pull. There were hundreds of things you could do that would get you bounced from flight training, but lighting a cigarette in the cockpit with flowing oxygen was right up at the top of "really stupid headwork" and was clearly guaranteed to remove a student, any student, officer or Marcad, from the program.

All was not lost just yet. While poor headwork can be grounds for dismissal, other than the lineman and the head of the flight equipment shop, no one of rank yet knew what I had pulled. If I used a lot of good headwork, perhaps I could figure a way out of the swamp.

I drove down to the supply shop and asked to speak to the NCOIC there. In such a case as this, you didn't even dream of asking an officer for a favor. The senior NCOs were of a more forgiving character. I figured that at some point in the past he may have fucked up big time and someone had helped bail him out.

I found such a brother in arms and he agreed that all I needed was a new mask and a new mike. If I came back and looked into the dumpster after closing hours, perhaps there would be a new assembly in a box waiting for anyone who happened to look in the trash. I was saved.

Sorta.

I wandered back to the squadron figuring that I had outwitted fate. But fate had something else in mind for me. I looked up on the board and saw my name scheduled for another hop. In the vernacular, I was fucked. I couldn't fly without a mask. I went to the duty officer and asked that I be removed from the flight schedule for the day.

The Navy and Marine Corps assume that when they offer our best and brightest young men the chance to learn to fly that said young men will always be ready and eager to fly. I was eager. I just wasn't ready. Not for another day. For the life of me, I can't remember what line of bullshit I used to convince them that I didn't want to DOR; I just didn't want to fly that day. I wasn't sick. I wasn't scared of flying. I liked my instructor. I just didn't want to fly.

Enlisted men lack the corncob-up-the-ass attitude so common among officers. I drove over to the supply shack after closing hours and rooted around in the garbage until I came up with the mask and new mike. Sure enough it was brand spanking new. Early the next morning I showed up bright and eager at the flight equipment loft and got the NCOIC to assemble the mask for me. Then I told the duty officer I was ready for any extra hops he could schedule me. I think those guys are still trying to figure out why Marcad Moriarty was so eager to fly one day when the day before he couldn't be crammed into a cockpit.

That entire saga taught me a most important lesson. I wasn't stupid, I could learn from my mistakes. Never again would I smoke in the cockpit without making sure the O_2 was safely switched off.

As students got a month or two into the basic jet training, the number of guys getting dropped from the program shrank. If you could safely fly the first 100 hours of what would be a 300-hour syllabus over an eighteen-month period, you pretty much had it made. Pretty much all the student pilots seemed to settle down and actually began to enjoy the training.

It always seemed to me that we were just shy of the hours we needed to be comfortable with any given flight requirement. I am certain the Navy had studied this and wanted to keep incipient aviators on the edge of their seats. You needed to sweat a little to make it as a pilot. But as time went by and I realized I could outfly most of my contemporaries, my confidence grew.

My belief remains that the cadets made better pilots than the college graduates did. We wanted those wings a lot more than the already commissioned officers. If a second lieutenant dropped out of flight school, he remained a second lieutenant. If a Marcad dropped out for any reason, he automatically became a lance corporal, grabbed a rifle and headed to Vietnam. That's no choice at all. I had no fear of combat in the air; I just wasn't thrilled about the concept of combat on the ground.

In addition to the need to exceed that I think all cadets had, we were younger by a couple of years so our reflexes were better. The Navy forbids cadets to marry, though a few were married. Married guys didn't feel as comfortable with flying on the edge, whereas cadets were perfectly comfortable with pushing the airplane to its limit and sometimes beyond.

Woody finished basic and transferred down to NAS Pensacola to do his carrier training and air-to-air gunnery taught in VT-5. I followed him by a couple of weeks. We were like an old couple by now.

But first I had to make a last pass at the bar to have one final drink. I wasn't about to gamble; I didn't want to push my luck. I walked in, sat down and ordered a drink. Before it arrived two guys, big guys, came up and stood on either side of me. The small one looked like a giant thug. The other was worse. One said in a deep voice, "The manager would like to have a word with you."

I wasn't perfectly comfortable with the meet-and-greet but I stood up and followed one of the fellows as he led me to a door I had never seen before. The other hulk followed me. In the room there was a big guy sitting behind a giant desk littered with piles of papers. He had one hand wrapped around a big cigar he took a puff out of now and again.

"Have a seat, Cadet Moriarty. I'd like to have a short word with you," he muttered with his feet up on the desk.

That set off my stall warning horn. How did this guy know my name? Nobody used credit cards in 1965 except for gasoline and I had no card to my name.

He continued, "We know what you have been doing."

I could feel my wings shudder as I approached an inverted stall. Did these guys really know what I had been doing? If so, I was about to get buried in the South 40.

"You been coming in and making come bets when you roll the dice and taking the odds every time. That tells me you know how to bet on dice. You never make the stupid sucker bets. But when some high roller takes the dice, all of a sudden you go the other way and bet the don't-come line. Whazz the matter, you think we are running some kinda clip joint here?"

I thought to myself, "Well, as a matter of fact," but realized that I might be smarter keeping my mouth shut.

"Good luck with VT-5. I'm sure you will be very successful in Pensacola on your carrier quals. But don't come back here. I'm tired of paying your way through flight training."

I wanted to point out to him that technically I really hadn't been taking the money from him and the table. Actually I was kind of taking it from the guys with the big wads of cash. But that was a nuance I wasn't sure he would understand or approve of.

My orders came in and I was on my way to Pensacola to do my carrier qualifications and start air-to-air gunnery. Flying was starting to get very interesting. The concept of belonging to a specific class was behind us. When you finished the training and passed the check rides, you got orders to your next station.

Chapter 9
VT-5 CARRIER QUALIFICATION AND AERIAL GUNNERY, NAS PENSACOLA

The old hometown looks the same as I step down from the train,
and there to meet me is my Mama and Papa.
Down the road I look and there runs Mary, hair of gold and lips like cherries.
It's good to touch the green, green grass of home.
Yes, they'll all come to meet me, arms reaching, smiling sweetly.
It's good to touch the green, green, grass of home.
The old house is still standing, tho' the paint is cracked and dry,
and there's that old oak tree that I used to play on.

Down the lane I walk with my sweet Mary, hair of gold and lips like cherries.
It's good to touch the green, green grass of home.
Yes, they'll all come to meet me, arms reaching, smiling sweetly.
It's good to touch the green, green grass of home.

[spoken:]

Then I awake and look around me, at the four grey walls that surround me
and I realize, yes, I was only dreaming.
For there's a guard and there's a sad old padre –
arm in arm we'll walk at daybreak.
Again I touch the green, green grass of home.
Yes, they'll all come to see me in the shade of that old oak tree
as they lay me 'neath the green, green grass of home.

Green Green Grass Of Home
Songwriter: Curly Putman
Copyright: Sony/ATV Tree Publishing, Tree International 1966

IN MAY OF 1966 I finished basic jet training at Meridian and transferred to VT-5 at Forest Sherman field at NAS Pensacola for my carrier qualification and air-to-air gunnery. For once Woodie and I weren't roomies but I knew that would change when we got to advanced training.

Shortly after I checked into VT-5, a request went out for a student to fly out to the *Lexington* and stay on board while the ship sailed to Galveston for Memorial Day celebrations on May 30. We weren't qualified to fly ourselves, so I jumped into the back seat of a T-2A and rode out to the carrier with an instructor doing all the work. The *Lexington* had left Pensacola and was a hundred miles or so to the west before we caught up. My first sight of her was from about 10,000 feet.

The instructor asked, "Do you want to see where we are going to land?"

What could I say other than "Sure." And then, "Oh, shit."

Imagine looking at a postage stamp from 10,000 feet. That's exactly what the *Lexington* looked like. A postage stamp. Just like a postage stamp but it was a lot smaller.

In hindsight it was a really good move on my part. I was getting a free ride. I didn't have to do anything except sit in the plane and not eject or set my mask on fire. The instructor did all the flying. He didn't even bother talking to me and that was fine. We came in over the carrier at 500 feet, broke smoothly, and by the time we got to the 180-degree position opposite our landing point he had completed the pre-landing checklist. He called the gear down, flaps down, hook down, and read off the fuel state to the Landing Signal Officer (LSO) controlling us.

It seemed to me he started his turn to the final approach path a little early, but when we did our Field Carrier Landing Practice (FCLP) passes on runways, those runways weren't doing 25 knots through the waves and the carrier was. The instructor made the approach and landing look like a piece of cake. I figured that if he could do it, I could do it.

I think we spent three days in Galveston, entertaining guests and people visiting the ship wanting to *ooh* and *aah* over the neat airplanes. Kids wanted to know if the planes had guns on them. So we lied through our teeth to them. American kids were gun crazy. Still are. By the end of the three days we were pretty tired of being asked the same questions again and again so we started trading planes. I was putting 20 mm guns on primary training choppers by the time the show finished.

But training got even better. The Navy could attach two 50-caliber gun pods to the wing stations on the T-2 and you could do aerial gunnery. That's so much fun they should make it illegal. The first time you press the firing button and two 50-caliber Browning machine guns start blasting away, you think you have died and gone to heaven.

All the air-to-air kills in World War I and WW II naturally were from guns. When aerial combat started in 1914 they used pistols, and eventually graduated to fixed 30-caliber machine guns. For the most part the Navy and Marine Corps used 50-caliber Brownings on the Naval Aviation fighters during World War II. In Korea they moved to 20 mike-mike (or millimeter) size guns, the bullets almost an inch in diameter.

At VT-5 we started with aerial gunnery and finished training with actual carrier landings. One aircraft tows a banner on a hopefully long enough cable. The banner flies vertically and has a target painted on it. The firing aircraft join up and fly up the left side of the tow plane, but have extra power and speed so that they can climb up to a perch position higher and to the right of the tow plane. Naturally that's called the perch.

You have a power and altitude advantage over the tow plane. When cleared, the firing aircraft lowers his nose to gain speed and turns into the banner. If done correctly, when approaching the banner in a firing position the firing aircraft would be at a 90-degree angle to the banner. At 1,000 feet you try to hold your gun sight pipper on the bulleye, and as you get closer and if you have a nice smooth pass, you open fire with both of your guns. You should be pulling 3-4 gees at this point so it was important to be smooth.

The guys in the armory paint the tips of the bullets and each firing aircraft has a different color. When the tow plane gets back to base, he releases the banner and it falls to the ground. The armory fellows count the bullet holes for each color and you find your score later, after you have landed.

It sounds a lot easier than it is. You might fire 150 rounds and get five hits. That's if you were really good.

If your plane started the pattern from the perch too slow, you ended up chasing the banner sometimes, as if trying to catch up with it. The banner pilots hated when that happened. If you were chasing the banner and were behind it, you were also behind them, and any rounds passing through or around the banner might well hit the tow plane. And they just hated that. If you were slow and at the wrong angle to the banner, that was called being "sucked." Actually I think being in the tow plane and having a student firing 50-caliber rounds at you was what sucked, but who am I to make up names for Navy traditions.

During WW II they used tracer rounds mixed with ball ammo: one tracer for every four rounds of ball ammo. At first they loaded the last twenty rounds as tracers so you would know you were out of ammo. Someone soon realized that if you saw the steady tracers and knew you were out of ammo, so did the guy you were shooting at. Maybe him knowing you lacked ammo was not such a good thing. That's like going in the bush in Alaska and wearing those bear bells on the laces of your boots. Do you really want to tell the bear where you are or would you rather keep it a secret?

At Guadalcanal the Marines and Navy fighter units engaged in heavy air-to-air combat. One bright young spark figured out that given where all his tracers hit, he should have been getting a lot more kills. He thought about it and realized that a tracer round had a different flight path than a ball round because the tracer was a lot lighter. Tracers don't follow the same path as ball ammo. So he had his guns loaded with nothing but plain ball rounds. His kills went up as a result, and soon Navy and Marine fighters all discarded the tracers entirely.

The T-2A came with a gun sight and every fighter I flew after that carried one. You knew what mil setting you needed for guns and you set it as part of your checklist. The gun sight compensated for the forces of gravity and if you pulled gee forces smoothly, wherever the pipper went, so did the bullets. In theory. I always thought the 50-caliber rounds were a lot like socks in a dryer. They just disappear.

I would gladly have paid the Navy to let me fly more air-to-air gunnery flights but they figured as long as student pilots knew the basics, that was sufficient. Once back in Pensacola our training began and we learned the subtleties of landing on an aircraft carrier. We finished hundreds of graded FCLPs and got ready to earn our spurs.

Navy and Marine pilots need to land on carriers. The training for such landings takes place on land, where student pilots take what is called Field Carrier Landing Practice. Naval doctrine calls for more of a controlled crash to get aboard a carrier than the Air Force's typical nice smooth landing. The distance between the four wires on a carrier is only 40 feet or 12 meters. If you land short you risk bouncing off the stern of the carrier, which really has to hurt. If you land long, you may as well keep going as you aren't going to stop with any wire holding you back. Your aiming point was the #3 wire but any of the four would stop you.

VT-5 proved to be a focused, concentrated form of training. The whole thing lasted only about six weeks. We flew hundreds of practice carrier landings. The pattern was only 500 feet, just as on a real carrier. We had to carry just the right power setting so our angle of attack was exactly correct for the slowest speed at which we could fly safely. All carriers sail into the wind and give you 15-25 knots of apparent headwind, but things happen quickly even at a 110 knots approach speed to a carrier.

VT-5 did the training in Pensacola because the carrier we would practice on was based there. It was the Essex Class USS *Lexington*, the *Lady Lex*. She had a slanted deck for landing and a straight deck for catapult takeoffs. Students were required to complete four arrested landings and four catapult takeoffs. Actually, once you landed on board, you weren't leaving until you got a cat shot. There was no alternative.

Having been through one carrier landing and catapult shot, I wasn't a real virgin. But still to this day, the tension of making a precision landing on a floating log out in the ocean and having to hit the #3 wire just so, makes me feel really alive.

And cat shots have been compared to your first orgasm. The pilot is sitting in the cockpit with his fist on the throttle, hoping he doesn't get a bad shot. You are going to waddle off the end of the boat into the drink if you have a catapult failure. All you can think about is that the lowest bidder built every part in that catapult.

Bam, and off you go. You pray that you have enough speed to keep flying and something like 1.8 seconds later your brain catches up with your butt and you start to think about actually flying. Every time you do it you wonder, "Will I make it this time?"

Somehow you do your four touch-and-go landings, you make your first couple of arrested landings. The LSO figures you need some fuel and the question is whether to go back to Sherman Field and refuel or continue. The weather is clear and you have done a great job of pretending you know what you are doing. He lets you do your last couple of arrested landings. Soon you get your fourth catapult shot of the day and you head for the beach.

I finished my carrier landings on June 14, 1966. When you finished your carrier qualifications as a cadet, your date of rank was then set. My date of rank as a second lieutenant was June 8, the same date the Annapolis class of 1966 of the Naval Academy graduated. That date would determine when I made first lieutenant and captain. Since seniority is both by date and by alphabetical order, if I had been named Adams, I would have made captain with less than six months in grade as a first lieutenant.

Aviation was turning into fun. We worked hard at perfecting exactly the right turns, speed and angle of attack for the carrier landings, but when you just made your first arrested landing on a carrier not much bigger than a postage stamp, you are floating on air for days. It's a tiny number of pilots who have ever landed safely on a carrier. The effects of a catapult shot should be a carnival ride, it's that cool.

I packed up my sea bag, loaded the Spitfire and headed for Advanced Jet Training at NAS Kingsville, Texas. I had my carrier landings and date of rank as a Brown Bar 2nd Louie.

Chapter 10
VT-23 ADVANCED JET FLIGHT TRAINING, NAS KINGSVILLE, TEXAS

If you love your Uncle Sam,
Support our boys in Vietnam,
Bring them home, bring them home.

It'll make our generals sad, I know,
They want to tangle with the foe,
Bring them home, bring them home.

They want to test their weaponry,
But here is their big fallacy,
Bring them home, bring them home.

I may be right, I may be wrong,
But I got a right to sing this song,
Bring them home, bring them home.

There's one thing I must confess,
I'm not really a pacifist,
Bring them home, bring them home.

If an army invaded this land of mine,
You'd find me out on the firing line,
Bring them home, bring them home.

Bring 'Em Home
Songwriter: Pete Seeger
Copyright: Pete Seeger

WHEN STUDENTS GOT TO Advanced Flight Training, they felt as if they were heading down the last stretch. There is something very real about doing carrier landings even on a slow, straight wing training aircraft. It requires real skill. And even half a dozen aerial gunnery flights begin to make the whole process more real.

I could both land on a carrier and take off. And if the VC ever attacked the US mainland using C-172s, I could probably shoot them down. I now knew how to fly. Our training wasn't about doing landings or turns without losing altitude, it was about using aircraft as the weapons of war the military intended them to be used as.

Vietnam continued to heat up. By now all the guys I went through boot camp with had returned from Vietnam. Many of them came back in aluminum boxes.

VT-23 began to receive as instructors pilots who had just returned from either a 13-month tour in Vietnam with the Marines or a six-month cruise off a carrier operating in the Gulf of Tonkin for the Navy pilots. We all knew we were bound for Vietnam, we just hoped it would last until we could get there and prove both our skill and our courage.

Those doomed to remain targets study tactics. Those destined to become warriors study war. Our greatest combat generals, Lee, MacArthur and Patton, all read dozens or hundreds of books on the history of war. They didn't give a shit about tactics; they wanted to know the enemy. When you know your enemy better than he does himself, you automatically know the tactics you need to know to defeat him.

We took courses on aircraft engines and avionics and aerodynamics, navigation, code and even speed-reading. We didn't study the history of war. And even more criminal of an offence, we didn't study the history of the Vietnamese. As a result, we pissed away the lives of 58,209 American kids.

My mother gave me and my twin brother the gift of reading before we began school. I read the paper daily when I was only five. I started reading full-length adult novels and non-fiction when I was eight. I don't know how she did it but she gave my twin and me a wonderful skill.

I figured that if I was willing to risk my life to save the brave South Vietnamese from the evils of Communism, I should at least read up on the country and its customs. The best books on Vietnam and the history of the conflict seemed to come from a guy named Bernard Fall, who first traveled to Vietnam in 1953. I couldn't afford many books but I joined a book of the month club during flight training. One part of the club included books on war. I read everything that Bernard Fall wrote on the war. At first he seemed to feel that America could and should fight demon communism. As the war continued Fall became more critical as he realized the US was duplicating the mistakes of the French before them.

During WW II, Ho Chi Minh saved the lives of a number of Allied pilots and smuggled them past the Japanese lines to safety in India and Burma. History estimated that he tied down two to three divisions of Japanese concentrating on fighting him rather than defending small Pacific islands from landing Marines. It is a small but vital factoid of history that what would later be called the Viet Minh under Ho Chi Minh actually accepted the surrender of the Japanese in Vietnam in September of 1945, there being no Allied forces handy.

France then insisted the US and Britain disarm Ho's forces and allow the Japanese to be issued arms until the country could be turned back over to the French. All during WW II it was the Vichy French that controlled the administration of Vietnam, under the control of the Japanese military. We fought the Vichy French in France prior to the defeat of Germany but turned Vietnam over to those who had been our enemy in France. We turned our backs on those who had been our allies during the war.

I was young, only nineteen, and still believed in the wisdom of my country's leaders. They were sure to know a lot more about Vietnam and the war than I did. Our president and leaders of the military only wanted the best for America. Once I got to Vietnam I soon learned that was bullshit.

Again, the first part of training in the TF-9J and AF-9J was the aircraft systems and basics. The TF-9 was a two-seat former fighter nicknamed the Cougar. The AF-9 was a single seat Cougar that students flew when they didn't need an instructor in the back screaming at them.

The F-9 had been a state of the art real fighter operating off carriers just after the Korean War. We can only guess how the plane would have done against its Russian and Chinese equivalent, the MiG-15, as the F-9 never saw combat.

But it had guns, and anything with guns just had to be cool. The

AF-9 carried four of the 20 mm cannons; the TF-9 carried only two 20 mm guns.

Woodie Patton had saved me a bunk with him in the brand new BOQ. Once again we were roomies. Woodie was getting into the role of becoming a fighter pilot. He was dating a lovely young lady from town and they became rather close. He came back from liberty one night telling me how he had stood up in the seat of his VW with his upper body through the sunroof so he and his lady could get really close. She lay down on the top of the car and he stood up in the car. It must have been pretty contorted. He needed to get with the program so he went out and bought a 1966 Corvette. Frankly I don't know how you get much closer you can get to a young maiden in a Corvette than a friendly hand job.

As students in Advanced, we began to delve into the real nuts and bolts of the use of aircraft in combat. We completed our training in advanced instrument flying. Then we moved on to two-plane formation followed by four-plane formation. We laid out 250-mile long low-level navigation routes that we had to fly no higher than 1,000 feet. The cattle in Texas hated the training command. Eventually we got up to loading the planes with a dozen Mark-76 practice bombs. These blue wonders only weighed 25 pounds apiece but carried a smoke charge that went off when they hit the ground.

We did both 30-degree and 45-degree dive attacks on targets laid out in the Texas desert. Two elevated manned stations marked the angle from their station so the exact landing point of each practice bomb could be plotted. At a central location, someone would plot both angles from the observing stations and mark where the bombs hit.

My assigned instructor during Advanced was a Marine aviator named Captain Pereira. He was just back from a 13-month tour in Vietnam as an F-4B Phantom pilot. He told me to focus on the air-to-ground work more than the air-to-air. While the Navy operating off carriers in the Tonkin Gulf had a very real air-to-air role as well as their traditional air-to-ground role, the Marines in Vietnam needed close air support.

The Marines had no air-to-air role during the Vietnam War. While John Wayne may have encouraged a number of young men to become Marine fighter pilots as a result of the movie *Flying Leathernecks*, the

Marine Corps had little of the air-to-air war. Marines delivered close air support to the ground troops.

Captain Pereira was really tough on me during the air-to-air training. The instructor would take a student out to the air-to-air restricted area we used for "hassles." The two aircraft would fly at the same heading and airspeed until the instructor told the student to make a 90-degree turn away from the instructor. They would turn at the same time and when the instructor judged that sufficient spacing existed, he would tell the student to start a turn back in, so the two aircraft were at the same speed and altitude but on opposite courses. When the two planes crossed, the fight was on.

In theory, a student who knew how to dogfight should eventually be good enough to defeat the instructor at least sometimes. In practice, especially against an experienced F-4B pilot, the student really never had a chance. Pereira waxed my ass again and again. He thought it was very funny. I never had a chance. I did everything as smoothly as I could but rolling-scissors or high-speed yo-yo or whatever I tried to use to defeat him just didn't work.

Air-to-air combat is not like running a manufacturing company where being #2 in your industry is just fine, or like finishing in second place in the World Series, a mark of excellence. Coming in second in air-to-air combat means you just died. If you were lucky, you went home in a cheap aluminum box and lovely young women wailed at your funeral about how they should have banged you and didn't.

I simply couldn't beat Captain Pereira fairly in an even contest.

So I cheated. After all, the point about aerial combat isn't about how you win, it's about winning and coming home to bang lovely young ladies.

At takeoff the AF-9 had a maximum weight of about 20,000 pounds with a pilot and full fuel. Empty weight measured a little over 12,000 pounds. Call it 6,500 pounds for 1,000 gallons of JP-4.

If we had an emergency and needed to land, we could dump fuel to get down to a safe landing weight. I kept that in mind.

Aircraft performance in two identical aircraft has a lot to do with aircraft weight. A 16,000-pound AF-9 will outperform a 17,000-pound AF-9 even if the blubber-butt 17,000-pound AF-9 is flown by a more skillful and more experienced former F-4B driver who completed a full

13-month combat tour in Vietnam. That is, if a Marcad who would hate to be the second best in an aerial combat battle flies the 16,000-pound AF-9.

When we flew two-plane air-to-air training flights, the instructor would take off first, and once he was well down the runway the student would start his roll. After the instructor gained sufficient altitude for a safe turn, he would start a turn toward the operating area and allow the student to catch up.

Captain Pereira called for takeoff clearance for a flight of two planes. The tower cleared us for takeoff. After Pereira ran up to full power, he released his brakes and started his roll. I would follow him by thirty seconds. I watched the clock tick over the thirty seconds and added full power, released the brakes and started my takeoff roll.

The RPM spooled up and I began to show some airspeed on my steed. I reached over and flipped up the switch to begin dumping fuel. I wanted to dump about 1,000 pounds before Pereira began his turn and looked around for me.

The tower comes up on the radio and announces that the number two aircraft that just took off appears to be losing fuel. Snitching bastards, can't they worry about other things than my fuel state?

I had to walk a very narrow line on this flight. We both started with 6,500 pounds of JP-4. I managed to dump 1,000 pounds so for all practical purposes, he started with 6,500 pounds, I began with 5,500 pounds. But as an instructor, he had to monitor my fuel state. I couldn't exactly tell him I was 1,000 pounds lighter than he was or he would have figured out something funny was going on.

Getting caught might have been cause for getting my young ass bounced from the training command and sent back to the Fleet Marine Corps. But I was determined to be the best fighter pilot in the world and that means not being #2 to anyone.

So every time Pereira asked me my fuel state, I figured what I should have had and lowered it a little at a time. When I should have had 6,000 pounds, I said I had 5,900 left. When I should have had 5,500 pounds, I reported having 5,200, and so forth.

We reached our assigned altitude to begin the "hassle" and made our turns. Actually I could really feel the better performance as a result of being a lot lighter. I needed far less power to keep up with Captain

Pereira. As we turned inbound I rammed the throttle to the stop, determined to win this fight. I did.

We had another four or five fights. I won every one. Even Captain Pereira commented on how well I had learned my lesson and how much better I was doing as a result of being so smooth. Yea, right.

The fuel gauges on the AF-9 weren't all that accurate. Below 900 pounds you really didn't know what you had left, so as I remember we were required to be on the ground at 600 pounds. It was written in rock: 600 pounds. On the deck.

The Cougar airplane was made by Grumman Aircraft, manufacturer of many of the Navy fighters during WW II. We called them Grumman Ironworks for the quality and durability of their planes. They built sturdy aircraft. We did not call them Grumman Fuel Gauge Works. Some subcontractor made the gauges. Some subcontractor no doubt won the bid with the lowest price.

Since Captain Pereira had gotten waxed by a student a whole bunch of times – and I know that was a first – he decided we would play rather than go directly home. I had done sufficient lying about my fuel state that I was only 300 pounds off what I really had. Pereira started attacking the tops of clouds with me in a close trail on him. I realized that he intended to land when he had 600 pounds. The temperature in the cockpit seemed to increase and I could feel the sweat stain on the back of my cotton flight suit.

When we landed at Kingsville I had 400 pounds of fuel left on the gauge. I hoped no one would notice my plane took on a lot more JP-4 than normal.

Pereira actually seemed proud of the fact that I cleaned his clock in one-on-one air combat. He told all the other instructors about how a student beat him. All of a sudden I became the go-to student if an instructor wanted to show how shit-hot he was. I didn't cheat but I beat all of the other students I fought against in air-to-air and most of the instructors. One hot shot instructor seemed just as determined to beat me as I had been determined to beat Pereira. He pulled eight gees on the plane and actually bent a wing trying to out turn me. Actually Pereira did a pretty good job of teaching me. Being really smooth had a lot to do with my success. If you've got the name you have to act the part.

As Woodie and I got closer to graduation we began to pick up the items we needed to be real Marine officers. One such requirement was a set of dress blues. All the towns surrounding Navy flight training had their specialty shops delivering exactly what the students needed at any given phase of training. The best uniform shops were in Pensacola and Corpus Christi, home to the multi-engine training for the Navy.

Woodie and I purchased our dress blues in Pensacola and were dying to actually wear them. In November of 1966 we got our chance. Each year the Marines celebrate the birthday of the Corps on November 10. I had been out with a nice young lady attending college at Kingsville. I asked her to the ball, to be held in Corpus Christi. Unfortunately she had already made a commitment to another Marcad. I asked out my second choice and she agreed to go with me.

One tradition of the Corps is that at every Marine Corps birthday party, the oldest Marine present cuts the cake and gives the first piece to the youngest Marine. During boot camp we had no Marine Corps birthday; after all, we weren't Marines yet. But in 1965 at Saufley Field in VT-1, as the youngest Marine I got the first piece of cake. In Corpus in 1966 I was the youngest Marine and got the first piece of the cake. That tradition followed me. In Vietnam in 1969, by now a captain stationed in Da Nang, I was still the youngest Marine.

The ladies of the Marines present at the Marine Corps birthday showed up in their finest costumes and all wore their best war paint. I got drunk, pined over my preferred date who was with someone else and managed to piss off not only her but also my own pretty much ignored date. Then we all went down to the bay to have a last drink on Captain Pereira's sailboat. I was convinced I could walk on the lines holding the boat to the pier but managed to fall in the water and almost drown. I did learn that really well made dress blues handle salt water quite well.

While I went through Advanced in Kingsville, one of my instructors tried to get on the Blue Angels flight demonstration team. The Navy had a theory that all Naval Aviators could fly any standard airplane with the Blue Angels, given some basic training in the maneuvers. You needn't be a super aviator gifted with the touch of velvet; all you had to do was be good at doing parties. The Navy figured that anyone could learn to do a smart rendition of the flight routine but it took a real pro to handle a good party.

So potential team members from around the country would fly into wherever the Blues put on a show and would hang out with them for the weekend. You needed to be as cool at handling cooing young women as you were at sipping fine rum to qualify. Being a handsome devil helped as well.

My instructor asked if I was willing to fly backseat with him to Asheville, North Carolina, where the Blue Angels planned a two-day show. Dumb fucking question. Ask an aviation cadet if he wants to fly halfway across the country under no training pressure at all just to hang out with the coolest guys in aviation. In one of my courses, the instructor tried to make the point that there was no such thing as a stupid question, only stupid answers. If you had a question about a subject, someone else might have the same doubts but be afraid to ask the question in fear of being made fun of. But that question really was stupid.

We landed shortly before the Blue Angels. At the time they flew the F-11F aircraft. We flew the Grumman F-9F that wasn't all that different than the F-11. Other than the fact we were painted in the colors of the training command and they were bright blue. We were sorta cool. We climbed out of the plane in our sweat stained flight suits and lounged around just as if we were part of the show.

The mayor of the town approached us and introduced himself. I have no doubt he had never met or heard of a Marcad before. I also don't doubt he forgot our names two minutes after meeting us. "Anything you want, boys. Girls, marijuana, beer, booze," he continued under his breath, "just let me know what we can get you and you will have it."

I'm thinking, "Maybe after I fight the war in Vietnam I should think about getting on the Blues. This could be a lot of fun." My eyes were as big as saucers.

One more qualification for the Blues is probably that the pilot should be single. I cannot imagine how any marriage would survive a couple of years if the husband were one of the coolest pilots in the world. Women were handing Blue Angel pilots in their bright blue suits their hotel room keys wrapped up in their panties. I couldn't help but wonder if it didn't get a little cold down there without some whimsies covering up the goodies.

Many of the students in advanced training knew what planes they wanted to fly once past graduation. When I went to Galveston for Memorial Day on the *Lexington*, I got to see the primary jet attack and fighter aircraft the Marines and Navy pilots flew. In one line I saw an A-4, an F-4, the A-6 and F-8. Compared to the rest, the F-4 was this giant monster ready to take on the world. I wanted to be guiding that beast when it did.

So one of the important classes in Advanced was when representatives from actual squadrons showed up to tell us just how wonderful their aircraft was to fly, and why we should be an A-4 or F-4 or A-6 driver.

The A-4 pilot got up and talked for fifteen minutes about the sensation of rolling into a 60-degree dive at 16,000 feet and pickling ten 500-pound bombs at 8,000 feet before pulling back the stick into a 4-gee pullout, all the while dodging surface-to-air missiles in North Vietnam. I wasn't real sure how I felt about the SAM-dodging part but the plane sounded pretty cool.

The F-4 driver showed us a short film of an F-4 going into full afterburner on one of the big carriers just before taking a cat shot, the plane fully loaded with Sidewinders and Sparrow missiles. Then he talked about how neat it was to get into a dogfight where one mistake would result in sure death, but since the US built the best equipment and had the most highly trained pilots in the world we could not be defeated. I saw myself as Snoopy taking on the Red Baron. I wanted the F-4.

We even had a C-130 pilot come in and talk about how boring it was flying the ungainly giant cargo plane the Marines used, but once a pilot completed his tour of service the airlines would be standing in line waiting to hire him. The other students and I looked at each other and rolled our eyes. Imagine something as boring as doing your 1,200th trip into New York's JFK airport when you could be whipping around North Vietnam with half the country taking pot shots at you.

The final speaker didn't have an actual aircraft he could brag on. His bird was upcoming. They called the deadly craft the Cheyenne and it would be the hottest attack helicopter ever built. Rather than taking ground fire into lightly armed Bell Huey helicopters, the Cheyenne could carry a Gatling gun, loads of rocket pods, and could stand off from a mile away and blow targets to kingdom come. It sounded pretty cool if you liked the idea of flying a plane with 10,000 moving parts all moving in different directions and built by the lowest bidder. We certainly didn't have any of those sorts of folks in our group.

Graduation day from flight training always took place early on a Friday afternoon in Corpus Christi. The students who had completed their training in NAS Kingsville or NAS Beeville or NAS Corpus Christi all had to make the formation at 14:00.

I only had a few flights to complete. By now I had caught up to Woodie, who needed one aerial gunnery flight to finish. I needed an instrument check hop, a two-plane formation, a four-plane formation and an aerial gunnery flight to complete the syllabus.

For almost an entire week the weather remained soggy. Finally on Thursday, December 1 the skies cleared. I flew two of my four remaining flights that day. On Friday morning I was on the flight schedule for two back-to-back flights. The scheduling officer determined he was going to get me my wings that day come hell or high water.

I took off on the four-plane formation flight at about 07:30, flitted about the sky for an hour and landed. Finally I only had one flight to complete, the air-to-air gunnery mission. The other four students and tow plane were in the air fifteen minutes before I took off.

Jumping into the AF-9 I had been assigned, I soon got permission to taxi, went out to the arming area by the runway hold short area and held my hands on the top of the canopy so the arming crew could pull the pins that armed my guns. I carried 75 rounds of 20 mike-mike per gun, or 300 rounds total. I made my takeoff roll and as soon as I could, I made a turn for the beach. In both Pensacola and off Corpus Christi, we did our air-to-air gunnery practice over water.

My plane was fifty miles behind the rest of the flight. They began their passes on the banner five minutes before I even caught up with the tow plane. I was still in a climb but even at full throttle I barely made more speed than the tow since I was still several hundred pounds heavier than him. I slowly passed him and turned to cross over him. A properly executed perch was 1,500 feet above the tow plane when you began your firing run but there wasn't any way in hell I had enough energy available to the plane to make it. I started from a perch at about

800 feet above the tow and banner.

Still I had little closure rate on the tow plane. I turned in toward the banner and began my turn in order to be at 90 degrees to it when I reached the banner altitude. It seemed to take forever for the banner to fill my gun sight. As smoothly as I could I made my pass and put the pipper right on the center of the banner. I fired and could feel the thuds of the 20 mike-mikes all firing at the same time. I made three or four passes at the rag before my guns jammed. The tow told me to head back to Kingsville as fast as I could.

It was about noon when I landed. The ops officer told me to forget the squawk sheet and get my uniform on so I could get my commission and get up to Corpus for graduation. He would fill it out for me.

I leapt in the Spitfire and sped to the BOQ. Woodie was already there, showered, shaved and looking spiffy. I wiped off the sweat and leaped into my brand new winter green uniform. Woodie and I hadn't actually been commissioned but we had put the brown bars of a second lieutenant on weeks in advance. We didn't know if we should wear the bars or not, given that we hadn't actually gotten our commissions just yet.

"Screw it, Woodie. Wear them. All they can do is make us lance corporals, shave our heads and send us to Vietnam," I said.

At that point I was quite glad Woodie had a 'Vette. We needed the speed to be able to make it to Corpus on time. We drove over to the Marine Detachment, where the OIC swore us in as second lieutenants in five minutes, and ran back to the car to go to Corpus.

We made it to graduation with five minutes to spare. The fifty or so other students graduating that week were already in formation. The aide to the Admiral doing the honors took our names and told us our places in the formation.

And so on the second day of December 1966 I became Naval Aviator number 24483. I was twenty years old. My orders called for me to transfer to the 2nd Marine Aircraft Wing at Cherry Point, North Carolina. Flight training had taken almost exactly eighteen months to complete, in 295 hours of flying in four different aircraft. I had made four carrier landings and catapult shots in the T-2 and another three in the TF-9J.

I'd had a couple of dates with the sister of the wife of one of the

Marine officers that went through flight training with me. The weather was a little nippy that day in December when we got our wings. I could see her and my friend's wife standing just inside the door staying warm while we were in formation outside in the sun and the chill.

I was thinking to myself, "Maybe I'll get lucky tonight."

The graduation ended. The formation broke up and we began to mill around as family and friends surrounded us. I felt a hand on my arm, and as I turned around another female I had dated planted a nice wet kiss on my mouth just as my friend's sister in law came up to us. The two women each realized they intended to surprise the same new brown bar Naval Aviator at the exact same time. Each thought to themselves, "Three into two won't go," turned around and left. I ended up with no date.

Dejected, I returned to NAS Kingsville with Woodie. We went to the club for our last happy hour and shared our completion of flight training with all our friends. One of the guys who had been on the air-to-air flight with me told me that someone on the flight had literally torn up the banner with dozens of hits. Since five or six hits was actually pretty good shooting and would knock down an aircraft, tearing up the banner had to be brilliant shooting.

I got to a phone and called the ordnance unit to ask whose bullets had mangled the banner. The fellow still in the shop said he didn't know who it was but it was someone shooting blue bullets. I had been shooting blue bullets. So on my very last flight in the training command I did something no other student had done in 1966. I hit the banner enough times to earn an "E" (Excellent) for aerial gunnery. I not only could shoot an M-14 and make expert, I could do the same thing with an F-9J and 20 mm guns.

I'd love to take credit and say it was my brilliance but actually it probably had more to do with the fact that my squirrel cage pattern around the tow plane was so much slower than the speed we normally flew that I had more time coming into the banner to shoot. Everyone else may have had three or four seconds of prime firing position; I had ten seconds or more. But it did mean that if you wanted to shoot with great accuracy, you didn't want a great closure speed on your target.

Chapter 11

VMFA-531 and VMFA-513, MAG 24 CHERRY POINT, NORTH CAROLINA

There must be lights burning brighter somewhere
Got to be birds flying higher in a sky more blue
If I can dream of a better land
Where all my brothers walk hand in hand
Tell me why, oh why, oh why can't my dream come true
There must be peace and understanding sometime
Strong winds of promise that will blow away

All the doubt and fear
If I can dream of a warmer sun
Where hope keeps shining on everyone
Tell me why, oh why, oh why won't that sun appear

We're lost in a cloud, with too much rain
We're trapped in a world that's troubled with pain
But as long as a man has the strength to dream
He can redeem his soul and fly
Deep in my heart there's a trembling question
Still I am sure that the answer gonna come somehow
Out there in the dark, there's a beckoning candle

And while I can think, while I can talk
While I can stand, while I can walk
While I can dream, please let my dream
Come true, right now
Let it come true right now
Oh yeah

I Can Dream
Songwriter: Walter Earl Brown
Copyright: Imagem U.S. LLC 1967

MY ORDERS REQUIRED ME to report to MAG 24 in Cherry Point, North Carolina just after New Year's 1967. MAG 24 consisted of an A-6 squadron, a C-130 squadron and a couple of F-4B squadrons. Since I was determined to be a fighter pilot, John Wayne notwithstanding, I wanted to arrive at MCAS Cherry Point a few days early so I could wait for a billet to open up in a fighter squadron.

As I write, I just did a Google search for MAG 24 to see where they are based today and what aircraft they fly. My point about the lack of sense in assigning women to combat is reinforced on the current home page of the Group. At the top is a picture and the name of a somewhat ugly looking fellow who is the Commanding Officer of the Group. Under him is a picture of a nice smiling fellow who probably is the Executive Officer. Next to him is another picture of a grim looking fellow who is the Sergeant Major of the Group. I've rarely seen a sergeant major smile unless he had just run over a puppy so I saw pretty much what I expected.

To my utter lack of surprise, under the command pictures, I find the picture of a young and attractive female Navy Petty Officer with the title of MAG 24 Uniformed Victim Advocate. Above her picture we got to the gist of her position. She was in charge of the "Sexual Assault Prevention and Response Page".

In 1967 we didn't have people worrying about sexual assaults, but then we didn't pretend women and men were exactly the same. We knew there was a difference. Looking at the ages of the dead on the Vietnam Wall points out that war is a young man's game. To be more correct now that I'm all gray, it's a kids' game. We send kids of eighteen and nineteen off to war to die believing their government cares about them. They are too dumb to be able to think for themselves. Why go shoot at someone who hasn't done anything to you, but who will shoot back if you piss him off enough? Only idiots or fools shoot at people for no reason.

Over the past fifty years our society – I'm hesitant to call it a civilization because we aren't there yet – our society has come to the absurd conclusion that we need women in combat so we can prove they are the same as men. Well, that's bullshit. There are 195 countries in the world. One of those countries feels that women belong in combat. All the rest restrict combat to men. Now granted, since the US has started

81 per cent of all the wars since 1945, we know a hell of a lot more about bombing the shit out of other countries than anyone else does. But if we are so enlightened, why is it that no one else gets it? Are our young women different than their counterparties in other countries?

A long time ago I was eighteen and nineteen and twenty and all I thought about was sex. That's how we make more generations. Young people think about sex all the time. They can barely wait to tear the clothes off their chosen partner. When you add in the spice of getting shot at or having to work in an especially dangerous occupation, you just add jet fuel to the fire.

Think about the future that will soon be here. Rabbits trained to be robots will operate aircraft carriers and submarines. What do you think the CO of those ships is going to be thinking about 24/7? That's right, he's going to be thinking about how to keep the cute little bunnies from fucking like rabbits because that's all rabbits think about, too.

I can't even imagine the rigors of command on a closed ship with a bunch of horny young men and a handful of horny young women. You might as well turn off the hot water system because they will all need regular cold showers.

The fact that the United States felt that it had both the right and the obligation to start 81 per cent of the wars in the world since World War II pretty much defines insanity, but to believe you can pack young people together without sex constantly rearing its head is beyond world-class stupid.

I'm not anti-women. Women can do most of the things men can. But until they can start writing their signature in the snow in their own handwriting when peeing, women do not belong in combat.

What have we gained with the sacrifice on the gilded altar of political correctness of the tiny bit of our sanity still remaining? I continue to hear the refrain of President Putin echo in my ears, "Do you realize what you have done?" Offering young women the opportunity to die for absolutely no reason at all in the same way we let young men die for nothing is not an advancement in equality unless you have lost your moral rudder.

If rape is a problem in any organization, you are asking people to do things together in a way nature doesn't approve.

In the Marine Corps you did not get an aircraft assignment out of flight training. You got assigned to a Marine Air Group and took whatever became open when you got to the base. With the Navy pilots, their scores counted right up until they finished flight school. The guys with the highest grades got their choice of aircraft. Everyone else got the leavings.

When Marines entered basic jet training, the need to compete in academics or flying stopped. As long as you passed all your check rides and academic courses, didn't burn up your mask smoking a cigarette or get caught dumping fuel on the runway during takeoff, you were pretty sure to graduate.

The only issue was really which coast you ended up getting sent to. The Marine Corps had a pretty well set-in-concrete rule that all Marine bases had to be located in the worst places in the country.

The Air Force put their bases in some of the best places in the US. You had your choice of being near San Francisco or Los Angeles. If you preferred the sun of Florida and fishing you could be assigned to MacDill in Tampa or Homestead, south of Miami. Those with young children might opt to go to Patrick Air Force base on the east coast of Florida so the little ankle biters can make regular trips to Disney World.

Navy bases allowed their aviators to fly out of Miramar, close to San Diego, or several bases in the San Francisco Bay area. On the east coast they planted airstrips in Key West and Jacksonville and Norfolk, Virginia for those who enjoyed four seasons.

What did the Marine Corps do? We put all our bases in the most godawful, military-hating places in the country. Yuma, Arizona; the biggest attraction there is the old Yuma jail where they put prisoners in cages about the size of a telephone booth so they could bake in the 120-degree sun. Cherry Point, North Carolina. The guys I flew with called it Cherryless Point because there wasn't a virgin female within 200 miles. I was stationed there for eighteen months and never once went out on a date with a local. By then, mud fences started looking pretty good.

For those who hated the flat and boring dripping heat of North Carolina, there was always the flat and boring dripping heat of South Carolina, at Beaufort. We did have one nice base located in El Toro, California. But you had to be senior to the Commandant Marine Corps to get stationed there. The Marine Corps closed El Toro after the Vietnam War on the grounds it was too nice a place to be stationed.

Every Navy and Marine Corps base used to have uniformed Marines guarding the gates. As we passed, we would comment, "In 190 years of guarding gates, the Marine Corps has never had a single gate stolen."

In 1997 the Marines stole a whole Naval Air Station when they commandeered the base at Miramar from the Navy. That's pretty cool.

Once at Cherry Point I checked into the BOQ. While in the training command I was warned to always check in a few days early so I could see which way the winds blew. I had my heart set on flying the F-4B fighter but every other new aviator wanted the same thing.

Early the next morning I went down to Wing to speak with the operations officer about what was available. It was a good move on my part. If I had checked in that same day, he would have had to assign me to an A-6 squadron since there were no spots in either of the two F-4 units.

The ops officer was Major Donald Waunch. Our paths would cross again and again during my time in the Marines. He recommended I come in each morning to see the status of open spots. It was good advice. I came in the next day and I had the choice of either VMFA-531 or VMFA-513. Major Waunch casually mentioned that he was going to be transferring to VMFA-531 in a couple of weeks, and that in his view it was a good outfit. So I took the open space.

Naturally, Second Lieutenant Patton also carried orders to Cherry Point. He arrived on the date he was supposed to show up and still got into 531.

Before we actually got to the squadron, the Group required us to go through an instrument flight refresher in a TF-9 unit used to bring people up to speed on instruments and procedures to be used in the Cherry Point region. Since we had been current in the plane a month before, it was like slipping on a familiar old pair of worn out jeans.

In the TF-9 used for instrument recertification at Cherry Point, we did five flights and a check ride before being turned loose to join the squadron we were assigned to. No longer treated as just a student and an aviation cadet of uncertain lineage, the increased status as a second lieutenant wore well. All the enlisted men saluted us, including the vast majority who were older. I went from a Private E-1 earning $78 a month to a commissioned officer and fighter pilot in just over two years in the

Corps. I had earned my wings and now it was time to earn my spurs, as I would do on every job I would ever hold.

The caste system was alive and well in the Marine Corps. Some of the obvious frills of status such as the swagger stick had been shitcanned. Carried during WW II and Korea as a measure of authority dating back as far as the Roman Empire, a swagger stick is a short version of a cane, used as an accessory to the uniform.

Finally in 1960, the Commandant, General David Shoup, announced in a comment on uniforms and accessories that "There is no need for gimmicks and gadgets." The swagger stick could still be carried if an officer felt he needed the validation of rank, but the use died almost immediately. I entered the Corps in 1964 and never saw a swagger stick being carried by anyone. Perhaps people realized that while the Romans looked cool in their mess dress uniforms while carrying the swagger stick, their empire also collapsed as a result of military adventurism.

When we checked into the base at Cherry Point we were assigned to single officer BOQ rooms. There was then a minor revolt among the junior officers about having to live permanently in what was in effect a nice motel room. Complaints were made up the chain of command about the quarters not meeting the regulations on space and quality. The Marine Corps bent and started giving junior officers the housing allowance their rank justified. We all moved off base into rented accommodations nearby.

I got together with a couple of other guys in the squadron and rented a three-bedroom place out on a barrier island. We were living in heaven. Gas for our gas-guzzlers cost twenty-nine cents a gallon. I think our total rent was $250 a month. I could drive back and forth the 25 miles to the base every day for about $50 a month in fuel. True, there weren't any women within 500 miles, but that's what they made airplanes for.

I don't remember the specific courses but we had three weeks of systems training on all the various parts of the F-4. The aircraft had a basic weight of around 30,000 pounds. That was 30,000 pounds of avionics and some of the most complex wiring and hydraulics known to man. We had to understand how each part of the plane worked and which of the hundreds of dials and switches made things go or stop.

Once we finished the ground familiarization course on the F-4 we had to do more simulator hours for both aircraft systems knowledge and instrument flight. That course consisted of an additional forty hours sitting in a multi-million dollar machine with some enlisted guy who in his heart hated second lieutenants, so he threw every possible emergency at the fledgling pilots.

I have deliberately forgotten how many times I crashed and burned in the simulator. Some things remain best ignored.

Both the Navy and the Marines flew the F-4 Phantom II built by McDonnell Douglas as a single pilot, two-man crew plane. We had a pilot in the front seat and an RIO (Radar Intercept Officer) in the rear cockpit. In the Air Force version of the aircraft they carried pilots in both crew positions. The Air Force bird had control sticks in each position. While the pilot in the rear cockpit had primary responsibility for tweaking and controlling the radar, in an emergency the rear seat pilot could land the plane.

The Navy and Marines gave the responsibility for use of the radar to especially well trained officers who wanted to fly but for one reason or another didn't become pilots. They became RIOs.

In my opinion, the Navy way made a lot more sense. Anything that blows a hole in a plane that incapacitates the front seat occupant usually takes out the entire aircraft. World War II aircraft were known for their ability to take damage, including engine damage. In one case, a B-17 was rammed by a Messerschmitt fighter and still managed to fly back to England safely. When the crew landed, the tail literally fell off the plane.

With modern jet aircraft from the 1950s on, the aircraft are so complex that one bullet in the right place could knock down the plane.

As opposed to life as a cadet, being a pilot and an officer in the Marine Corps in the 1960s ranked high on the "neat things to do" list. As a result of having two-man crews, the F-4 squadrons had almost twice the number of officers that the single seat squadrons such as the F-8 and the A-4 had. So the collateral duties got spread out a lot more.

All Navy and Marine officers have a primary MOS that shows what they do for a living. I was an F-4 pilot, a 7521 MOS. But we would be assigned other duties depending on what classes we had been through or any specialty we were qualified in. In between doing my instrument refresher in the TF-9 in January of 1967 and making my first F-4B flight in March of 1967 I got sent to ALO (Air Liaison Officer) school in Norfolk, Virginia. There we did training so we could control naval gunfire from ships offshore, fire artillery batteries and control air strikes. We were really getting into the fun stuff. In Vietnam I would end up controlling everything from 81 mm mortars to the 16-inch guns on the battleship *New Jersey*. So I also had a secondary MOS as an ALO. I didn't have or need an office; I didn't have to monitor any other troops. I didn't have to do anything except stand by every few months to be called up with the duty battalion stationed at Camp Lejeune, North Carolina.

All of the services maintain a certain level of readiness at all times. The Marines had a duty battalion on standby on both the east coast at Camp Lejeune and the west coast at Camp Pendleton. In case of a national emergency requiring the use of troops *right now*, the duty battalion could be packed and prepared to fly, combat ready, in 24 hours. While I was stationed at Cherry Point, about fifty miles north of Camp Lejeune, standing by was more of a theory than a practice. If we were called up, I needed an hour to get to Lejeune.

Finally the big moment came. I had wanted to fly the F-4B since the first time I saw one. It did a better job of turning JP-4 jet fuel into noise than any aircraft ever built. Equipped with twin J-79 GE engines capable of putting out a total of 34,000 pounds of thrust, the plane could do Mach 2.2. I wanted it. On March 14, 1967 our crewman slipped me fully equipped into the rear seat of the only two-stick F-4B we had. My instructor took me out to bore holes in the sky for an hour and a half, just to get a feel for the bird. I was in heaven.

We landed, debriefed and prepared for another flight. While I flew seventeen different planes in my six years in the USMC, I didn't fly the other high performance jets like the A-4 or A-6. So I can't comment on how they take off, but I know their thrust to weight ratio was a lot lower. The basic weight of the F-4B was just over 29,500 pounds and at full afterburner we produced 34,000 pounds of thrust. Taking off with full wing drop tanks, the plane only weighed about 48,000 pounds.

Once cleared for takeoff, we would taxi onto the duty runway. At that weight we could release the brakes and go into full afterburner with the stick fully in your lap. We eased the stick forward as we gained airspeed until we felt the nose lifting off the runway. I remember a

48,000-pound plane using something like 2,500 feet of runway to take off. Landing was entirely different; if you were heavy it was going to take a long time to get stopped.

We got ready for takeoff. Nervously I pushed the button on the side of the stick that controlled the nose wheel steering to wobble out to the runway. I completed my flight checks and called for takeoff clearance. I eased out onto the runway, stopped the plane, and did a final instrument and control check just as if I actually could think that far ahead with the stick of the world's hottest fighter between my legs. We got permission to take off, the instructor said he was locked in and ready. Off we went.

An F-4B takes off the same way a plane gets shot off a carrier. You have so much power that you have this giant shove on your butt. The next thing you realize is that you are doing 200 knots and you had better get the gear up damned quick. You pop the gear handle up and flip up the flap switch. If you are not careful, you are already though 5,000 feet.

With two wing drop tanks on the F-4B you are carrying about 18,000 pounds of JP-4. We rarely carried the 600-gallon centerline drop but almost always used the 370-gallon tanks on each wing. In full afterburner and at low level below 10,000 feet we could burn up all our fuel in twenty minutes. It was actually easy to figure fuel burn and time left. Basically we set the power at 6,000 pounds an hour. Depending on your altitude, you could fly for almost three hours. I'm not sure the butts of many pilots could handle the hard pack of the survival kit we sat on for that long, but the airplane had a three-hour range.

That was the most awe-inspiring flight I ever made. Here I was, twenty years old, in the front seat of the hottest fighter aircraft in the entire world, burning jet fuel like I didn't have to pay for it. I had handsome uniforms with which to impress the pretty girls, got paid to fly, and lived right on the nicest tourist beach in North Carolina. I didn't have a worry in the world.

Glancing around, I looked at really old people in their fifties and sixties and thought, "Golly, I hope I never get that old. I hope they shoot me first." I couldn't imagine having a body falling apart, bad hearing and only distant memories of the morning hardon. I would have far rather died first. But at sixty-nine I look at the 20 and 25-year-old kids and think about how I'm so much happier to be my age than theirs.

If they knew anything about the world we built for them, and the debt trap that their grandkids will have to climb out of, they would hang all the old farts from the nearest yardarm.

I flew about ten flights in the F-4B in March of 1967 before the squadron left for a three-week stay in Yuma, Arizona for the air-to-ground training that we did every quarter.

When we arrived in Yuma I had the weekend off, so I jumped on a courier plane going to NAS Miramar so I could visit with a companion from pre-flight who was going through fighter training at Miramar. His name was Troy Nicks and he was going through the Navy fighter weapons program.

I woke up on the Sunday morning while Troy and his wife Judy were at church. I felt sick and was passing blood. When they got home they realized something was wrong and took me out to the Sick Call at Miramar. The doctor walked into the room and looked around to see just how sick the people were that he needed to attend to. He took one look at me and told me to go into his office for an examination at once.

It turned out that I had a bleeding ulcer and needed immediate medical care. Troy took me to the Naval Hospital San Diego at Balboa. They admitted me and started pumping blood into me.

In 1967 medical authorities believed that ulcers were caused by stress. I qualified I suppose for that diagnosis, as flight training is stressful. But ulcers are not caused by stress. You can't cure them with bland diets. A type of bacteria causes inflammation of the stomach lining. The disease is easily cured today with a heavy dose of intravenous antibiotics. Back then no one knew that.

I continued to bleed. They put a second needle in my other arm and started feeding me blood through both arms. I had no idea how critical my state was. I think I went through twenty pints of blood. That's two full refills. Getting that many transfusions can kill people all by itself. I had the giant advantage of being young and in prime health. With the exception of the ulcer, of course.

My doctor made the decision to carry out a partial gastrostomy. They would cut out half my stomach and hopefully the worst that would happen is that I would bleed out only half as fast. The doctor made one more inspection of me while a corpsman was shaving my groin and chest hairs in preparation for the operation. He saw how pale I was turning and made the decision to operate at once. He also instructed the corpsman to install needles in both ankles, so I had blood going in four places at the same time.

I died.

Really. I died.

I went through the whole out-of-body experience. I floated above the bed and got to watch the corpsman shave my groin with a razor. I wanted to tell him to be careful around the family jewels. I didn't exactly hit the roof; I was just floating around looking at all the interesting things going on in the room.

I did inspect the metal lockers we kept our clothes in. Whoever else inspected them hadn't been doing a very good job. When you are floating near the roof, you can see all the dust on the tops of the lockers that people have been ignoring. For a hospital, they weren't all that concerned about cleanliness. My drill instructor at either boot camp or preflight certainly would have caught the dust.

It seemed like it was time for me to leave so I sort of floated away to a dark tunnel that had a very bright light at the end. I was pretty sure it wasn't Johnson's "light at the end of the tunnel." When I got there a bunch of people I was related to but had never met before greeted me. I had a wonderful feeling of contentment and freedom from pain and worry.

Then a bureaucrat or someone came along and told me that I couldn't stay even though everyone wanted me to stay. I had things that I had to do so I was sent back.

I woke up in a hospital bed missing half my stomach but having this giant scar up my chest. I don't remember telling people about the dust on the lockers but I did chat with my doctor. He said that I had actually died on the operating table. He seemed shocked when I told him that I knew.

To this day I don't understand what happened. I've read other descriptions of the out-of-body experience and they are all about the same. I felt a great feeling of peace and contentment. In any case, when you have gone through the whole process, you no longer fear death. It's one of those "been there, done that" experiences.

The hospital kept me for a week or so and then I flew back to Cherry Point to recover. I was up and about shortly but couldn't fly as pilot-in-command until I could pass my flight physical. Literally there was a fair danger that I would never fly as a Marine pilot again.

But part of the reason we send kids off to war is that they recover the quickest. My health soon recovered and I was eager to fly.

Without a full medical and return to active duty, legally I couldn't fly as pilot-in-command of any Marine planes but there was no such restriction on flying copilot on aircraft requiring two pilots. Given the choice between a copilot and a wet soggy sandwich, I would make the same choice as everyone else; I would opt for the wet soggy sandwich in a heartbeat. But beggars can't be choosers and another lonely weekend in Cherry Point would have driven me over the edge. I went to the H&MS (Headquarters & Maintenance Squadron) and asked the operations officer if they needed copilots for any of their trips coming up.

Ask a man in the desert dying of thirst if he wants a drink of water and you will get the same response I received. The ops officer acted as if I had just handed him the Holy Grail.

In each Marine Air Group there is a headquarters squadron that has a bunch of strange aircraft. They are old and used but still serviceable. When colonels and generals want to take a cross-country, they call the H&MS and schedule a flight. Of course, most often this is on weekends. Or some Wing-wienie will need a trip somewhere to get his four hours that month to qualify for flight pay. Most often they need copilots. And since all the married guys want to spend quality time at home with the mother of their kiddies and the little ankle biters, copilots are about as rare as chickens wearing necklaces of hens' teeth.

So every weekend I went somewhere. I flew the US-2B, the UC-45, the T-33, the T-1, the C-117, the T-28 and the UH-34. Without a doubt, there wasn't anyone in the entire Marine Corps qualified in as many airplanes at the same time. You need to remember, I didn't have to pay for the fuel or the lunches and I got a paycheck twice a month. This was exactly like dying and going to heaven.

At the end of one week the operations officer of the H&MS unit called and asked me if I could do a trip to Washington DC, leaving Saturday morning and coming back Monday. I needed to ask the duty officer at VMFA-531 if I could be off half a day on Monday; he had no problem with it.

I could sense something in the tone of voice of the ops officer from H&MS. He was trying to tell me something without saying it. He asked if I could make the trip, I said yes, and I showed up bright and early Saturday morning.

One thing I learned early on in my short career as a copilot is that the PIC is usually both senior to you and lazy. I was a second lieutenant. Hell, everyone in the Marine Corps was senior to me. But when the PICs got to the airplane they wanted it already preflighted, fueled, lunches ordered, a weather brief ready to read, and if I knew where we were going, to have a flight plan filed. In short they wanted all the crap done they should have been doing themselves. But keep in mind; they were all senior to me. So this Saturday morning I preflighted the plane, I ordered lunches, I filed a flight plan, the weather brief was ready and we had full fuel.

Then the shit hit the proverbial fan. The Commanding General of MCAS Cherry Point drove up to the operations building with the red flag on the fender of his car showing his two stars. This was Marion Carl, the fifth highest scoring Marine Corps ace during WW II. He fought at the Battle of Midway and shot down two Japanese aircraft on his first mission.

At Midway, the Marine defenders sent up 28 aircraft. Only ten survived to land and only two of the 28 planes could be patched up to fly another mission. He was in one of the two. Marion Carl as a captain at Midway earned the Navy Cross, the second highest decoration for valor. At Guadalcanal he shot down an additional 16.5 Japanese planes. He was the first of 118 USMC pilots to become an ace.

When the car with the general's flag on the bumper drove up, my heart stopped. For a silly moment I imagined that he would be my PIC on my cross-country. But when General Carl got out of the vehicle, he was wearing his dress greens uniform. Nobody flies in dress greens. But I was more than a bit nervous even being around someone so senior. He was the senior officer on the base and I was probably the junior officer at Cherry Point.

He walks up to me, standing at attention in my green Nomex flight suit. He glances over at the plane and then looks at me. The guy was about six foot three inches tall and I'm five foot eight, so he looks down as if he's peering at a midget.

"You flying this, Lieutenant?" he growled.

I was still holding a salute that he hadn't yet returned. I had never actually met or saluted a general before. I wasn't totally comfortable with what I was supposed to do other than wanting to crap in my pants.

"Sir, I'm waiting for the pilot. I'm just the copilot."

He returned the salute. I could drop my salute and just stand there like a brick until he was good enough to go away.

"Plane preflighted?" he asked in a grunt.

"Yes, sir," I stammered in response.

"Got fuel?"

"Yes, sir, it's fully fueled."

"Lunches?"

By this time I was getting a terrible feeling in my stomach. He didn't act as if he had some general interest in the status of the plane; he acted like it was his plane. And as Commanding General of the Wing and the base, I suppose it was his airplane.

"Yes, sir."

"Flight plan filed?"

"Yes, sir."

"Well, what the hell are you waiting for?" he finally asked.

In surrender to my worst fear, I responded with great hopes for the future, "Sir, I'm waiting for the pilot."

"Humph. What the hell do I look like?" he demanded.

I thought about it for a minute or two so I could give him the best answer I could.

"Well, you look like a living legend in the Marine Corps. You look like one of the bravest and most skillful pilots at the battle of Midway. You personally were responsible for convincing the Japanese Task Force commander that he needed to have his planes unload the torpedoes that they had been armed with on the four Japanese carriers and reloaded with bombs so the airfield at Midway could be bombed a second time. That delay in changing weapons on the planes meant that the American carrier Task Force led by Admiral Ray Spruance was able to catch the Japanese carriers with aircraft being reloaded and refueled on the deck. The Japanese lost the battle because of the bravery of a Marine Corps Captain named Marion Carl.

"You look like the Marines' first ace, a winner of the Navy Cross and a guy who shot down 18.5 enemy aircraft. You look like one of the most experienced Marine test pilots in history and the first Marine to fly supersonic. You look like the fighter pilot I'd like to become."

I thought all that.

I didn't say it. I'm not fucking daft. I did spend a lot of time thinking about how maybe this is what the operations guy was trying to warn me about and didn't have the guts.

You can't fly piston airplanes wearing Marine dress green uniform. So General Carl pulled a well-worn orange cotton flight suit out of the trunk of his car and slipped it over his dress greens. You can't fly in dress greens unless you put on a flight suit over them, I suppose.

He got in. I got in. He didn't say a word, just mangled switches and set instruments as if he had been doing this fifty hours a month for the last year. I would never see another pilot quite as comfortable in a plane as Marion Carl. Any plane, any time. He didn't fly them, he wore them.

I would fly a number of trips as Marion Carl's copilot. I never lost my absolute and total feeling of terror at the idea of flying with the Base Commander. He flew. I sat and occupied the right seat. He did all the radio work. I sat in silence. On every trip he did about the same thing. We would file an instrument flight plan, and just as soon as we could fly in visual conditions he would cancel the instrument flight plan and continue under visual flight rules (VFR).

He never made a single VFR position report as you are supposed to. He left it up to me to make sure to cancel the flight plan at the end of the trip. We would go up to 10,000 feet or whatever the correct altitude was for our direction of flight. Then he would go to sleep. He never said a word to me. I would wait until the aircraft slipped ten degrees or so off course and as casually as possible I would ease my hand under the yoke and have it drift back to our correct course. I was in a total panic. I wouldn't have dreamed of taking the yoke in both hands and flying the plane. I think he would have broken my wrist if I tried. Clearly he was the pilot. He did the flying and I was in charge of flight plans and lunches.

We would cruise along for a couple of hours with me making tiny corrections. Just about the time we needed to begin our descent, he would wake up, shake a little to get the blood moving again, and he would grab the yoke. No one, no one else flew an airplane when Marion Carl was aboard.

When I got back from the trip on Monday, I went over to the 531 hanger to check in and see what was going on. The duty officer told me I was in big trouble and I needed to see the CO (Commanding Officer) as soon as I got back. I went to his office and tapped on the door.

"Lieutenant Moriarty, you are an F-4 pilot. You do not have my permission to fly any aircraft for any unit other than VMFA-531. No more cross-countries for any reason. Do we have an understanding?" he barked.

"Sir, yes sir." That's all I could say.

"Get out of my office. NOW."

I guess I had been told. My career as a copilot seemed doomed to destruction.

Later that week I got a call from the H&MS operations officer, again asking if I was available for another cross-country to Pensacola, Florida. I filled him in on what my squadron CO had said. The ops guy seemed disappointed that he had lost a wingman of sorts.

Ten minutes later I had another notice to appear in front of the squadron CO. I wasn't looking forward to it. I gingerly entered his office.

"Ah, Lieutenant Moriarty, it's so good to see you. Go ahead and have a seat. Would you like some coffee?" he asked in the most pleasant of voices. I was wondering where the aliens had taken the real CO who had breathed fire at me earlier in the week, and if they were going to return him.

"I've just had a conversation with General Carl and he was wondering if you were around this weekend and if you could fly with him. I told him that I would check and make sure you were available to him anytime he needs you, day or night. Do we have an understanding?" he asked in a soft voice.

"Sir, does this mean I can fly anything any time with the H&MS?" I thought I should at least try to expand the flight envelope.

"Of course. We are proud of having General Carl's copilot in our unit and you can do anything you want, any time you want." He smiled and we drank our cooling coffee. I hate coffee but when the CO gives you a cup, you drink.

I would learn later that every potential copilot on the base was terrified of Marion Carl. He never talked, he just snarled. And since they all wanted to kiss ass and get promoted, he hated them and they hated or feared him. I was a second lieutenant. I was terrified of majors and anything higher, so I couldn't possibly be more scared if I was flying with JC himself.

I also found out that not a single pilot had ever touched the yoke while flying with the general. I know he let me fly the plane but I always thought that he liked me because he always got a smooth flight.

One day, coming back from Michigan flying the US-2B, one of the chip warning lights came on for the left engine. The chip lights in the R-1820 engines were magnets with electrical wires that would short and show a light when there were metal particles collecting on the magnet. It was an indication there might be a serious engine problem coming. Regulations required an immediate landing at the nearest suitable airport and inspection by a mechanic.

We were humming along VFR at 9,500 feet. General Carl was sleeping; I touched the yoke now and again to maintain our heading. The light came on. He woke up. He looked at the light, looked at the engine, looked at the temps and oil pressure and unscrewed the light. We flew on and continued our leg back to Cherry Point.

Marion Carl qualified as a warrior. Perhaps it rubs off, but he was the smoothest pilot I ever flew with. He certainly understood what rules to obey and what rules you could ignore.

Phantom pilots who couldn't fly the front seat were pretty useless. Don Waunch had arrived in VMFA-531 and became operations officer. He liked the fact that he had a good pilot he could shove in the back seat of the F-4 so he used me to help other struggling pilots. I went on a bunch of cross-countries with senior officers who were transitioning to the F-4 before being transferred from desk jobs to commanding squadrons in Vietnam. I soon realized most of the pilots simply weren't all that good. They could take off and land but they weren't smooth.

The squadron also sent me to every oddball school that Group needed a warm body for. One of the schools was the month-long Army Basic Intelligence course at Fort Holabird, Maryland.

The basic intelligence school the Army taught was the first course that every intelligence officer or spook in the Army or Navy or Marines went through. I got there in early June of 1967. The first thing the instructor did was to assign every student a country to study, with a report to be prepared on the war-making capability of that country. I was assigned Israel.

That turned interesting. Israel began the Six Day War on June 5 by having its Air Force destroy the entire Air Force of Egypt in a surprise attack. I got notice that the duty battalion at Camp Lejeune had been put on standby and might well be called up for immediate action in the Middle East. I'm sitting in Maryland and I'm supposed to be ready to get on a plane in North Carolina in six hours if called up. I got in touch with the operations officer of the duty battalion and told him where I was. He told me that if they got notified to mount up, he would send a plane to pick me up. I was less than six hours from war on a front that I never even thought might be at risk of war.

My report on the war-making capability of Israel determined that since the army was made up with a small core unit and a lot of reserves called up from civilian life and business, Israel had to end the war in no more than a week or its financial system would collapse. And of course that's exactly what they did.

I was in Baltimore when the reports came in of the "accidental" attack on the USS *Liberty* by the Israeli Air Force and Navy. Israel killed 34 American servicemen and civilians aboard the US spy ship and 171 more were wounded.

Israel protested that it was all a mistake and that they didn't intend to attack the US warship. Crewmembers on the *Liberty* remain convinced the attack was deliberate. Israel of course had committed a number of attacks on US interests over the years, including the Lavon affair in Egypt in 1954 and the Pollard case where a Zionist spy did billions of dollars' worth of damage to US intelligence work.

The attack on the USS *Liberty* showed the highest casualty rate of any attack on any US Navy vessel in history, with seven out of every ten crew either killed or injured. We knew it was deliberate. Israel wanted to send the US a message and was trying to drag the US into helping them fight the war.

I wish I had been the admiral in charge of the USS *Saratoga*. If I had been in charge, I would have ordered every fighter and bomber on the *Saratoga* to be loaded with a full combat load. I would have sunk every vessel in the Israeli Navy bigger than a bathtub. And if anyone had tried to attack my planes I would have shot them down.

Warriors don't necessarily do what they are ordered to do; they do what is right.

Much of the chaos in the Middle East today can be directly traced to America's blind and mindless support of anything Israel wants to do. In 1947 America had no enemies in the Middle East. By 1948 we had no friends.

Our class at the Basic Intelligence school consisted mostly of about 95 Army second lieutenants, all college graduates who had just been drafted. To a man they figured being a spook was a lot safer than commanding a grunt platoon out in the jungle. One giant difference I soon recognized between the Army and the Marine Corps was that even in 1968-1969, at the height of the war, Marines wanted to get into combat. The Army draftees made it crystal clear they had no intention of actually going into combat if they could avoid it.

We had three Marines in the course, with an artillery captain stationed in Hawaii and a staff sergeant from Pendleton. Like all the courses I took in the Marines and during flight training, we were graded on a constant basis. The captain and I partied every night during the entire course. He had a car and we would drive down to Washington DC, where the ratio of young women to young men was about five to one in our favor. I remember many nights where we stumbled back into the BOQ at three in the morning, still half drunk. Our classes started at 0800 hours.

At the end of the course, he was number one in the class, I was number 3 and the staff sergeant came in number 5. The Army pukes hated us.

While the Army guys teaching the course were nothing short of brilliant, with the best instructors I would ever see, the essence of intelligence is pretty simple. Ignore what you are told, for people are liars and often mistaken. Pay attention to what you personally can see and think about what it means.

I think that any warrior needs to know the basics of intelligence. It helps to have accurate information when battle approaches.

I got back to the squadron in late July and sat in the back cockpit for another month before passing an intense flight exam to requalify as a pilot. In August I got my clearance and could hop back in the front seat of the F-4.

On September 8, 1967 I had fifteen months time in grade as a second lieutenant and received what was pretty much an automatic promotion to first lieutenant. My twenty-first birthday was the next day.

F-4 aircraft cost a lot to fly. As a first tour aviator, as the fledgling pilots were referred to, we were lucky to fly 15-20 hours a month. Since I had been granted papal disposition by the squadron CO to continue my H&MS flying, I often flew more hours monthly in other planes than I did in the F-4, which was supposed to be my primary craft.

My love life eventually improved. I was living on the beach twenty-five miles off base. One of my roomies used to drive up to Washington DC and park at National Airport. He put on a worn flight suit and wandered around the airport until he spotted his prey, any young and tired-looking stewardess who looked like she had just returned from a long flight. He would engage the young woman in conversation. It was like a hawk stalking a field mouse. Soon he would have her laughing and somehow would convince her to take him home for the weekend.

I don't know how he did it but he seduced a lot of young stewardesses that way. I'm far too shy to ever have such a conversation but it seemed to work for him. He didn't actually lie to them but the whole exercise was for him to get them to take him home, and once he was on their turf, he swooped. His name was John Halbig.

John was your garden variety Marine aviator slut. He would bang a venetian blind if it stood still for him. In any case, he brought one pretty young maiden down for a visit to Cherry Point for a weekend. She and I needed one glance to fall in love. John didn't know what was going on but she and I were making intense plans for getting together just as soon as we could.

A couple of weeks later she had a weekend off and flew down to spend it with me. John had planned to go on a cross-country and we intended to make the most of it while his back was turned, but at the last moment he decided to stick around to see my date. He thought I was dating the roommate of my intended. So once her flight arrived we spent a weekend in New Bern, locked in a motel room until John left.

I visited Washington DC every weekend she was home for months. Our relationship continued until she transferred back to Seattle.

As pilots we stood more than a fair chance of being shot down and captured by whoever was the enemy of the day. Back in 1967-1968 the enemy of the day was North Vietnam. In 2015 we change our enemies more and faster than we change our underwear. You have to turn on CNN to see who we are bombing today.

In any case, the military trained us for the bad things that could happen to us. One bad thing that could happen is to be shot down and have to survive in the jungle where it's really hard to find a McDonalds and there literally are no Burger Kings. To "have it your way" might mean cutting down a palm plant and chewing on the innards. So all of the junior pilots went through a three-month survival school. Maybe it wasn't really three months. Maybe it was less than a week, but just seemed like three months.

Mike Murphy and I got orders to the school at the same time. We discussed the school and our tactics for getting through it well in advance. Mike was three months behind me in flight school but as a result of my medical down time, we got orders to Vietnam at the same time and would get orders home on the same date. He lived in New Bern, NC while we were in VMFA-513 together but we stayed close friends.

I think the purpose of survival school was to make you as uncomfortable as possible out in the woods. The 15-20 of us going through the school were taken out in boats down the river near Cherry Point and dropped off on a spit of land. We had to make our way through a line of instructors waiting to beat us with sticks, simulating capture. This was just the start of the fun. Mike didn't like getting beaten any more than I did so we paddled our way past the line of instructors, landed at what seemed a good spot and came up behind them.

We could hear the instructors screaming at the students and the howls of anguish from the students when they were captured. We didn't have any cigarettes with us. We had been forbidden to take money, food or cigarettes with us before the boat ride. But if we had had cigarettes, we would have been smoking as we sat under a tree and chatted about the world in general.

Mike was the kind of guy all the other pilots hated. Handsome, charming and witty, if you walked into a bar with him to swoop down on some lovely ladies, you were going to be SOL (shit out of luck). We told Mike he should have carried a stick with him to beat off the panting hotties. If there were ten women in a group and you and he made a pass on them, you didn't even get the rejects. They all wanted him.

I flew with him on a couple of hops. He was good at flying too. I hate people like that.

Eventually we made our way to the rendezvous point where all the students who had managed to evade capture met up. I think we were allowed some parachute cord, a survival knife and a flint to start a fire. Well, it was too hot for a fire, we had nothing to cook, and every piece of game larger than a mosquito had been killed and eaten many years before.

We had to build some short of shelter and survive for a couple of days on what we could find to eat. Mike and I determined that what we would like to kill and eat the most would be a baloney sandwich on white bread. So we hiked out of the training area that we were strictly forbidden to leave. We walked up to the highway to New Bern. It was about a ten-mile hike, but who counts when there is a baloney sandwich waiting for you at the finish line?

We found a roadside bar. Mike called his roommate to tell him where we were. Thirty minutes later Mike's roomie showed up with baloney, cheese, a loaf of bread, and we were in heaven. The roomie wasn't much of a provider and missed the mustard and mayo, but we were hungry. The sandwich tasted of ambrosia.

We packed up the remains of the bread and took the cheese and baloney back to the POW camp. We didn't sell sandwiches to the rest of the group. We weren't quite that mercenary but it probably was because none of us had any cash. The instructors had a shit fit when they found the empty plastic bag the bread came in. The students undergoing the course all looked at the sky and whistled Dixie and pretended to be innocent.

Mike and I figured we should go up to Washington DC for New Year's. Mike said we could stay with his parents in their apartment. I knew his dad was in the Air Force but didn't have any idea that Mike Murphy Senior was a major general. He served as the congressional liaison for the Air Force. That's one of the most important positions in the Air Force. I thought he would be some B-52 pilot or staff wienie and here he was, one of the most powerful men in Air Force blue.

Before we set out for a night on the town, Mike started telling his mother and father the entire saga of how we had cheated during survival school, first by swimming around the enemy lines and then hiking out for baloney sandwiches. Mike's mother most enjoyed the story of the sandwiches. She suggested we should have been eating something with more nutrition. Mike's dad was laughing. He totally enjoyed the story. I was just sitting there looking stupid, hoping the general didn't blow the whistle on our mischief.

"So what do you think?" Mike the Marine asked of his father.

To my great surprise, his dad responded, "You idiots did exactly the right thing. The purpose of survival training isn't to teach you how to obey the rules; it's to teach you how to disobey the rules. It's about survival and you survived."

Warriors need to know how to survive.

Mike was a warrior. He earned three Distinguished Flying Crosses flying the F-4B in Vietnam. I don't know the details. There was little an F-4 could do that was worthy of those little pieces of ribbon. I didn't know any F-4 pilots getting DFCs for anything, much less three of them. The majors liked to write each other up for an award when they had made both a successful takeoff and a successful landing on the same flight, but junior captains didn't get awards unless they earned them.

Mike left Vietnam on the same set of orders I originally had in 1969 with a transfer to Yuma, Arizona. He applied to fly with the Blue Angels. He became the sole Marine pilot with the Blues in 1970. In July of 1973 his aircraft collided with that of the team leader and both of them were killed. Mike was only twenty-nine. My memory of him is frozen in time with him never aging. He remains forever young.

Mike had the greatest career you could have as a fighter pilot. He got his wings when he was twenty-four, went into combat and flew over 300 missions in Vietnam, earned a fistful of awards and medals and died looking good in the hottest fighter in the world, flying with the Blue Angels. If they made dying while practicing for an air show as a Blue Angel a carnival ride, ninety per cent of Marine pilots under forty would sign up for a go in the hopes of catching the brass ring.

If Mike hadn't died that day he would have become the first Marine pilot to be made CMC (Commandant of the Marine Corps). I miss him a lot.

By the beginning of 1968 most of the pilots past their first tour (i.e., the officers with between four and twenty years of active duty) had completed a full 13-month tour in Vietnam. Among the chopper drivers the attrition rate was catastrophic. The guys in the CH-46 and CH-34 helicopters felt like sitting ducks in their magnesium-skinned potential bonfires with rotors. They couldn't wait to get back to the land of the giant PX to turn in their wings and resign from the Marine Corps.

Faced with an excess of high time F-4 pilots and a shortage of senior captains and majors in chopper units, the Marine Corps in their infinite wisdom transferred 28 of the most highly qualified F-4 pilots into chopper outfits. VMFA-531 went from having a top-heavy set of officers to a unit with a bunch of low time lieutenants. And again the Marine Corps in their infinite wisdom wanted to turn VMFA-531 into a training squadron. Since by now most of the junior guys were qualified in the F-4, about 20 of us got orders to VMFA-513. It was pretty meaningless. We went to work in the hanger next door and wore a different squadron patch on our leather flight jackets.

By the time I got my orders to Vietnam I had amassed about 210 hours in the F-4. I left for Vietnam in July of 1968. In all of my flying in the F-4B from January of 1967 through July of 1968, ninety-five per cent of the training was in air-to-air combat. I did qualify in both the Sidewinder heat seeking missile and the Sparrow, the radar guided missile, unlike many of my contemporaries. But I never dropped a bomb or napalm in the US. The closest we came was dropping the Mk-76 practice bomb at ranges in Yuma.

My unit in Cherry Point trained me to be a fighter pilot but did not train me to use the F-4B as a bomber. As the military often does, they train for the last war. In the case of Vietnam, the last war was Korea. And we weren't really even trained for Korea; we were trained for Guadalcanal in WW II. It was cool calling ourselves fighter pilots but the Marine Corps didn't have a fighter role in Vietnam. We were still being trained primarily in air-to-air as late as mid-1968, three years after the war became a US ground war.

As I made the transition from a pilot in training to a pilot in fact, my pleasure in the art of flying increased.

In the H&MS unit I flew a lot of different airplanes with a wide variety of other pilots. Some of my flights in the C-117 remain memorable. The C-117 was a Douglas built, stretched C-47 built for the Navy in 1944. Every C-117 that I ever flew in was older than I was.

In May of 1968 one of the pilots from Wing that I had done some flying with in the C-117 called me and asked if I wanted to do a three-week trip in the C-117. I had to decline because 513 needed to go to MCAS Yuma, Arizona for the quarterly air-to-ground training. He laughed and said that we were taking the plane in support of the squadron, which needed to have troops taken to Yuma for support and moved around the west coast for training. Naturally I agreed.

I began to realize the flight might be a little unusual when he showed up at 0800 on the day of our departure with a trash bag filled to the brim with beer cans. When I glanced at the bag, he just smiled as he said, "Don't worry, they are all empty." Just as if everyone going on a 2,000 mile cross-country carries around a bunch of empty beer cans.

We were two pilots and a couple of enlisted guys as part of the crew. They would help with aircraft fueling and maintenance. The major, and my memory fails me at the issue of his name, told the crew chief to carefully put the bag of empty beer cans up forward in the cockpit where they would be handy.

The troops that we were moving showed up, we had fueled, picked up lunches for all and filed our flight plan. Off we went. The C-117 never flew higher than 10,000 feet and I suppose it cruised at 180-200 knots. We leveled off on our first leg. After a few minutes of stable flight, the major told the crew chief to take three or four of the empty cans, open the cockpit door and toss them down the center aisle to the back of the plane, and then to slam the door shut. He did, and we could hear the sound of beer cans bouncing down the aisle.

Fifteen minutes later, we repeated the process. I was grinning by now. There was no telling what the snuffies in the back were thinking as they saw a couple of dozen beer cans getting tossed out of the cockpit every hour. Later in the flight, I went to the back to pee. The plane had a urinal attached to the rear bulkhead. We had an entire group of young Marines with white faces strapped tightly into their seats. After 20 or 30 empties had bounced down the aisle, the guys got it and started laughing. They knew this was going to be a fun trip.

Since we had long legs on the plane and two pilots doing rotations on the legs, we could get a lot of flying done in a day. We did six-hour and eight-hour days all the time, and as much as fifteen hours on one day where we needed to cover a lot of ground.

We went to Olathe, Kansas on the first leg and dropped off a dozen troops going to a course there. We picked up another dozen who had just finished the course. Since we pretty much owned the airplane and had a handful of fuel chits that would get us fuel at any military base in the US, we went everywhere we felt like going. The next stop was Buckley Air Force Base in Colorado, where we fueled up. Then we toddled our way up to Whidbey Island in Washington.

We were going to be there overnight so I had contacted Clara, my airline stewardess friend, to see if she could come up and see me. She said that she really wanted to get together with me so I promised to call her when I landed. Clara had transferred from her base in Washington DC to Seattle to be closer to her home.

I had a big surprise when I saw her after she drove up from Seattle. She was pregnant. Of course that created a problem I didn't know how to sort out. We had talked about marriage but I knew I was going into combat and wasn't prepared to marry before I went. Having a baby on the way changed where we stood but didn't change how I felt about marriage.

I don't know to this day if I did the right thing or not in not getting married. I have met a lot of guys who have been in exactly the same circumstances and did get married. My observation is that it rarely works. Marriage is for people who want to spend the rest of their life waking up to the company of the other. To enter into marriage because someone got pregnant isn't the best of reasons.

Clara stayed overnight and we talked. She didn't try to pressure me at all and was ok with having the baby and giving it up for adoption. Since she was the one most affected, all I could do was allow her to make all the decisions. She had the baby about the same time I got to Vietnam in late July of 1968. I would have married her when I came back from Vietnam but during my first 13 months she found someone new and married him. I got the proverbial "Dear John" letter in Vietnam. I don't know if I was broken hearted or relieved.

At some point in the trip we actually flew to Yuma and I got a week's flying in the F-4B, doing what I was being paid for. Then the fool major and I took off again for another two weeks of touring the entire west coast in our own private airplane using fuel paid for by the wonderful and generous taxpayers.

The major had an older brother who owned a dental practice in San Diego and had a dental assistant he was dating. I think there is some sort of rule that says that all dentists have to bop their dental assistants. In any case, the major invited his brother and the brother's girlfriend to join with us on a trip from San Diego to Las Vegas for the weekend.

We had been flying with the same crew for three weeks. They knew us, we knew them, and everyone agreed we could keep our mouths shut. We landed at NAS Miramar and took a large flight suit for the brother and a small flight suit for the girlfriend into the ops office. They changed and walked out to the plane with us as if they were part of the crew. And I suppose in a way they were.

The major and I alternated the flying. He flew one leg, I flew the next. While he stayed in the left seat for all the legs, it was as easy to fly the C-117 from the right seat. It was my leg to fly. We fired up both engines, called for our flight plan and taxied out to the duty runway.

Over fifty-some years of flying, I have discovered that all pilots are goofy. Except me. They do some really weird things. Naturally I don't. The major liked to use full flaps for landing the C-117. The C-117 could land on a 1,500-foot gravel strip if you used full flaps. But we landed on military runways 12,000 feet long at Miramar. You could land and take off six times on a strip that long. Remember, I told you he was goofy.

The tower cleared us for takeoff. I eased my way out onto the duty runway and ran the power up. Everything looked good so I released the brakes and we were rolling down the runway. Except the plane was acting really doggy. It sort of bobbled along and gradually the speed came up. I raised the tail and eventually the plane left the ground. But even at full power it wasn't handling right.

Then the crew chief tells me, "We still have full flaps down."

Well, that resolved that problem. Some twit didn't go through the takeoff checklist properly and we just took off with full down flaps.

The major and I looked at each other and laughed. The ceiling was about 800 feet and the only good thing was that we hadn't gone IFR yet. He inched the flaps up a little at a time and the speed began to recover. Eventually the airplane started acting like a real plane with two engines.

An hour and a half later we were taxiing up to the ramp at Nellis AFB for the weekend. We were a little concerned while we were at NAS Miramar that someone might see the long blonde hair flowing from under a Marine utility cover at Miramar and want to know more. But the Air Force is convinced all Marines are insane. They never batted an eyelash.

I'll throw this in while I'm talking about Marines landing at Air Force Bases and what they thought about us. On the previous squadron sortie to MCAS Yuma for weapons training I was given the chance to fly one of the squadron F-4B planes to Yuma. You couldn't make it in a single leg so you could do an overnight anywhere from Houston to Chicago and drift into Yuma the next day. Lieutenant Ben Crawford, who was my roommate on the beach in North Carolina, was my RIO for the trip.

We chewed the fat on where to go for the night. Neither of us had ever been to Oklahoma City so we filed a flight plan for Tinker AFB in Oklahoma. It took a couple of hours of flight. The operations people sent a follow-me vehicle out to guide us into our parking spot. We shut the plane down for the night and hitched a ride with the follow-me truck into operations. I went in and filled out a request for fuel and got us a ride to the BOQ for the night.

The next day we called the ops department for a ride to the field. Once we got there, I went in for a weather briefing and filed my flight plan. Now I'm 5' 8" and Ben stood about 5' 7". He was the only officer I ever met of any rank in the Marine Corps who was younger than I was. So he was not only younger, he was actually a little shorter.

I filed the flight plan and went to the duty driver so he could take us to the plane. Ben and I wore our green Nomex flight suits with a leather patch over our left chest with our names and rank on it, and we had our covers on with our rank and the Marine Corps insignia showing we weren't Air Force wienies.

The driver wouldn't take us to the plane. He told me to check with the duty officer. I went to the duty officer.

"What's up? We just filed our flight plan and we need a ride to the plane. Your driver tells me he won't take us. It's half a mile to the plane and I'm not walking. We also need a ladder and a start cart for an F-4," I said in a commanding voice.

"Who do you guys think you are kidding? Are you ROTC or Civil Air Patrol or what? I am not stupid enough to believe you are the pilots of an F-4, even a Marine F-4."

I was pretty dumbfounded. I'd never had anyone actually refuse to accept my rank or the fact that I had an airplane on his ramp. So I showed him my ID card saying, "I'm a Marine second lieutenant, that's my fucking airplane and I want a fucking ride to it so I can leave."

He wasn't buying it, not for a moment. He simply could not believe that two Marine second lieutenants in his operations office actually wanted to fly their airplane off his base.

I got nowhere with him. In his mind he knew we were frauds and he wasn't about to let us on the tarmac. He even threatened to call the Air Police and have us thrown off the base. I rummaged through my brain bag for the information sheet we had been given at the squadron in case we got in trouble. I gave the ops officer the squadron duty officer's phone number and told him to call. He wouldn't even do that. He was convinced we were kids playing a trick on him.

"Look," I said. "That's my airplane, you have the squadron phone number. Either call them and verify who we are or I'm going to crawl across that counter and kick your ass. That's my fucking airplane and you need to straighten up and fly right or you are going to get your ass kicked and you can explain how a Marine kicked your butt." Not for nothing did I listen to the DIs in boot camp so I could chew ass when I needed to.

He began to realize that maybe it was our plane. He wouldn't call the number I gave him but went through the operator on the military phone network to ensure he got the VMFA-513 duty office. The phone call went through and he began talking to the duty officer.

"I've got two assholes here trying to go out to one of your airplanes. It's an F-4B, number 152XXX and these two clowns are playing at being officer and pilot," he began. "What are their names? Let me check."

"Gimmie your ID cards," he demanded.

Ben and I slid them across the counter to him.

"Well, one is Second Lieutenant Robert Moriarty and the other says Second Lieutenant Benjamin Crawford. I know damned well they are fakes because these two are just kids," he continued. His face began to turn white. "Yea, they look like kids. Right? Right. You mean they are kids. Really? It's their plane? Are you sure? Yes, sir. Sorry to have bothered you, sir. Yes sir, immediately."

He seemed to have gotten the word. I found out later that everyone in the squadron duty office just about peed in his pants laughing at the conversation. The reason we looked just like kids was that we were kids.

The squadron assigned one of our F-4s to the smallest and youngest two guys in the squadron and the Air Force wasn't about to let us have our plane. We took shit about that for many months.

In Las Vegas we had the entire weekend to party. We had a couple of Marine pilots, a dentist brother of one of the pilots and a hot young dental assistant with a great sense of humor. We checked into one of the hotels right on the strip and changed into our civvies. The young dental assistant looked even hotter in her party clothes.

We drank, we played 21, we shot craps. I taught everyone my system for betting on craps. The odds the big casinos gave were better than the actual odds so we won a fair bit of cash to pay for the weekend. We were young, stupid, and glad to be alive.

Eventually all good things end, and the weekend passed. We flew our extra two crew back to San Diego and eventually made our way back to Cherry Point to rejoin the real world.

In late May of 1968 I finally got my orders to Vietnam. Most of the guys I went through flight training with had undergone transition to the F-4 and had been in-country for months. Now it was my turn. My orders called for me to report to Treasure Island in San Francisco for further assignment as required. It meant Vietnam.

Ben Crawford and John Halbig had already left for Vietnam so I canceled our lease on the house on the beach and closed it up.

Plate 01. Spring of 1964: In my last year of high school in Fort Worth I was elected Senior Class Treasurer. It's the kind of thing officer selection boards in the Marine Corps liked to see in officer candidates. *Credit:* AHHS

Plate 02. Volunteering for the Marines in September of 1964 was the first decision I ever made in my life entirely by and for myself. *Credit:* USMC

Plate 03. When I began the Marcad program in May of 1965 I was 135 pounds of twisted steel and sex appeal. Or so I thought. *Credit:* USMC

MORIARTY 139½ 5'7" II SHAFFER 143 5'7" III

6 MORIARTY 142 5'8" II GALLER 141 5'6" III

Plate 04. Avroc Shaffer beat on me for three rounds of three minutes apiece. As Churchill once said, "Never, never, never give up." You don't have to be better than your opponent; all you have to do is outlast him. August 1965. *Credit:* USN

Plate 05. There was something really cool about climbing into a jet trainer when you were only 19 years old. Or any other age. December 1965. *Credit:* USN

Plate 06. Woodie Patton and I managed to find any trouble in the neighborhood for years. December 1965. *Credit:* USN

Plate 07. The first time I climbed into the cockpit of a T-2A I looked at all the dials and gauges and thought I'd never figure them all out. Since then I've realized it was pretty simple. December 1965.

Plate 08. The AF-9J was a real fighter of late Korean War vintage. When you armed the four 20 mm cannons you knew you carried some real firepower. November 1966. *Credit:* USN

Plate 09. The proudest day of my life was December 2, 1966 when I became Naval Aviator #V-24483 in Corpus Christi, Texas. It was less than two years before that I had graduated from Boot Camp in San Diego. *Credit:* USN

Plate 10. I got to Vietnam and combat in the F-4B in VMFA-542 in July of 1968. I was 21 and the youngest fighter pilot in the world. I had been a roommate with Ben Crawford in Cherry Point. Joe Featherston and I still stay in contact. *Credit:* Joe Featherston

Plate 11. The F-4B was designed as an interceptor in the 1950s. It held the "time to climb" record for its weight category for many years but left a trail of smoke you could see for 20 miles. We would have been far better off in Vietnam with a turboprop version of the A-1 Spad. July 1968. *Credit:* Joe Featherston

Plate 12. But the F-4 did a far better job of turning JP-4 into smoke and noise than any other aircraft ever designed. July 1968. *Credit:* USMC

Plate 13. The O-1 was the most combat-effective aircraft the Marines used in Vietnam. You can see in the background just how much damage we did to Northern I Corps. The entire province looked like the surface of the moon. November 1968. *Credit:* Bob Stamper

Plate 14. Bob Stamper and I were close friends and flew one interesting mission together, taking on some rocket sites. When we went out with an M-60 machine gun or M-79 grenade launcher we called it trolling. The NVA thought we could see them, so always shot back. Actually we couldn't see anything but could hear them when they shot at us. 1968/1969. *Credit:* Bob Stamper

Plate 15. The Army Bird Dogs stationed at Dong Ha were a slightly browner shade of green than the Marine Bird Dogs. The NVA knew they couldn't control air as close as the Marine planes could, and they took a lot more losses than we did. *Credit:* Bob Stamper

Plate 16. Greg Nelson flying an O-1G. You can tell it's a Golf by counting the rocket pods. The Golf model had only four rockets, while the Charlie version carried six. If you could cruise at 100 mph you were doing really well. 1969. *Credit:* Bob Stamper

Plate 17. Steve Palmason next to a Charlie model. He won a Silver Star for attacking an NVA unit under a low overcast where it was impossible to call in close air support. He even dropped ammo to the trapped Marines below when they ran short. He saved the lives of a lot of Marines. 1968.

Plate 18. Major Drayer taught me how to control air and checked me out in the O-1. I think the VMO-6 field grade officers were among the best I flew with in the Marines. 1968.

Plate 19. Larry Adams in the front with John Hagen in the rear seat. John had the best eyesight of any AO I ever flew with. He was colorblind and could see right through camouflage. 1969. *Credit:* Bob Stamper

Plate 20. Jim Lawrence stayed on active duty and transferred to the Air Force to fly the A-10. That plane was a lot closer to what we needed in Vietnam than what we flew, but the Air Force hated it because it was too simple and too cheap. 1969. *Credit:* Bob Stamper

Plate 21. Gunny Lockwood (on the right) kept the Bird Dogs flying. We had the only O-1s in the Marines and he had to do a lot of behind-the-barn deals with the Army and Air Force to keep our few airplanes airborne. 1969. *Credit:* Bob Stamper

144

Plate 22. Typical ordnance load for the UH-1E, here with VMO-6 in 1967. *Credit:* USMC

Plate 23. From the left: Larry Adams, unknown, Bob Moriarty (with my back turned), John Hagen, Dick Webb. *Credit:* Bob Stamper

Plates 24 (above) and 25 (below): O-1 Charlie. *Credit:* Bob Stamper

Plates 26 (above) and 27 (below): O-1 Golf. *Credit:* Bob Stamper

Plate 28. I was a 22-year-old captain when stationed with WERS-17 in 1969/1970. *Credit:* USMC

Chapter 12
VMFA-542 DA NANG, REPUBLIC OF VIETNAM

Come and sing a simple song of freedom
Sing it like you've never sung before
And let it fill the air, tell the people everywhere
We, the people here, don't want a war

Hey there, Mister Black Man, can you hear me?
I don't want your diamonds or your game
I just want to be someone known to you as me
And I will bet my life you want the same

So come and sing a simple song of freedom
Sing it like you've never sung before
And let it fill the air, tell the people everywhere
We, the people here, don't want a war

Seven hundred million are you listening?
Most of what you read is made of lies
But speaking one to one, ain't it everybody's sun
To wake to in the morning when we rise?

Now Brother soldier Nixon are you busy?
If not won't you drop this friend a line?
And tell me if the man who is plowing up your land
Has got the war machine upon his mind

Simple Song Of Freedom
Songwriter: Bobby Darin
Copyright: Carlin America Inc, BMG Rights Mgmt US, LLC 1968

IT'S COMMON TODAY to talk about heroes. We bandy the word
about so much that it has worn to the point of being meaningless. If

everyone is a hero, nothing is heroic.

There are heroes in life. They take chances, go against the grain and stand for something rather than falling for anything. They fight for what is right, not what is popular.

Bobby Darin was such a hero. Troubled with a bad heart because of repeated bouts of rheumatic fever as a child, he knew he would die young. His singing career took off in 1958 at the age of twenty-two when "Splish Splash" sold over a million copies. Darin sang bubblegum music for teenagers. With maturity and with the war in Vietnam expanding daily, in 1968 he released his first and only anti-war song.

Bobby Darin was part of the establishment. When he sang "Simple Song of Freedom" it marked a turning point in the war just as important as when Walter Cronkite spoke on February 27, 1968. The song cost him airtime and a lot of money but he did it because it was the right thing to do.

Walter Cronkite closed his CBS News Special On February 27, 1968 and totally changed Middle America's perception of the Vietnam War.

> *Mr. WALTER CRONKITE (Anchorman): I wrote a three-minute closing for the program, which seemingly, without reluctance, our stern and uncompromisingly fair news president Dick Salant approved.*

> *Tonight, back in more familiar surroundings in New York, we'd like to sum up our findings in Vietnam, an analysis that must be speculative, personal, subjective. Who won and who lost in the great Tet Offensive against the cities? I'm not sure. The Vietcong did not win by a knockout but neither did we.*

> *Then, with as much restraint as I could, I turned to our own leaders whose idea of negotiation seemed frozen in memories of General McArthur's encounter with the Japanese aboard the battleship Missouri.*

> *We've been too often disappointed by the optimism of the American leaders...*

both in Vietnam and Washington, to have faith any longer in the silver linings they find in the darkest clouds. For it seems now more certain than ever, that the bloody experience of Vietnam is to end in a stalemate. To say that we are closer to victory today is to believe, in the face of the evidence, the optimists who have been wrong in the past.

To say that we are mired in stalemate seems the only realistic, if unsatisfactory conclusion. On the off chance that military and political analysts are right, in the next few months we must test the enemy's intentions, in case this is indeed his last big gasp before negotiations.

But it is increasingly clear to this reporter that the only rational way out then will be to negotiate, not as victors, but as an honorable people who lived up to their pledge to defend democracy, and did the best they could.

This is Walter Cronkite. Good night.

We have no such leaders today as Walter Cronkite. Mainstream media lacks leadership. The mass media more closely resembles the propaganda wing of the military-industrial complex. Reporters tell stories with a straight face that they know are lies. And our young men die for nothing while the mainstream media wave flags as if they are pom pom girls showing us their panties.

In 2003 the Dixie Chicks, a popular female pop and country music group, played a concert in London some nine days before the US invasion of Iraq. Lead vocalist Natalie Maines said to the audience, "We don't want this war, this violence, and we're ashamed that the President of the United States is from Texas." That was heroic and cost the band millions of dollars in lost revenue.

It wasn't the public who stopped listening to the Dixie Chicks; it was the right wing fanatics who controlled the mass of radio stations that put an embargo on their music.

Freedom is the right to be critical of those who lead you. Or anyone else. The only people you are never allowed to criticize are your overlords when you become a slave.

The President of the United States, in theory, works for the good of the citizens of the country. If he can't handle complaints, he should resign. We don't need less criticism; we need more, a lot more. The war in Iraq was illegal according to every tenet of international law. Everything Americans were told by the government turned out to be just as big a lie as those told to drag us into the war in Vietnam. Natalie Maines showed us what a hero and a warrior look like. We should be awarding medals for bravery to those like her who stand up for what is right rather than what is popular.

My time to put up or shut up came in July of 1968. My orders called for me to report to Treasure Island for a flight to Okinawa but were changed as I was enroute and I was told to report to March AFB. I checked into the BOQ and waited for my flight. I was nervous. Everyone wonders how he will respond when the bullets start flying. Yet I was excited at the same time. As a highly trained F-4B pilot I knew I should be able to handle anything the NVA or VC could throw at me. But still, you never know until the bullets start flying.

Time came to board the flight. We stopped in Hawaii for fuel and then continued on to Okinawa. All Marines on their way to Vietnam stopped first at Camp Hansen in Okinawa for a few days to acclimate to the steamy and hot weather of the orient. The Marine Corps issued us new utilities and checked that our physicals and shots were up to date. They wanted to know that if we were killed, we were in good shape beforehand.

Then the big moment came, the last leg to Vietnam. On the flight I chatted with the stewardess. She said the flights broke her heart. She took planes filled with kids into the country and flew prematurely aged men back to the world in planes only partially filled. The stewardesses knew that for every empty seat on the plane leaving Vietnam, some mother's son was coming home in a cheap aluminum box.

We didn't know what to expect when the doors on the plane opened in Da Nang. I had a Randall survival and attack knife on my belt. If we were overrun I could at least fight a last ditch battle.

The air of Da Nang smelled of human waste, rotten and decaying vegetation. I will never forget the smell. Temperatures stayed in the high nineties with humidity near 100 per cent. We climbed down the baking aluminum stairs peering from side to side, looking for enemies about to attack.

The motto of the military should be "hurry up and wait" because you always have to wait for some corporal to finish filling out a list before you can do anything. I knew I was being assigned to MAG 11 and to VMFA-542. But we had to check in at Wing and that took a day or two, and we needed shots and that took a day or two, and we needed to be issued gear and that took a day or two. Finally a jeep took me over to MAG 11 where I gave them copies of my orders and eventually I made it to VMFA-542.

I wasn't all that overjoyed to recognize the CO when I checked in. Both Woody Patton and Ben Crawford were in 542 but the CO was Henry Vitali. When I was still with 531 in Cherry Point he was one of the Pentagon desk jockeys I had to fly with. I was in the back seat and he flew as PIC. We took a cross-country flight to Tampa and he tried his very best to kill me. I flew with a lot of pilots who weren't good pilots but a really bad pilot was about as common as Mormons running bars. Hank Vitali was not only a bad pilot, he was a rotten pilot.

It was no wonder, for he was ancient. He had to have been over forty years old. Fighter pilots throughout history have been young. Vitali was well past it.

When in early 1968 the Marines moved all the senior majors and light colonels from the F-4 to choppers, they still had to fill billets in units in Vietnam requiring field grade officers. So rather than pick from the most talented and experienced Phantom drivers, they took a bunch of desk jockeys who had done nothing but administrative work for the last ten years and put them in command of fighter squadrons.

At VMFA-531 they were told to give Vitali twenty hours in the plane, call him qualified and send him to Vietnam. They did, and he was about as good as any other pilot with twenty hours in the plane, which is to say not very good at all.

The Marine Corps tends to attract insecure people who have a need to prove themselves to others. I'm not going to apologize for saying that; it's just as true of me. But if those same people prove to be good ass-kissers, they get promoted up the line and eventually promoted way beyond their capabilities. However, by this time they have a lot of rank, so rather than bullshit their way through a problem the way the rest of us do, they pull rank and insist they are correct because they are of higher rank.

Every officer in the Marine Corps has a fitness report done every six months by his CO. Call it a report card. To retire at fifty per cent pay requires the officer to be promoted to at least the rank of major in less than twenty years. Since all that the "lifers" thought about was retirement, they needed to be promoted so they could make at least their twenty years' service. If they managed to stay for thirty years, they got 75 per cent of their basic pay as retirement. But they had to be promoted even higher during those thirty years.

The up-or-out system came from General George Marshall. After WW II he felt that we needed younger officers in charge, in order to have a cadre of multi-skilled officers who could expand their service rapidly with troops produced through the draft for mobilization for war. As a result the focus changed, from a high value being put on useful skills to a military overloaded with more generals than necessary and an utter obsession with promotion. Today we have more admirals than ships.

Fighter pilots weren't fighter pilots any longer; they became ass-kissing paperwork shufflers. It's far worse today, with every general absolutely surrounded with a cadre of high-grade officers devoted to seeing that his every wish is fulfilled at once.

We fight a lot of wars, we just never win any. Any war worth fighting is worth winning. Any war not worth winning is not worth fighting.

People of high rank who got there through kissing asses, which is most of them, want to be surrounded by butt lickers. Vitali was one. As an FAC flying the Bird Dog later, I controlled flights led by him several times. He couldn't hit his ass with his elbow but every time he flew he demanded the FAC give him a write-up so he could put himself in for an award. I'd guess that two-thirds of the awards handed out to pilots in Vietnam were to majors and lieutenant colonels and I'd guess ten per cent or less were deserved.

The worst case of ass-kissing I ever heard of was MacArthur awarding then Congressman Lyndon Johnson a Silver Star for flying along on a bombing run against the Japanese in Papua New Guinea. Later it came out that his plane actually had to turn back to base with mechanical problems and never came within a hundred miles of the target.

Vitali was a marionette and wanted to surround himself with marionettes. He did. VMFA-542 had a distinct split between the junior officers, comprised of lieutenants and captains, and the senior captains and majors. First tour pilots fought the war. The second tour pilots talked about how good they were. If you had the misfortune to be in a squadron led by a marionette, you just kept your mouth shut and put up with it.

I still have my VMFA-542 squadron yearbook from November of 1967 until November of 1968. The squadron spent less than a year in-country. During that entire year only one crew was lost. While the F-4B turned fuel into noise and smoke better than any aircraft ever designed, our role as bomb droppers flying close air support was one of the safest jobs in the war.

One of the first things virtually every Marine or soldier did when he arrived in-country to begin his tour was to make or get a copy of a short timer's calendar. Everyone checked off the days they had remaining in Vietnam. You could always start a conversation just by asking, "How short are you?" Virtually everyone knew exactly how many days they had left on their tour.

I didn't care how long I had left. It was a war. Warriors fight wars. They don't count the days they have left in the country. I never had or even wanted a short timer's calendar.

In every combat environment there are a hundred different wars going on at the same time. Marines flying the F-4B dropping snake and napes in the Arizona Territory southwest of Da Nang didn't fight the same war as the Air Force 366th Fighter Wing (Gunfighters) flying an air superiority role over Hanoi, even though we all flew out of the Da Nang air base. Grunt captains slashing though triple canopy jungle chasing the wily VC didn't see the same war as a B-52 pilot flying 13-hour missions out of Guam who never came closer to Vietnam than six miles above the ground.

Our squadron had 31 crews, guys who flew together on a regular basis. The F-4B was complex enough that you really needed to fly with the same guy as much as possible for better crew communication. My normal RIO was Claude Pyatte from near Asheville, North Carolina.

Claude didn't make any bones about it; he was a real hillbilly.

I arrived in the squadron about July 20. Wing procedures called for pilots to spend at least a week getting used to the heat and humidity before flying any combat missions. I would learn later that my daughter, Susan, was born on July 25, 1968.

Pilots needed to be eased into their roles in combat. Since most of the training in the States revolved around air-to-air work, literally we needed to do on-the-job training as pilots using the F-4 in a close air support role. We had zero training in close air support in North Carolina but ninety-eight per cent of what we did in Vietnam was air-to-ground in support of ground troops.

In hindsight all militaries make some godawful stupid decisions. During Korea and up until 1965 the Navy and Marine Corps used a plane designed in the waning days of WW II called the A-1 Skyraider, or more popularly, the Spad. The plane carried fuel for 6.5 hours but oil capacity limited the time aloft to only 6.25 hours. You could load the plane from stem to stern with ordnance. It carried more than its own weight in ordnance. Pilots loved it because if you didn't nail the pilot between the running lights with something bigger than a 20 mm, the plane could take hits all day long and never blink.

The Spad was the greatest airplane ever invented for close air support. So the Navy and Marines gave them away in 1966 just as they became needed. They flew all their A-1s out to Arizona and left them to rot in the desert at Litchfield Park.

The US has a nasty habit of dumping our unwanted and unloved military crap on third world nations. In the case of the Spad, we gave 150 of the A-1s to the South Vietnamese to operate in the VNAF. The South Vietnamese thought the Americans had lost their minds. They had been using the T-28 carrying two bombs to cover their troops. Now all of a sudden they could start and end three or four wars with just the ordnance on a pair of A-1s.

While the Air Force may have the ugliest uniforms in the entire known universe, they aren't stupid. They inspected all the rejects from the Navy and Marine Corps out in the desert and said, "Well guys, since you don't seem to want these used pieces of crap, we will take them off your hands."

The biggest problem the Air Force had was their pilots snickering on the radio when they called for takeoff from Litchfield Park. The Air Force pilots couldn't believe such a great airplane was so unloved. They laughed at us.

The Navy and Marines replaced the A-1 with the A-6 Intruder in 1964 and 1965. While the jet powered A-6 could carry 28 of the 500-pound bombs at a time, it was pretty useless for close air support. When we needed the A-1 the most, the VNAF and US Air Force had our entire fleet because no one in the Marine Corps had either the guts or the intelligence to change already made plans.

When I was flying the O-1 Bird Dog in Quang Tri, just south of the DMZ, we were in one of the most dangerous areas in Vietnam for FAC planes. If we flew over the A Shau valley, we took AAA on every mission. The Air Force operated west of us with the Spad, in the southern part of North Vietnam and in Laos, near Tchepone. That was the most deadly AAA combat environment in aviation history. The only plane suitable for such an environment proved to be the Spad. The Air Force just loved the Spad.

We had a bunch of F-4B squadrons with everyone running around talking about what great fighter pilots they were when we didn't have a fighter role. The best close air support aircraft the Marines operated was the A-4. The A-4 carried half the ordnance load of the A-1 and had less than one-quarter the fuel endurance.

The damned fools in the Pentagon who made the decision to shitcan the A-1 should have been court-martialed. Marines died for lack of a decent aircraft carrying ordnance and guns to give them close air support. Pilots died because their aircraft couldn't take hits. A single 30-caliber bullet from an AK-47 could knock down a Phantom or Skyhawk if it hit in the wrong place.

I've been pissed for 47 years at the stupidity of that decision. Even today, the Air Force brass hates the A-10 aircraft because it's not complex and expensive. The military-industrial complex has utterly taken control over the United States economy. Congress consists of a bunch of ignorant and corrupt pimps who have been bought off by everyone and anyone willing to donate to their reelection campaigns.

I'm not shocked at politicians being corrupted. It happens on a continuous basis throughout history. But a Congress critter serving a single two-year term can retire with a fully funded million-dollar retirement. Just how much money do those silly corrupt bastards intend to steal? If we made it an absolute rule that Congress couldn't vote to fund any combat unless a simple majority of Congress could identify on an unmarked map just where the enemy of the day was, peace would rule the world.

Since the Air Force literally stole the very best close air support aircraft right out from underneath the Navy and Marine Corps and got away with it, some Air Force captain wearing that terminally ugly blue uniform decided to add insult to injury by suggesting the Air Force install 7.62 caliber Gatling guns in surplus C-47s to use for close air support.

It turned out to be the second greatest close air support aircraft ever invented. I saw the plane used only once; they were based way south of us. It sounded like a zipper being undone. ZZZ*ZZZZ*. The story was that the plane could put one round in every square foot of a football field in three minutes. It wasn't actually that good; it only pumped out 18,000 bullets a minute. But it would break up an attack faster than any aircraft ever built. The Air Force had it. We didn't. We used the C-117 and C-47 for hauling VIPs around.

In combat it's always important to understand just what it is that you are trying to accomplish. The A-6 cost a lot more than a surplus A-1 so more money went to the guys building military planes. But the A-1 was the plane we really needed.

In 1965 when we went to war in southeast Asia we could have and should have taken the basic airframe design of the A-1 and slapped a turbo-prop engine on it. It would have been about as hard to do as learning how to fall off a bicycle. Cessna could have done it in a week. But it wasn't expensive or complex so the military didn't want it and Congress wouldn't pay for it.

Actually, for the work we are doing in Afghanistan and Iraq today, an updated Spad would be the best aircraft. The military-industrial complex sold Congress a pig in a poke when they convinced them to spring for drones. Nothing beats the Mark-1 eyeball in an aircraft. While drones have better vision than pilots, their field of vision is severely restricted.

Some whistleblower just revealed that in Afghanistan the drone operators looked for very tall men to attack in the hopes of whacking

Osama bin Laden. One drone operator found such a specimen and got permission to attack the suspected OBL surrounded by his troops. He fired his missile and killed a schoolteacher surrounded by his class. Of course he looked tall, he was an adult with a bunch of children around him. Just one more "victory" in the unending Forever War.

The best and most important lesson I learned in Vietnam was never to create enemies faster than you can make bullets. The entire drone program seems designed to turn the entire world against the US. It's working.

When I returned from Vietnam in 1970 I went to Southern Methodist University for a semester. I flew out of a little strip south of Arlington and got to meet the fellow who designed the Huey Cobra gunship. He took two other engineers, and for $1 million put together the Cobra out of spare parts from the Bell UH-1B and engine. It went into service in 1967 and proved to be a great weapons platform.

If one officer in high command in the USMC had the balls and the brains to see what any midget could, we could have had a replacement for the A-1 in less than a year for probably under $1 million a copy. The Huey Cobra succeeded because the company came up with the plane and ignored the procurement programs demanded by the military.

But the way our procurement system works, we need to feed thousands of military retirees now working for the big aviation manufacturers and we need time to think about what we are doing. The total piece-of-shit Lockheed Cheyenne program took ten years to build ten airplanes. It cost hundreds of millions of dollars. The aircraft proved utterly unsuitable for combat.

We are doing exactly the same thing today with the F-35 program. The planes don't fly, can't carry weapons, burn up the decks of the aircraft carriers they are supposedly designed for and cost $400 million apiece. That's the dumbest fucking airplane project in the history of the known universe and nobody has the guts to kill the project. It will never fly a single flight in combat, it's so useless. And because it has such short combat legs, half that of a World War II fighter, it has doomed the entire US aircraft carrier fleet. If we ever attempt to use them in combat against a real military power, they are going to be floating upside down in the first five minutes of battle.

We have potential enemies who have anti-ship missiles with a range of 1,000 km. The F-35 has a combat range of 500 km. So a rowboat carrying a Silkworm missile could take out the best and biggest aircraft carrier the Navy has in service.

But the military-industrial complex loves the plane. That's the greatest reason to kill any procurement program all by itself.

After a week or so getting used to the climate in Vietnam, I made it onto the flight schedule for a night TPQ mission over Laos. Ground-based bombing used by the Marine Corps in Vietnam consisted of a special form of radar called the TPQ-10 system. With it we could attack any target in an aircraft loaded with low-drag bombs; typically the radar operator on the ground would control us carrying ten of the 500-pound Mark 82 bombs.

The aircraft flew at about 20,000 feet at a relatively slow speed like 300 knots since we had no threat from AAA at that speed and altitude. The TPQ operator would have a specific target's coordinates. He would plot the specific characteristics of our bombs, feed in data such as wind and temperature and tell us when to drop. It was not unlike a GCA (ground controlled approach) where once he got a positive identification on our aircraft, he would have us make minor changes of speed, altitude or heading. When everything came together and we were at the drop point the controller would order us to pickle our bombs.

I don't know what the limits were on the use of the radar. I suspect we never dropped closer than a couple of miles from any friendlies. But for a new pilot in-country, it was the easiest and safest combat mission you could fly. For fun they had us fly over Laos, because while Laos was an extremely dangerous place to be flying at 10,000 feet or lower, at 20,000 feet you may as well have been flying Eastern Air Lines into Miami.

Even junior pilots such as myself got more flight time in 542 than we had in North Carolina, but we still were lucky to get on the flight schedule more than once a day. The squadron had eighteen airplanes assigned to it. One was the "hanger queen", doomed never to fly. If maintenance could keep ten in the air on the same day they were doing an exceptional job.

I wasn't getting the flight time my body required in 542 so I went over to the local H&MS to see if they had any need for pilots. That turned out to be a stupid question. A good copilot was of even greater value in Da Nang than in Cherry Point. I made a deal with them. If they would give me the good hops, they could give me the middle of the night flare drop flights that no one wanted. They not only agreed, they upgraded me to PIC of the C-117, the S-2F and the C-1A. I was the only first tour PIC of those planes in the Marine Corps.

One of the better VMFA-531 F-4B pilots that we had lost to choppers in late 1967 was flying out of Marble Mountain in the CH-46. I went over to Marble Mountain to see him. Major Megan was one of the finest pilots I ever flew with in anything. He invited me along as a gunner on a typical day's flight. Little did I understand what I was getting into.

We took off from Marble Mountain about 10:00 am or 1000 military time. We would fly to one combat base out in the Arizona Territory to the southwest of Da Nang and pick up some supplies, and then we would take them to another base. Megan knew where all the bases were, and the safest way to approach and take off from them. We did that for most of the day.

Once we picked up a sling load of lumber. It wasn't loaded correctly. The load began to oscillate, then the plane began to oscillate.

Megan called back to me to look at the load and tell him if it was safe or if it could cause major problems with the plane. I leaned out and looked at the load. The swings were getting bigger and bigger. One of the beams in the load of lumber was about to punch a hole in the fuel tank on the side of the CH-46. I told Megan and he said, "Watch it for a minute."

He must have hit a button up front because all of a sudden the load dropped from the plane, on a suicide mission. We splattered lumber all over the rice paddies below. He wanted me to mark the position the next time we flew over so they could send out a Marine truck to pick up the lumber we dumped.

When we went over the next time it looked like an ant farm below, with tiny pieces of lumber going in all directions. The locals figured they needed the lumber more than the Marine Corps did and in an hour it had all disappeared.

During the briefing prior to the flight Megan told me that they had eighteen planes in the squadron. At least one aircraft from the unit had taken hits every day for the last year. At best they could launch 12-15 planes in a day. So at the very least, every pilot in the squadron flew in an aircraft that got hit by gunfire twice a month. I started understanding why the chopper pilots were so eager to get out of the Corps when they got back to the world.

But as dangerous as he made it out to be, I didn't see any sign of enemy action the entire day. We did 20 or 30 supply runs and the only thing we were going to die of was boredom.

The plane had two pilots, both officers; a crew chief; and two gunners for the 50-caliber guns, one on each side. I spelled the crew chief on the Browning now and again. Dusk began and we had one more run to make into yet another small LZ. Megan told me to keep my eyes peeled because according to him that was the time of day the VC liked to start shooting at the choppers. I took it with a giant grain of salt.

The aircraft spiraled down in a combat approach designed to keep the plane from a predictable path. Flying straight and level on the same heading is a great and quick way to die in combat. Just as we touched down on the zone I saw what looked like fireworks starting. It was a really beautiful spray of red, like a scarlet fire hose. Except it was 12.7 mm tracers coming right at us. Megan goosed the plane and off we went, hopefully faster than a speeding bullet.

He hadn't been kidding. The tricky little VC were waiting for us in an ambush. The gunner on the Browning behind me blasted away, a few seconds of fire at a time. I was actually very glad I didn't have to shoot. I couldn't tell the difference between where the Marines were and where the VC were.

I made another trip over to Marble Mountain to see my brother Jim, who was stationed with VMO-2 in early August of 1968. He worked in the avionics shop but went out on gunship flights regularly as a gunner. I caught a lift with someone headed that way.

Marble Mountain was near the South China Sea and got shellings and ground attacks on a regular basis. After the war ended, we learned that the VC around Da Nang used the mountains as a rest and recuperation (R&R) center during the entire war. I've been back there twice and taken a tour through the mountain. The VC had a perfect view, from where they watched every aircraft's arrival and departure.

In 1969 a World Airways Captain landed a DC-8 in the dark of night on the tiny strip there, confusing it with the far longer twin runways at Da Nang about five miles to the west. World had to remove the seats and take on a minimum fuel load to get the plane out of the field the next day.

Marble Mountain was close enough to the real war that I wore a flak jacket and carried a snub nosed .38 revolver in a shoulder holster in case of problems. Generally when you were in potentially dangerous areas it made more sense not to have officer rank insignia on your cap.

As I sauntered into the VMO-2 area, a sergeant major came rushing up to me with his knickers in a twist. "Moriarty," he demanded in a huff, "what did I tell you about carrying non-issued weapons?"

I looked at him as he shouted my name. He seemed to know me but I had never seen him before in my life. He continued in a high pitch, "No snub nose pistols for you. Those are for officers and I don't know where you stole the damned thing, get rid of it. If you think you need to run around carrying a weapon, get an M-16 from the armory. Who do you think you are, anyway?"

Actually that was a very good question. "Sergeant Major," I asked in a polite but strong voice, "are you talking to me?"

His face turned a bright red as he answered, "I'm going to have your ass, you fucking wiseacre. Who do you think you are kidding?"

I lifted the flak jacket from where it covered my single silver bar indicating I was a first lieutenant and showed him my rank. "Sergeant Major, I think you have me confused with someone else. I have a snub nosed thirty-eight but it's an issue weapon and I will keep it. Thanks very much," I replied calmly.

He turned pale and began to sputter. "Sorry sir, but you look just like this feather merchant we have in the squadron named Moriarty. I swear you look like his twin brother. My apologies, sir. He's always carrying weapons he isn't qualified to carry and I thought you were him."

"Actually, Sergeant Major, I *am* his twin brother, but I'm an F-4 pilot with VMFA-542 at Da Nang over here to see him. Will you give me directions to where I can find him?"

The power of group think in the Marine Corps is so powerful that Jim could have pinned on a set of lieutenant bars and the sergeant major would have been saluting him instead of me, and gotten away with it.

A few days later Jim came over to the VMFA-542 ready room. He was wearing his utility uniform and a set of sergeant insignia, as was correct, seeing that he was a sergeant. He was sitting on the side of the ready room and I was facing forward in the front row. If you walked into the ready room from the back, you could see him but couldn't see anything of me but the back of my head.

I heard someone walking into the room. He stopped with his back to me and hands planted on his hips in an aggressive manner. It was the CO, Lieutenant Colonel Vitali.

"Moriarty, what the fuck are you pulling now? I'd like to see you as a sergeant but you are out of uniform and I'm going to have your ass."

I didn't really know which Moriarty he was talking to so rudely but I thought I would let Jim respond. Since we were indoors we didn't salute, but Jim stood smartly to attention in the presence of a senior officer. Me? I didn't give a damn. I wasn't going to stand to attention just because Vitali walked in.

"Sir, I am a sergeant and I am wearing the correct insignia for my rank. Perhaps you have me confused with someone else," Jim responded. Now that was cheeky. True, but cheeky.

"Your name is Moriarty, right?"

"Sir, yes sir." Now Jim was going to kiss up to him while in the process of deceiving him.

"You are in my squadron, right?" the Colonel continued to press.

"No sir, I'm flying with VMO-2 at Marble Mountain." I could hear him starting to grin. He was really getting into this.

"Sergeants don't fly gunships, unless things have changed recently." Vitali continued wandering down the wrong path.

"Sir, I don't fly them. I'm not a pilot, I'm a door gunner," Jim continued.

"What the fuck? We have a pilot named Moriarty, he's a lieutenant and an F-4 pilot as far as I know. Who the fuck are you?" Vitalli said.

I reached up and pulled on Vitali's shirt sleeve. "Skipper, I'd like to introduce you to my twin brother, Sergeant James Moriarty of VMO-2."

Vitali looked at Jim and then at me. Then looked at Jim again and back to me. "Well I'll be fucked. You do look like twins."

"Skipper, that's because we are twins. Jim is a sergeant because the Marine Corps found out his parents were married and demoted him."

Vitali chewed on that for a few minutes before stomping out of the ready room in a huff. We weren't the closest of chums.

August of 1968 brought a lot more flight time in combat in the F-4B. As the new skipper Vitali wanted to impress the Group CO who wrote his fitness report, so he pushed maintenance to get as many airplanes flying as possible. Everything in the Vietnam War was about generating numbers. How many sorties, how many bombs, how many bunkers destroyed and enemy dead.

You don't win wars by generating statistics. You win wars by convincing your enemy to change his ways. But no one ever discussed the fact that the Vietnamese had been fighting for their independence since 1930. All they wanted was to be free.

If Kennedy or Johnson or Nixon had ever read Bernard Fall, we could have saved the lives of 58,209 American kids and the $700 billion cost of the war. Fall knew we were on a losing path. Ironically he would be killed in the area he called "The Street Without Joy." Later in the war I would know The Street Without Joy intimately.

America began to get serious about Vietnam in 1964. The Gulf of Tonkin Resolution bullshit had nothing to do with anything the North Vietnamese did to our ships in the Gulf of Tonkin. It had to do with the fact that our thugs running South Vietnam were losing the war. They were losing the war because they were corrupt to the bone and the villagers hated them and the utter corruption of their government.

Americans either forgot or never learned that in the Geneva Accords of 1954 ending the French involvement in Vietnam, the US, France, the USSR, the UK and China all agreed that there would be a temporary line of demarcation at the Ben Hai River. Vietnam would be separated into two zones, the north zone controlled by the Viet Minh (who had defeated the French at the final battle of Dien Bien Phu) and the southern zone controlled by the State of Vietnam, then headed by former emperor Bao Dai.

A free general election in both zones would be held eighteen months later, by July of 1956, to create a unified Vietnamese country.

The US then refused to hold the election because our thugs would have lost.

Ho Chi Minh admired the US and modeled his Constitution and Declaration of Independence after ours. But the State Department had a fit over the fact he called himself a communist and accepted support from both the USSR and China.

We didn't have to fight him, and forty years after the fighting stopped in 1975 it's easy to see they were never our enemy. They just wanted to be free. We were the terrorists who invaded their country and tried to tell them what to do. You couldn't drive a jeep down the road in Da Nang without the kids flipping you the finger. They weren't kidding. When they got old enough they intended to pick up a rifle and kill as many Americans as they could until they made the price too high for us to bear. It worked.

On the night TPQ flight that we did just to say we had been in combat, something happened that I never expected. I was totally taken by surprise.

TPQ missions were always single aircraft flights. We carried our full load of ten low-drag 500-pound bombs. You don't drop anything else from 20,000 feet. As I began my takeoff roll, I worried about bombs falling off the plane. But that was only because I had never taken off loaded with ordnance. I got permission to take off. I released the brakes, although even fully loaded, when you kicked in full afterburners you had so much power that you were going to move even if the brakes were fully locked.

The stick was full aft, that's how you made a takeoff in the F-4B, stick full aft and ease forward as you gain airspeed. The brakes came off; the power levers went around the horn into full afterburner. Most of the takeoffs I would ever do, we were actually slightly over our maximum takeoff weight. But the F-4B only needed perhaps 3,000 feet even with 105-degree temperatures on the runway. The aircraft gained flying speed, the nose came up and we were airborne. You tapped the landing gear lever up and put the flap lever up once you had sufficient flying speed. So we were airborne and safe. When you had 300 knots, you came out of afterburner.

Most of the takeoffs were to the south at Da Nang. The field had two north-south runways and we used the south runway most of the time. The field had a full Marine Air Group, and the 366th Tactical Fighter Wing of the Air Force, and some Army O-1 and O-2 observation squadrons. The south end of the runway ran right up to the neighborhood we called Dogpatch. It was made up of thousands of homemade shacks providing housing to tens of thousands of

Vietnamese civilians who had fled the countryside to avoid being killed by either one side or the other in the name of freedom. In 1968 Da Nang airport had a takeoff or landing every two minutes.

By now I was a mile or so from the field and passing through 1,500 feet when I saw what looked like a roman candle going straight up, slightly to the left of my flight path. For a minute I wondered what it was when the lights went on under my brain bucket. I realized someone was shooting a 51-caliber machine gun straight up, trying to shoot me down. This was my first flight and already someone was trying to kill me.

Like Paul on the road to Damascus I went through an epiphany as I thought, "That guy's trying to kill me. What the hell did I do to piss him off? Why does he want me to die?"

During boot camp, ITR and flight training there is always the unspoken actions of the enemy but no one ever actually tells you, "They are going to try to kill you." So the first time bullets come right at you and you know there is someone out there who desires your death, you are taken aback and literally have to wonder, "Why's he trying to kill me? My momma loves me and would be very disappointed if I flew home in a box. What did I do to piss him off? Clearly he has some kind of attitude." You have some faint clue that being in the military might be dangerous but the first time bullets come your way, it still comes as a surprise.

The fact that you are in an F-4B loaded with ten low-drag bombs that you plan on dropping on his country estate escapes you. He's trying to kill you because you are trying to kill him. That sounds really simple but that's the one difference between those who have been in combat and those who never heard a shot fired in anger. There is a difference. Those who enter into combat in any form despise the rear echelon pogues who do everything in their power to avoid combat. We called them REMFs, for Rear Echelon Mother Fuckers. There was no greater insult. In the past forty-five years since I came back to the world, I've seen guys I soon realized had been Remington Raiders, office clerks. I wouldn't say it but I would think, "You REMF."

After a couple of the get-together TPQ missions we began the real war of dropping close air support to troops in contact with the enemy and who needed our help.

We carried a wide variety of weapons. Bombs came in 250-pound,

500-pound, 750-pound and 2,000-pound sizes. Most often we used the 500-pound Mk-82 bomb, which itself came in two varieties. It used the same fins either way it was used, but if the fins were set to open it became a high-drag bomb designed to be used from a low angle and low altitude delivery. If you didn't open the fins it became a low-drag bomb that you might drop in either a 45-degree or 30-degree dive. When the Navy operated in a high AAA threat environment up north of the DMZ, they typically used a 60-degree dive delivery.

The higher the angle of dive, the higher you began your approach and the higher you dropped. And the distance from the ground was the greatest. Those 60-degree dives gave you the worst accuracy. So high-drag bombs released at 500 feet in a 10-degree dive might go through the door of the hooch that was your target. If you were in a 60-degree dive you might pickle at 9,000 feet, and if the guy in the hooch even heard the sound of the explosion, you were being very accurate.

A variation of the bombs was called a "daisy cutter." When we needed a landing zone created, the best way to do it was to send in a team armed with chain saws who would cut all the trees down in a 30-40 meter wide circle so choppers could land. The VC and NVA naturally objected to us coming into the 'hood so we didn't do that. Instead we installed 36-inch long fuse extenders on 750 and 2,000-pound bombs. The fuse blew up the bomb when the fuse hit the ground. The bomb then went off 36 inches above the ground, and like cutting daisies, it made an instant landing zone. A daisy cutter is a long fuse that can be used on any size bomb; it is not a big bomb, as reporters confused it in Iraq War 1.

We used a lot of napalm. It came in 500-pound and 750-pound aluminum tanks. The Air Force used the 750-pound napes. We used the 500-pound napes. You always dropped it in a low angle 10-degree dive. The canisters had all the aerodynamic efficiency of a toilet bowl, so two dropped at exactly the same altitude, speed and time might hit fifty yards apart. But nape was an area weapon.

You did not want to be in the glide path of a napalm delivery. It was nasty. Basically it was JP-4 mixed with a thickener that gave it a jelly-like consistency, so it burned like jet fuel and it stuck to whatever it hit. According to the Geneva Conventions it was also illegal, but who cared? Peaceniks in the US felt that the supplier of the powder that you mixed with fuel to make napalm, Dow Chemical, was committing war crimes. They were not far off the mark.

We carried both the 2.75-inch folding fin aircraft rocket and the five-inch Zuni. The 2.75-inch rockets could be loaded in pods that carried either seven or nineteen rockets. Zunis came four to a pod. Zunis came standard with contact fuses but on occasion we used radar heads that would make them explode just above ground level for an airburst.

The wingman of the one F-4B that VMFA-542 lost in the year they were in combat has always believed that their Zuni rockets exploded right in front of their plane. That is what killed Captains John Lavoo and Bob Holt. It's possible that the radar head of one rocket "saw" another rocket just ahead and exploded. The wingman reported no ground fire at all; he thought the rockets were at fault. That's a sad way to lose a plane and crew.

We had a ceremony at Arlington for John Lavoo in 1999 after they found the remains of the aircraft and sent them back to the US. I told his daughter, who was only three at the time of his death, everything I could remember about her father. I knew him from VMFA-531.

We could carry a Hughes Mk-4 20 mm gun pod on the centerline station of the F-4B. For ninety per cent of the targets I had in Vietnam, the 20 mm gun was the single best weapon to use.

When the air war started in 1964, the Air Force soon realized that giving up guns and going to an all-missile fighter meant loss of opportunity. In Korea, US pilots claimed to have knocked down 10-12 MiGs for every US loss. After the war, studies showed that the real kill ratio was a far more modest two enemy aircraft shot down for every US plane. In the early days of air-to-air combat over North Vietnam the ratio was a dismal 1:1 or worse.

Aerial combat tactics devised by the US after Korea called for BVR (Beyond Visual Range) missile shots, where the US aircraft fired long-range missiles long before they could even see the enemy. Since we had Air Force and Navy aircraft in the same area at the same time, a number of US planes were shot down by other US planes in the early days of aerial combat starting in 1964. We soon fell back to the WW II and Korea concept of requiring visual confirmation before any missiles were fired. As a result, aerial combat regressed to turning and burning hassles where guns proved to be the best weapons. While the Navy still flew the A-1 Spad, they even had two kills against MiG-15 jet planes shot down by the internal 20 mm guns in the wings of the A-1.

The most advanced US fighter was the F-4 and it carried no internal gun. You could carry a 20 mm gun pod. The Air Force used a six-barrel 20 mm Gatling gun. The Navy and Marines used the two-barrel Mk-4 Hughes 20 mm gun. If the pilot fired too long a burst with the Hughes gun pod, one of the barrels would eventually jam and the gun became inoperative.

Pilots in my F-4 units hated the Hughes gun pod for any work, whether close air support or air-to-air. I loved it because it was the perfect weapon, only temperamental. It was a perfect example of a weapon procured to feed money to Hughes rather than to acquire the best gun. Clearly the Air Force 20 mm Gatling gun was the best gun ever used by American forces.

The Air Force even went to McDonnell Douglas and requested an internal 20 mm gun. They got it. The Marine Corps used the F-4 from 1962 until the retirement of the last aircraft in 1992 and never demanded an internal gun. Such incredible stupidity should always be rewarded but rarely is.

We also carried CBUs (Cluster Bomb Units) in canisters that were dropped the same way we dropped low drag bombs, in a 30 or 45-degree dive. At a certain altitude above the ground, the canisters would open the same way a clamshell does, and spread the bomblets in a donut-shaped pattern. Our CBUs carried as many as 2,000 bomblets in each CBU canister.

If you ever had enemy troops caught out in the open, CBUs were the best anti-personnel weapons to use. Unfortunately CBUs are like herpes, being the gift that keeps on giving. In Laos, Cambodia and Vietnam dozens and more, mostly children, are still being killed each year some forty years after the war. Estimates say that as many as twenty-five per cent of the bomblets failed to arm properly when released and are still killing people today.

In my eighteen months of training in Cherry Point before going to Vietnam, I did zero training in close air support. Nada. None.

We did do some air-to-ground work with the Mk-76 25-pound practice bombs in 30 and 45-degree dives. The practice bombs were inherently inaccurate and did not reflect the reality of dropping real bombs in combat. Looking back through my training records, I see I had a 108-foot CEP (Circular Error Probable). That meant that my bombs missed the target by an average of 30 meters. Still pretty close.

For the Marine Corps overall, with low-drag bombs in combat conditions, the CEP jumped up to over 500 feet. So every bomb dropped by us in South Vietnam missed by an average of 150 meters. Since the frag pattern of a 500 or 750-pound bomb is not more than 50-75 meters, it meant we missed all of our targets on average.

That's why I loved the gun pod. We never had hard targets in South Vietnam. We weren't hitting power stations or refineries or dams, we targeted bunkers and 50-caliber gun positions. In 1,150 hours of combat I never attacked a target bigger or harder than a good-sized outhouse. A 20 mm gun would have been perfect most of the time for the targets I went after. But we didn't have an internal 20 mm gun through abject stupidity of procurement, and the squadron didn't like loading the Hughes Mk-4 because the pilots didn't use it correctly.

That's a lot like using water bombs in grammar school when you really needed a peashooter.

When I began to get onto the flight schedule and started dropping ordnance for close air support, initially I wasn't very good. I never hit friendlies; good FACs never allowed you into a position where you could hit friendlies. You never flew over your own troops. But I would drop retarded high-drag bombs 250 meters long or napalm 200 meters short. I scared the hell out of a lot of VC and NVA but that's all. Most of that was due to a lack of training.

Gradually I got better. My RIO, Claude Pyatte, was a giant help. When I flew with him, he fed me the information I needed to hit the target. All of our close air support missions were two-plane sections. Some were planned, to support a particular unit that we knew about in advance, and a lot were flights where we operated out of the hot pad.

Being scheduled for the hot pad meant that you had a particular ordnance configuration; typically snake (high-drag bombs) and nape for the closest of close air support. We would have a section leader and a wingman. I was way too junior to be a combat section leader at first. We preflighted our assigned aircraft and went to sit in an air-conditioned trailer until we got a call to launch. We wore our full set of flight gear;

Nomex flight suit, Gee-suit, survival vest equipped with a couple of survival radios. We carried a .45 automatic if you wanted and for certain a snub-nose .38 loaded with red flare rounds.

We were on a five-minute notice. When notified to launch, we had to be on the runway and rolling within five minutes. The flights off the hot pad always turned interesting because the only guys who needed us were the guys who needed us *right now*. They would have troops in contact and required our ordnance or Marines were going to die.

The Marine Corps had three different wars going on at the same time. The 3rd Marine Division operated from just south of the DMZ to Phu Bai. They were based at Dong Ha and ran operations all over Northern I Corps. MAG 11 based out of Da Nang supported the 3rd Division as well as the 1st Marine Division. By and large the 3rd Marine Division fought uniformed and organized units of the North Vietnamese Army. While there were some VC in Northern I Corps, they were a tiny factor in the war up north.

The 1st Marine Division was based west and southwest of the Da Nang airfield. Their primary enemies were local indigenous units of the VC. Now and again the 1st Marine Division went up against uniformed NVA but their primary enemy was the VC. That was a tough and challenging war because it had no fronts. You had no idea of who was friend and who was enemy. Even that changed when the sun went down.

MAG 12 and MAG 13 flew out of the Chu Lai airfield some fifty miles to the southeast of Da Nang. MAG 13 was primarily an F-4 group with three F-4 squadrons but they also had an A-6 squadron. MAG 12 was an all-A-4 unit with three A-4E squadrons. MAG 12 and MAG 13 supported Marine ground forces all the way from Hoi An, southeast of Da Nang, to Leatherneck Square just below the DMZ.

I flew a lot of hot pad missions in support of the 1st Marine Division around Da Nang. The grunts of the division were in contact with the enemy for much of the length of their 13-month tours, or until they got killed or wounded. They had a tough war against a determined enemy.

One flaw, in my view a fatal flaw, in books about being in combat is that for the most part they are written by lifers, the guys who wanted nothing more than a fat retirement check at the end of twenty years' active duty. As a result, there are a lot of books written by squadron and battalion COs and few written by the guys who really fought the war.

Of the 58,209 American kids who died in Vietnam, more 20-year-olds died than any other age. Since it takes at least six months of training after someone joins the service voluntarily or is drafted, the weight of the war was on the lance corporals and corporals. I know that in the Air Wings, it was the junior officers who did most of the fighting. I'm told and I believe that it was the second lieutenants and platoon commanders who suffered the greatest losses among the grunts on the ground. So we heard from the guys who watched the war, not from the guys who fought the war.

Few books on combat reveal the depth of feeling the combat troops had about the REMF, the majors and lieutenant colonels back in the rear coming up with great ideas for operations that would get a lot of their men killed. The combat troops hated them. Wing and Division headquarters in Da Nang got all the steaks and fresh vegetables. The further out in the field you were, the worse the living conditions and the chow.

In VMFA-542 I lived in half of an air-conditioned Quonset hut with one roommate. We had our own personal refrigerator for storing beer and snacks. My roommate and I would kick in some Vietnamese piastres and spring for our own hooch maid twice a week. They would do a wonderful and cheap job of your laundry while drinking all your gin and replacing it with water.

In Quang Tri with VMO-6 I lived in a wooden SEA (South East Asia) hut with twenty other guys. We had no air-conditioning, no hooch maids, and the food the Wing didn't want. We pissed in the tubes that 105 mm ammo came in and crapped in four-man outhouses. That was a lot of fun.

I flew an average of one mission a day in 542. The squadron liked to get people out of country as much as they could, so I soon got orders to a week-long vacation going through a Water Survival School in northern Japan on a forty-acre base we took from the Japanese. At the time few Japanese spoke English, so we pointed to things we wanted to buy. You got 360 yen to the dollar so everything was cheap. Everything was either "number one" if it was good or "number ten" if it was bad. A well-educated and experienced Marine would speak perhaps fifteen words of Japanese. We knew even less Vietnamese.

We had seven-day R&R trips to exotic destinations such as Bangkok, Hong Kong, Tokyo, Manila, Sydney and Hawaii. There was an unspoken but rigidly enforced rule that the only guys who got R&R in Hawaii were the married pukes.

As far as the troops were concerned, the only purpose of R&R was to get laid. The junior enlisted guys almost all opted for Manila and Bangkok where there were thriving centers of prostitution and massage parlors where you were guaranteed to leave with a happy ending.

I wanted Sydney, based on the recommendation of my good friend and fellow scallywag Lieutenant Joe Featherstone, our squadron supply officer. We flew down to Sydney, checked into the best hotel in town and went to a mixer on the first night of the R&R. I connected with a couple of Army chopper pilots that I at least had something in common with. We met a handful of nurses that promptly picked out their mates for the next week.

I remember with great fondness sitting in a restaurant with the group of pilots and nurses. My intended reached under the table and put a firm grip on my knee and announced she could stay out late because she didn't have to go to work the next day. Perhaps when we got up, the two of us could go to the beach. She made it clear to me that she would shake me to wake me rather than call me.

She took me home that night and had her way with me. When we got up the next day we made plans for going to Bondi Beach. She suggested that I return to my hotel to shower, shave and pick up my swimsuit. She would have her boyfriend pick me up and the three of us would spend the day together. That sort of took me off guard. I wasn't all that eager to make the acquaintance of the boyfriend of the woman I had just spend the night with.

I could imagine the conversation, "Did you just sleep with my girlfriend?" he would ask.

And I would reply, "Not a wink. Not a single wink."

Bondi Beach is everything you will ever hear about it. We hit the beach and then went to a party later in the afternoon. There were about ten guys, each with their girlfriend, and there was me, now flying solo. The guys were all fascinated with the idea that I had been flying Phantoms in combat only two days before.

I looked around the house where the party was taking place. I was in the living room surrounded by ten guys. But I had just left the squadron two days before where I had been surrounded by fifty other guys. I wasn't interested in talking to guys; I could do that any time. I wanted female companionship.

I wandered into the kitchen where all the females were. After a few moments of silence caused by a male entering their domain, they started asking me questions. Not about war, but about my family and where I was from and what I wanted to do after Vietnam. In fifteen minutes I had the women hanging on my every word as if I was the most charming and interesting person they had ever met.

I thought it was something I was saying and doing. Actually it wasn't. Australian men were probably the most chauvinistic men I would ever meet. They thought women were sperm receptacles, little more. They had no more interest in listening to women than listening to the mating call of a branch of coral reef.

Then our threesome went to an Australian supper club. I've not seen anything similar anywhere else in the world. These were private clubs pretty much funded by the revenue from the hundreds of slot machines scattered around the club. There was a swarm of people having dinner and drinks in the club. They had entertainment and even a comedian.

Before the show started, the announcer came over the mike and said that the club had a very special guest, an American who had traveled all the way from the US to Vietnam to Sydney just to see the club, and they should give an especially warm welcome to the American Marine pilot fighting for their freedom in Vietnam. I looked around because whoever the guy was, we had a lot in common.

He was trying to honor me. "I want to extend a very warm welcome to First Lieutenant Robert Moriarty, a US Marine flying the F-4 Phantom." I watched in shock as the entire club stood and gave me a standing ovation. Over the course of the evening – and many free drinks, for it was impossible for me to pay for a drink – I learned that Australians still believed it was the 1st Marine Division who fought the Japanese at Guadalcanal and saved Australia from being overrun by the Japanese army.

I don't know the tradition now, but at the end of the evening everyone stood. First they played the Marine Corps hymn and then *God*

Save the Queen. I felt greatly honored.

I made the acquaintance of several other nubile and willing young women over the course of the next week. Australian men have no idea of what they are missing.

At the end of the week, as the 150 or so young men gathered to get on the buses back to the airport to return to Vietnam, I saw a sad sight. Many of the young American enlisted men thought the only way to find a bed partner was to pay for it. Australia had virtually no prostitution at the time; the women gave their love freely, as I had learned. At the bus there were a lot of 30-year-old women with boyfriends trying to shove money into their hands. The women couldn't understand why anyone would think they needed to pay for something freely given. But for a 20-year-old Marine, his first and last sex came from Tijuana when he had to pay to lose his virginity. They believed you either had to marry a woman to have sex or pay her.

Later in October of 1968 I came the closest I would ever come to ejecting. I went out on a normal TPQ mission. Da Nang weather proved to be pretty soggy, with low ceilings. The mission was over Laos and when we got back to Da Nang we had to hold while other aircraft landed. Then one guy landed with bombs on board and one came loose. The tower closed that runway, and all of a sudden we had more aircraft in the pattern than they could land safely and timely.

My fuel state was too low for me to divert to Thailand, which would have been by far my first choice. I had just about enough fuel for one GCA; I had to land. The controller brought me in and when I was about three miles out told me that the field was closed, as someone had blown a tire on landing and was sitting in the middle of the runway. We had a loose bomb on the right runway and a broken airplane on the left runway and I had no fuel.

I was instructed to complete the missed approach and to climb to 2,000 feet to the northeast by five miles of the Da Nang Tacan and then to eject.

My response was simple. "Fuck that. Keep me coming down, I'm going to land on the taxiway."

The tower came up and repeated the instruction to fly over the bay and eject about the time I broke out of the overcast. They refused to give me permission to land on the taxiway.

I was in the clear, I could see the runway, I could see the taxiway so I lined up to land. The tower said, "You do not have permission to land on the taxiway. Take your assigned heading and altitude and eject. Do you understand?"

I did. I said, "Fuck you. I'm landing. This is my airplane and I'm not putting it in the water because your runway is fucked up."

We landed and continued to taxi down the strip to the VMFA-542 hangers. Halfway there we ran out of fuel. Now the airport really was closed.

Early the next day Colonel Vitali wanted to see me. I knew for sure he would thank me for saving one of his birds that cost taxpayers $4.5 million. Maybe there would even be a medal in it for me for saving the plane and two American lives.

"Lieutenant, were you told to take the airplane over Da Nang bay and eject?" he snarled.

"Yes, sir. But I knew I could put it on the taxiway. I was so low on fuel; I may not have been able to climb to 2,000 feet. Given the circumstances I think I made the right decision."

Vitali continued, "You were given a direct order. Why didn't you obey it?"

I felt as if he was transmitting on one frequency and I was receiving on another. Was I in some alternative universe? I just saved an airplane and I'm getting my butt chewed.

"Get the fuck out of my sight. If you are given a direct order, you obey it. Do you understand me, Lieutenant?" he demanded.

One of us clearly didn't have a clue. In 1999 when we had the ceremony at Arlington for John Lavoo, the fellow who had been my RIO that day came up to me and thanked me for saving the plane. He came back to the US after his tour in 542 and went to flight training. Eventually he became an airline pilot and retired when he was sixty.

We used a Martin Baker ejection seat in the F-4B. It was pretty much guaranteed to mess up your back. So if we had done what we were told to do, we would have lost the airplane and probably ruined ourselves physically. And that's all dependent on the Sea Air Rescue being able to find us out in the bay in the middle of the night. I did the right thing. Warriors know when to obey orders. Even more importantly, they know when to disobey orders.

I flew one mission with T. R. Moore. Moore was a major, full of himself. I think he was ops officer or maintenance chief. In any case he was a big swinging Richard in the squadron, at least in his own eyes. We carried a load of 500-pound bombs, ten of them. DASC handed us over to an FAC operating just north of the Hi Van pass between Da Nang and the city of Hue, about 45 miles northwest of Da Nang.

I don't remember the target very well; maybe it was another "trees in the open" mission. We finished dropping our ordnance using a 30-degree dive to drop all the bombs in three or four passes as requested by the FAC. When I joined on Moore's wing we looked each other over for damage. He seemed to be streaming fuel from underneath his aircraft.

"Ringneck 009 lead, this is Dash-2. You are losing fuel from what looks like your main tank. I can see a hole in your belly." I spoke into my mask and transmitted to him.

Then it got interesting. We couldn't have been more than fifteen miles north of the field. Moore declared a mayday and requested a straight-in emergency landing with the crash crew standing by with foam. I didn't understand the panic. If we had been a hundred miles from the field with no idea of how bad the leak was, it could have been serious. But from ten miles away he could have practically shut the plane down and glided his lead sled home.

He landed, pulled off the runway and shut the plane down while still on the taxiway. Maintenance promptly sent a tug to drag it back to the hanger. By the time I landed and taxied in for hot refueling, Moore was holding court in the ready room, telling tales of how the entire hillside exploded with gunfire and he was lucky to make it through all the flying steel. That was very funny because I was flying the same pattern on the same target and I didn't see anything. The FAC never even reported any AAA or automatic weapons fire.

But you can't argue with facts. Major Moore did have a big hole in the bottom of his aircraft and it came from somewhere.

He was scheduled for R&R to Hawaii. He left the day after the mission and returned a week later. Maintenance had by then found the iron that made the big hole in his plane. They mounted it on a plaque to present to him when he got back. It seems that he had made a low pullout and the hole came from a fragment of his own ordnance. We didn't hear any more about how the hillside had erupted in gunfire.

By now I had been in the squadron for several months. Claude Pyatte and I each understood how the other worked and we were a smooth team.

Vitali kept pushing Wing to come up with an air-to-air role for VMFA-542. As a sop to him, the Navy agreed that 542 could fly the MiG Combat Air Patrol off Haiphong on November 2, 1968.

The Navy flew two different CAP locations. They had a pair of fighters stationed permanently over their carriers. That was the Ship CAP. Also they had a pair of fighters flying a racetrack-shaped pattern off Haiphong during daylight hours. That was the MiG CAP. Should the Air Force aircraft always stationed over North Vietnam indicate a takeoff of MiGs, the Haiphong CAP could be vectored into position to engage them.

Then on November 1, President Johnson announced a temporary ceasefire for everything north of the DMZ. US aircraft would not fly any bomber or fighter missions over North Vietnam until further notice. That ceasefire remained in effect all of the time I was in Vietnam.

But at 542 we were ecstatic. Any time our forces made a change, the North Vietnamese would try to determine the limits of the change. The CO put the word out that there would be an all-hands effort by the maintenance department to get as many aircraft ready for air-to-air combat as possible. That wasn't all that many. In several of our planes, the radar didn't work. It didn't matter at all for normal close air support missions but would be critical for air-to-air.

While the squadron had a full complement of heat-seeking Sidewinder missiles and radar-guided Sparrow missiles, all of them had made 200 carrier landings and then been transferred to us by the Navy, knowing the chance of us ever firing them was near zero. After all, the Marines didn't have a fighter role assigned to them, so why would they need air-to-air missiles that actually worked? But for a single day, we were to be a fighter squadron for real.

Naturally the first sections of aircraft went out according to the seniority of the pilots. Squadron CO leading the first element, the Squadron XO would replace him, and down the line. Much to my great pleasure and surprise, Claude and I were on the flight schedule to be on station at 1130 hours.

A section of two fighters would go up and relieve whoever was flying the racetrack pattern off the port of Haiphong. Haiphong unloaded all the Russian, Chinese and even Canadian ships sending supplies to North Vietnam. Trucks then took the cargoes to Hanoi via the Paul Doumer Bridge, constructed in 1902. American forces tried to drop that bridge dozens of times before some bright sparks did some measurements and realized we were using bombs too small in size. The Navy and Air Force lost dozens of aircraft to AAA guarding the bridge before laser-guided bombs finally destroyed it in 1972.

The section of fighters would fly the racetrack pattern at 25,000 feet in a giant oval until they ran short of fuel, and would be relieved by yet another section fully loaded with fuel. In theory one section would be in the racetrack pattern while the second section did aerial refueling off a Marine C-130 located further off shore. The closest we were supposed to get to North Vietnam was twelve miles, unless they committed some act of aggression such as an attempted pass in the direction of the carriers out on Yankee Station.

As the day grew longer, the aircraft problems mounted up. Missiles wouldn't tune. Radars gave up the ghost. Airframes got tired and gave up. It looked as if our day in the sun as a fighter squadron might be doomed.

Finally it came our turn for Claude and me to launch. I was the wingman, I don't remember just who the flight lead was. We flew the 300-odd miles to station.

Claude and I were in luck. Our radar tuned, we could pick out targets 45 miles away, close to the limit on the F-4B. We had four Sparrows on board; three of them tuned and said they were ready for combat. That had to be some kind of a record for the radar-guided missiles. We had an additional four Sidewinders. They all tuned as well. I also had one of the Mk-4 Hughes 20 mm gun pods to fall back on.

The takeoff and trip to station took about 45 minutes. As I remember, our pattern would be about 25,000 feet. MiGs might get above us to gain an altitude advantage but for the most part they liked to keep the battle below 15,000 where they had the turning advantage.

I talked to Claude and explained what I was going to do. I wasn't going to say anything about the gun pod or Sparrows tuning because anything that we transmitted to Red Crown, the Navy control for the MiG CAP, also went straight to Hanoi.

Our flight lead checked in. "Hello Red Crown control, this is Ringneck 533 with a flight of two aircraft. Lead has two Sparrow, four Sidewinders and 45 minutes time on station. Dash-2 has four Sidewinders, negative radar or Sparrows, also 45 minutes loiter time."

Claude and I snickered to each other. Anything to lead the enemy into underestimating our potential.

The pattern ran for 25 miles north, then a turn to the south, 25 miles to the south and a turn back to the north. While the flight was terminally boring, it could get exciting in a hurry. We counted on Red Crown to feed us information about any MiGs that might get airborne from the airfields surrounding Hanoi. It seems pretty strange today but during the American Vietnam war, we were forbidden to attack any of the fighter airports or the port of Haiphong.

For a warrior to be forbidden to attack his enemy makes no sense. We could attack any MiGs once they got airborne. We just couldn't attack them on the ground. And it was ok for the North Vietnamese to unload weapons at Haiphong, as we couldn't target them until they left the port area. It wasn't a real war except for the dying of young Marines.

When our fuel state got down to below 10,000 pounds, Red Crown would have the next section relieve us. Then we would fly out to the tanker and gas up with a full load. You wanted as much fuel on board as you could carry. We had the 370-gallon drop tanks on each wing. If we needed to clean up, we could pickle them and get down to fighting weight with one press of a button.

Our section did two tours on the MiG CAP and went to refuel, and that was when the gods of war smiled upon us. Our flight lead developed a hydraulic leak and had to return to base. He asked if we were willing to stay on station until another flight could relieve us. We had just come off the tanker with a full load of fuel.

"Dash 2, this is Ringneck 533 lead. Are you willing to stay on station until we can get another section up here? I understand your radar is down and you can use Sidewinders but there is no one else who can do it for another thirty minutes," he transmitted.

Claude and I were jumping for joy. The only thing in life worse than a copilot is a flight lead in an air-to-air environment that wants to shoot down what by all rights should be *your* MiG.

I smiled and responded, "Ringneck 533 lead, this is Dash 2. We are fine. Most of the Sidewinders seem ok. We will probably be fine."

I wasn't really talking to him; I was talking to Hanoi flight ops, hoping they would take the bait. By this time Claude and I had been airborne for over three hours. Our butts were sore. But we were counting on the North Vietnamese to think they had a single aircraft barely armed and with a tired crew who really weren't up for combat. Like hell we were.

We did our 25-mile leg to the south and began our turn to the north. Claude says over the intercom, "Mo, you might want to chill the 'Winders, I've got a pair of aircraft bearing 340 at 45 miles. No, make that three planes."

I wasn't about to give away our secrets just yet but I called Red Crown. "Red Crown, this is Ringneck 533 Dash 2, do you have anything airborne? It seems pretty boring up here."

"Ringneck 533, Red Crown. Do you read?"

"Red Crown, Ringneck 533, loud and clear. Go ahead."

"Ringneck 533, we have three aircraft that just departed Phuc Yen now climbing. Speed indicates probably MiG-21s. We will keep you advised."

Claude and I were about to wet our flight suits. The gooners were falling for our trap.

"Claude, when we do our next turn to the south, I'm going to put it in burner and do a climb and keep coming around 360 degrees. They won't be expecting us to stay in the turn. If I am right, they will be boring out to us and we will have an energy advantage on them like crazy. I want to set up for a Sparrow and as soon as the donut closes I'm going to light it off. I want you to lock up the flight leader. I'll take him out first and count on the other two to start worrying about which of them I am going to take out next."

The Sparrow missile required a constant radar lock from the firing aircraft until it hit. It was a good BVR missile but a rotten dog-fighting missile because you often would lose your radar lock in a dogfight. No radar lock, no Sparrow kill.

In a dogfight with one aircraft against three enemy planes, actually the single ship has the advantage. The flight lead of the enemy flight is focused on targeting you but his wingmen are focused on staying with him, not worrying about what you are going to do next. For taking out the flight leader, who had no idea I had him on radar, I had live Sparrows that tuned perfectly and were the best weapons for a standoff fight. He would still be floating down in his 'chute while his wingmen were wondering what the fuck just happened to him.

Claude and I came to the north end of our pattern at twelve miles off the coast of Haiphong. I started my turn to the east and shoved the twin throttles to their stops. I had my fuel selector set to burn out my wing tanks as soon as possible, because if we started turning and burning I was going to pop them off the plane. I kept up my rate of turn and rolled out with the MiGs on my nose at about thirty miles. All they had to do was keep coming and cross the twelve-mile legal border and they were mine.

The flight did fall for my trap and were coming after me, but something in my behavior told someone that maybe this battle wasn't going to be quite as one-sided as they thought. I was supposed to be a victim yet I wasn't acting like a victim, I was acting just like I was about to kick ass and take names. Just inside the twelve-mile arc, they made a steep turn to the west and blasted back to home plate.

If it had been October 31 and if we hadn't had the twelve-mile restriction I could have blasted the flight leader out of the sky and gone after the wingmen to see if I could carve them up as well. I had the entire fight under my total control though they didn't realize it. But we did have the restriction, and when they turned back to North Vietnam I couldn't go after them.

Rats.

In the entire American Vietnam war from 1955 until 1975 not a single Marine pilot flying a Marine plane shot down a North Vietnamese plane. True, two Marines on exchange duty with the Air Force did shoot down MiGs, but those Marines flew Air Force planes. Claude and I were one of maybe ten Marine crews who ever had a MiG on their scope, if that many. I went through flight training with dozens of Navy pukes who went on to fly the F-8 and F-4 off carriers and none of them ever had a MiG on their scope.

Claude and I had three of them dead to rights and couldn't fire.

Rats.

Eventually someone relieved us on station and we flew back to Da Nang. We were really hoping that we could do a couple of victory rolls over the Da Nang airfield but it was not to be. This flight would be one of 125 missions I flew in the F-4B and it was my only actual fighter mission.

With all the time on station and refueling three times, we had 4.6 hours in the bird that day. That was my longest flight in any aircraft ever. Not in terms of sitting in a plane but sitting on a concrete survival seat pan.

By now Vitali and I had taken measure of each other. I couldn't stand him and he thought little of me. Since everyone who wore wings in the USMC wanted to be a "fighter pilot", junior officers rarely lasted over six month before being transferred to some silly ground job. It was the typical stupid Marine Corps thinking of the time. You should take your best and most competent pilots out of the cockpit and put them in a ground position.

Probably the worst job in the Marine Corps at the time was to be assigned as a ground FAC with a grunt unit in Vietnam. These were air wing crew, either pilots or backseaters, sent out to the field to tromp around with the grunts. You were responsible for coordination with the chopper groups to get supplies flown out to your unit. When you had casualties you needed to talk helicopters into your position for medevacs. As a pilot and an officer you found yourself neither fish nor fowl. In most ground units the radio operator for the FAC could do as good a job as the FAC, or better. In many cases the FACs became infantry officers when the battle started and the bullets started flying.

One guy I flew with in 531 spent six months out in the field with a grunt unit southwest of Da Nang in the Arizona Territory, known for the constant gunfights. In one battle, he and an NVA soldier mere feet from him were trading hand grenades back and forth until one of his took out the NVA soldier. I think there was some sort of rule we covered when we went through flight training that said pilots weren't supposed to get within grenade range of the enemy. If there wasn't, there should have been.

While Vitali was looking around for the very worst job he could find for me, I looked for a decent billet. It's the nature of warfare. While you make your plans on how you are going to outwit your enemy, he's busy doing exactly the same thing to you.

One day in mid-November I was up in the MAG headquarters

talking to the personnel officer. I wanted to know what jobs there were for junior officers who weren't needed in the fighter outfits. Casually he mentioned a request from Wing for four pilots to be sent to Quang Tri to work as FACs flying the O-1 Charlie and the O-1 Golf with VMO-6. Each MAG was to send in the name of two potential candidates.

That was it. That was the perfect position for me. I had been through ALO (Air Liaison Officer) school shortly after I got my wings. Being a Bird Dog pilot would be perfect. I had already learned how to control naval gunfire from ships offshore and how to work artillery batteries.

So the envelope consisted of three MAGs each submitting the names of two pilots, for Wing to pick the four best qualified. The MAG 11 personnel officer told me that he had already picked the two pilots to be submitted from MAG 11. I asked if either of them was trained as ALO. I had the MOS. So he looked in their records, and neither of them was qualified. He took a pencil, scratched out one name and inserted my name, serial number and rank. In five minutes his clerk had typed up the new response to the Wing.

When the enemy is about to roll into your six o'clock position and shoot you down, you need to use every bit of skill and skullduggery you possess. There may have been four guys at MAG 12 and MAG 13 just as eager to avoid real combat as I was, so I stacked the deck. They were in Chu Lai, fifty miles away, and I was half a mile from Wing.

Actually, my entire career in the USMC prepared me for being an FAC with VMO-6. I had been a real grunt, an 0300, albeit for the shortest of times. I could shoot. I went through intelligence school. And best of all, I actually could fly tail dragger aircraft. I had a lot of time in both the C-117 and the C-45.

I snuck over to Wing and found the assistant personnel officer, a major, and made my pitch. I had done my six months in the F-4B so I knew the limits of aircraft and ordnance. I was tail dragger qualified; I was an 0202 intelligence officer and an ALO at the same time.

The major actually thought I was doing him a giant favor. Here I was, probably the most qualified first tour pilot in the Marines for flying the O-1 in combat. He dictated the orders picking the four pilots to be sent to VMO-6. My name was at the very top.

When I went back to VMFA-542 that afternoon the personnel

officer hinted that Vitali was looking around to find a good spot for me as a ground FAC. I smiled. By the time he found the worst position for an aviator with either the 1st or 3rd Marine Division I would be flitting around overhead in a Bird Dog.

This was one case where youth and vigor overcame old age and treachery.

A week later my orders came in from Wing, assigning me for duties involving flight operations and training with VMO-6 in Quang Tri. The CO handed them to me with a look of both great surprise and even greater disappointment. In between grins I attempted to pretend the orders were as big a surprise to me.

I was on my way to flying combat in a real warbird, the O-1 Bird Dog, with the best mission in the war.

Chapter 13
VMO-6, QUANG TRI, VIETNAM

War, huh, yeah, What is it good for?
Absolutely nothing
War, huh, yeah, What is it good for?
Absolutely nothing
Say it again, y'all

War, huh, good God. What is it good for?
Absolutely nothing
Listen to me

Ohhh, war, I despise
Because it means destruction of innocent lives

War means tears
To thousands of mothers' eyes
When their sons go to fight
And lose their lives

I said, war, huh,
Good God, y'all
What is it good for?
Absolutely nothing
Say it again

War
Songwriters: Barrett Strong and Norman Whitfield
Sung by Edwin Starr
Copyright: Sony/ATV Music Publishing LLC 1969

I MADE MY LAST FLIGHT with Claude Pyatte (or anyone else) in the
F-4B on November 18, 1968; a close air support mission near Da Nang.

It was one of seventeen flights I made in the F-4B in the entire month. A couple of days later I would have my initial flight in the Bird Dog in Quang Tri. That first flight in the O-1 took place on November 22. I would fly more combat in a single week in the Bird Dog than I was doing in the F-4B in a month. It was a marriage made in heaven, the O-1 and me.

I took a couple of days to turn in my gear and to check out of VMFA-542. I was able to catch a ride on the pretty much daily run from Da Nang to Quang Tri in the C-117 as a result of my flying with the H&MS unit at Da Nang.

Checking into VMO-6 showed me an entirely different side of the war. When I went to the medical facility to turn in my medical jacket, they had just treated two crewmen from an OV-10 that had taken hits that day. The pilot was injured badly enough that he had already been flown to Da Nang for medical care. The AO in the rear seat was also named Moriarty, Timothy Moriarty. The 50-caliber rounds through the canopy cut him up around the face from the Plexiglas shards. Clearly there was a lot more combat happening in Quang Tri than in Da Nang.

The four fixed wing pilots selected by Wing checked into VMO-6 at about the same time. One I had known in flight training, Jimmy Reese. He was in a preflight class about two months behind me so should have made it to Vietnam six months before me. But while going through advanced flight training in Kingsville, one weekend he and his roommate got totally wasted. Jimmy climbed out on a ledge outside their room and fell three floors to the concrete below. It would have killed him had he not been utterly hammered.

We had a former F-4 pilot named Al Parker that came up from Chu Lai and an A-6 pilot named Stevens. They were both captains. Al Parker came from F-4s at MAG 13, John Stevens had been an A-6 driver out of MAG 11 in Da Nang.

When I got to the squadron, the O-1 unit with VMO-6 was sort of a redheaded stepchild that didn't really belong to anyone. Marines had first used observation aircraft in the role of a member of the air wing team as early as 1944 and they had proven their value to the infantry. In the three VMO squadrons in the Marines, the units had UH-1E gunships and O-1C Bird Dogs in 1964.

But in its wisdom the Marine Corps planned on leaving their O-1 aircraft behind. Some were even given away to Civil Air Patrol units as discards. Combat needs in and around Da Nang in 1965 showed the need for Marine pilots controlling Marine fixed wing aircraft, so a half-dozen planes were brought to Vietnam, but the Marine Corps literally did not have a spot in a squadron for them. From 1965 to 1968 the Marines had an O-1C detachment assigned to an H&MS unit. It floated around the country, used where it could be used.

By the middle of 1968 someone finally figured out that we had the planes, we had the pilots, and we needed to assign the small unit to someone. So the O-1s returned to VMO-6 where they started out in the first place.

At some point the Marine Corps woke up and realized that for Marines to get the most benefit from close air support, they needed Marines controlling them while flying Marine aircraft. I don't know how they did it but we stole 5-10 airplanes from the Army and called them the O-1G. It was slightly lighter than the O-1C and had a smaller engine but it flew just fine. We used four of the 2.75-inch smoke rockets on the O-1G and six with the O-1C.

If there is a God in heaven, and I'm not sure either way, she has a sense of humor. I went from being a sort of useless appendage similar to an appendix in VMFA-542 to being highly valued in VMO-6. I had been through ALO School and that helped. I had been through Army intelligence school and that helped. I flew tail waggers with the C-47, the C-117 and the C-45, and that helped.

The OIC of the O-1 detachment – we were still called that even when back in VMO-6 – was Major L. J. Drayer until he rotated back to the States and was replaced by Major D. T. Sites. Both of them left the Bird Dog pilots alone as much as they could. We didn't need to be led; we were already the best there was.

But Major Drayer took me under his wing for training. He threw me in the backseat of one of the Bird Dogs and took me out to familiarize me with the area. When we returned to Quang Tri he intended to have me do touch-and-go landings until I had a feel for the plane. All tail draggers want to ground loop; we lost more aircraft to inexperienced pilots ground looping them than to combat.

I had no instruments in the back of the plane, just a stick and throttle, but the airplane seemed pretty stable. Major Drayer told me, "I want you to focus on setting your attitude with your tail just above the ground, pull the power back and let the plane settle on the main landing gear. You do not have to let the tail wheel down. But once you are firmly on the mains, add full power and go around. We'll do this until you get comfortable flying a tail wheel plane."

"Wilco," I responded.

I pulled the power most of the way back; I did want to keep some power on. I dipped the wing into the wind and cross-controlled the rudder and ailerons so I could maintain directional control. When I thought I was an inch or two above the runway, I pulled the power all the way aft. The left main squeaked as it touched down. I kept the cross controls in and the right main still airborne as I smoothly added power to go around.

Major Drayer grunted into his lip mike as he punched the intercom button. "You little fucker, you've done this before. How much time do you have in the Bird Dog?"

"Actually, including today's flight," I responded, "I'd make it an even forty-five minutes."

"Don't you dare bullshit a bullshitter, you've flown this plane before," he insisted. "I know an experienced pilot when I fly with one."

"No, I haven't. I've never been in one before. I do have some time in the Beech 18 and the C-117," I maintained.

"Just how much time in those planes?" he continued to quiz me.

"Maybe fifty hours in the C-45 and two hundred in the 117."

"You little fucker, you sandbagged me. You have more tail dragger time than I do! You just became the maintenance test pilot and the instructor for the new guys. You jet jocks aren't worth shit in a tail wheel airplane because none of you ever flew real airplanes before. You think you are so smart; well, you just became the senior instructor. See if you can find the runway again and I'll buy you a beer."

He was dead right about jet jocks. The first and last piston engine airplane most of us flew was the T-34 in primary flight training. The T-34 was draggy enough that when you pulled the power back it fell out of the sky. The Bird Dog was pretty similar to a Cessna 170. They floated down. Jet jocks really had giant problems controlling the plane and keeping directional control in a strong crosswind. At anything greater than fifteen knots if you had full flaps down, you were going to lose it and go into a ground loop, where the tail wanted to flip around and lead you instead of following you like a good plane should.

So in the Bird Dog I flew a single airplane familiarization flight and completed one practice landing. I would do all the fam flights from then on. But learning how to control air strikes took more time. I made my first flight in the O-1 on November 22 and didn't actually begin to control air strikes until November 27.

I suppose now would be a good time to define "close air support". When you drop ordnance, it is either close to friendlies or not close. With platforms such as the B-52, with formations of as many as 27 airplanes dropping 117 of the Mk-82 500-pound bombs each, you don't want to be dropping close to friendlies. Those formations had area size targets. But when troops are in direct contact with the enemy, often you need to drop within 100-200 meters of their position.

No matter who your enemy, he is going to figure out your tactics and capabilities and will try to outwit you. While you are busy making serious plans to defeat him, he is doing the same thing, planning on how he can kill you. In Vietnam, the VC and NVA realized that the closer they came to our ground troops, the safer they were from aerial attack. From a book learning point of view, anything closer than 500 meters was danger close, but literally every close air support mission I ever saw used the limits of the ordnance to determine just how close you could safely put the ordnance.

The bombs we used the most were the Mk-82 500-pounders. You didn't want to be dropping them much closer than 150-200 meters from friendlies, else you start to kill your own people. I liked the Mk-81 a lot more; it was a 250-pound bomb so you could sidle up a little closer to the friendlies. Nape was always a pinpoint weapon, used as close as 50-100 meters if the dropping aircraft knew for certain just where the friendlies were. We used rockets to good effect but the F-4s and A-4s couldn't carry many of the five-inch Zunis and they didn't pack much of a punch in comparison to 250 or 500-pound bombs. The 2.75-inch rockets were area weapons for when you caught the enemy out in the open. That didn't happen all that often.

The very best weapon we could use for close air support was a 20 mm gun but as far as the military was concerned, it was way too low-tech. The military-industrial complex wasn't going to get rich off of guns so we lacked the right close air support planes. FACs rarely used 20 mm because no airplanes carried many rounds of ammo.

As an F-4 driver I knew most of this before going to VMO-6, but learning the difference between how the Navy used the F-4 and how the Marines and Air Force used it was critical to being a great FAC.

Navy aircraft included the A-4, the A-6, the A-7 and the F-4. After the bombing halt called by Lyndon Johnson on the November 1, 1968 we had access to far more Navy planes but they lacked both the fuel range and the ordnance to give us the kind of support we needed. In order to operate off carriers, they carried perhaps 50 per cent of the load similar land based aircraft carried.

While all Marine pilots were carrier qualified during flight training, the Marine Corps operated no fixed wing aircraft off carriers during the Vietnam War. With the sole exception of a Navy unit flying the OV-10 near Saigon, the Navy flew all their fixed wing airplanes from carriers.

Since the Navy pilots had been operating in a very high AAA threat area when attacking North Vietnam in the Hanoi area of battle, all they ever wanted to do was make a single pass and leave. We called it "one pass and haul ass." Accuracy suffered greatly and basically we couldn't use the Navy planes for real close air support; the pilots simply weren't qualified.

VMO-6 was the most bastard squadron in the Marine Corps. We had I think eighteen UH-1E gunships armed with four forward-firing M-60 7.62 mm machine guns as well as two nine-shot 2.75-inch rocket pods. The Hueys operated as gunships to support CH-46 aircraft going into hot LZs. The Hueys weren't there to kill nearly as much as they were to convince the NVA to keep their heads down until the choppers could finish loading or unloading their cargo.

By and large the gunship pilots were on their first tours. We had a few more senior captains and a major or two, but by and large, flying helicopters in Vietnam wasn't a popular occupation. By their aerodynamics, the only way choppers even flew was because they were light. Flying thin-skinned and vulnerable airplanes, the chopper drivers knew they were targets. The CH-46 aircraft replaced the UH-34, which was powered by an R-1820 piston engine that sat in front of the two pilots. Nothing on earth short of an atom bomb was going to pass through one of those engines. With the CH-46 the engines were on the top of the plane and nothing protected the pilots. The pilots saw themselves as bullet stoppers for the engines and it should have been the other way around.

The Hueys flown by VMO-6 had only giant Plexiglas windows that wouldn't stop a determined BB gun assault.

In August of 1968 VMO-6 began to get the first of the OV-10 observation aircraft. In order to stop the high number of trained and experienced helicopter pilots from leaving the Marines, Washington DC realized they needed some sort of bait. The chopper pilots pretty much refused to fly multiple tours of duty in Vietnam in such dangerous aircraft as they had flown before. It wasn't just that they were dangerous; it had far more to do with the fact that the pilot was little more than a target. You weren't taking the fight to the enemy; you were sitting there waiting for him to finally improve his aim well enough to hit you.

So in their infinite wisdom the Marines promised the second tour former chopper drivers that they could transition to fixed wing aircraft via the OV-10. I think we had about a dozen of the new planes, all flown by former helicopter pilots. Similar to the UH-1E, the Bronco carried four forward-firing 7.62 mm M-60 machine guns and two 19-shot 2.75 inch rocket pods. The Bronco pilots could control air strikes using WP rockets out of one pod fired one at a time or could deliver high explosive 2.75-inch rockets from the other pod.

The OV-10 thus had a dual role, as an observation aircraft replacing the aging O-1 and as an offensive aircraft with minor offensive capability compared with the A-4 or F-4. I don't know, but I don't think the plane filled either role that well. As an observation plane they were much faster than the O-1, and that's a real limitation. We flew low and slow. We could both hear and see the enemy. As an attack platform they didn't carry much ordnance. The Navy used the OV-10 with 20 mm guns and it proved far more effective.

The question was always: is immediate but limited ordnance more or less valuable than bigger ordnance delivered a few minutes later? As far as the grunts were concerned, they liked the OV-10 for keeping heads down but they loved the F-4 for killing the enemy.

Finally VMO-6 had the ten or so remaining O-1 aircraft in the inventory. No stateside squadrons had Bird Dogs any longer. And I don't think there were any stateside-trained O-1 pilots who ever flew as FACs. All of the Bird Dog pilots I knew were former fixed wing pilots from fighter and attack squadrons.

By November of 1968 the old hands in the Bird Dog, like Captain Chuck Saunders, Captain Tom Irvine and First Lieutenant Stephen Palmason, had all flown 300-400 missions and were ready for orders home.

It's hard to imagine just how much power our government put into the hands of people in their early twenties. By now I was twenty-two. I was the youngest but the rest of the Bird Dog pilots were only twenty-four to twenty-six years old. The government handed us ultimate power. When a Marine Bird Dog went out into battle he determined who lived and who died. We owned the battlefield. Everyone worked for us. The artillery fired where we told them to shoot, the fixed wing dropped exactly where we told them to drop. Navy ships fired the rounds we demanded and where we wanted them. When it was time for an emergency extraction, the choppers went in when we told them it was safe. If you shot at us, you died.

We were nothing more than a bunch of highly trained and motivated kids. The observation pilots controlled all of the air war, while among officers the grunt junior officers did all of the fighting on the ground. We had the power of life and death. When the NVA threatened Marines, we killed them. We liked our Marines; we had gone through boot camp and training with them. Not for a moment would we want to change places with them, but their lives were in our hands.

The O-1 was the lightest tactical aircraft in the Marine inventory, and the oldest. It was also the most deadly. The F-4 may have carried a lot more ordnance and done a better job of turning jet fuel into noise and smoke, but it was an O-1 that controlled that ordnance and ran the battlefield.

Steve Palmason and I would share an apartment after my return from Vietnam while I went to school. I even dated his sister when I moved to New York. Shortly after I arrived in VMO-6 he earned a Silver Star for a mission that reads like it came out of a movie.

Steve launched on November 25 for a normal O-1 mission with an observer in the rear cockpit. When he checked in with Dong Ha DASC, the controller for his area told him to report to a grunt unit that was in close contact with an NVA unit and had taken several casualties. When Steve made contact there were two CH-46 helicopters orbiting below a low ceiling. There were no OV-10 or Huey gunships available, dusk was falling, and due to the low ceilings it was impossible to call in fixed wing aircraft.

Steve took charge and used the CH-46s as gunships. Each machine had two 50-caliber machine guns, one on each side. Steve worked with the grunts to figure out where they were taking fire from the NVA and then marked the targets for the CH-46s, which made strafing runs on the NVA. Every time he fired a smoke rocket the NVA presumed fixed wing aircraft would shortly be swooping down on them with nape and snakes, but it was only choppers using their internal guns.

Since it was late in the day and dark approached, everyone agreed the choppers needed to pick up the wounded and get them to medical care. The 46s had run low on 50-caliber ammo and the grunts were running low on M-16 ammo, so Steve fired the rest of his WP rockets and dumped several smoke grenades he had in the plane with him to create a smokescreen for the chopper going into pick up the wounded. He even made a low pass to drop the two bandoleers of M-16 ammo he carried in the plane to the infantry troops.

All the while the NVA were blasting away at him and the choppers.

Jeff Stack was his AO that day, and throughout the flight he was blasting back at the NVA with his M-16 from the back seat. In addition, Jeff had an M-79 grenade launcher with him in the plane and as the CH-46 pulled out of the zone, Jeff continued to fire grenades at the NVA position.

If Steve hadn't done everything that he did, those Marines would have died. There would have been no criticism of him for orbiting overhead and saying he couldn't do anything for them. That happened all the time. But Steve Palmason was a warrior. Warriors do whatever the situation calls for to protect their men. Marines stayed alive that day who wouldn't have done, but for the actions of Steve and his AO. The NVA are still trying to figure out what the nutcases in the O-1 were trying to do.

Steve went on to become the very first pilot hired off the street by Herb Kelleher, founder of Southwest Airlines. Kelleher brought together several small regional airlines in Dallas to form Southwest

Airlines. Steve soon became chief pilot and flew for thirty-two years with the airline before retiring in 2003.

I don't remember who it was that trained Jim Reese. He was one of the four guys who went to VMO-6, including me. On the morning of December 2, 1968, less than a week after getting qualified in the O-1, First Lieutenant James R Reese and his AO Rich Latimer were shot down and killed. Jim was the class clown during flight training but he was also the guy everyone loved for his insanity. I miss him a lot. He was only twenty-six years old.

That same day, Al Parker was up in the DMZ next to the Ben Hai river when he got shot up. He took a round right in the wrist that hit his watch but returned to Quang Tri safely.

By now I was pissed. One good friend had been killed and one of the guys I came to VMO-6 with wounded. I found a willing AO, signed out an M-60 machine gun and loaded my plane with half a dozen boxes of 7.62 ammo loaded with four ball rounds and one tracer. I wanted the NVA to know I had them in my sights. We flew up to the exact coordinates where Al Parker had taken his hits. I told the AO to lock and load and blast the shit out of the tree line on the other side of the river. He did, and we had hot brass flying all over the cockpit.

At that time the only way you could get permission to drop ordnance in the DMZ or in North Vietnam was if you first took fire. Sure enough, the NVA didn't like getting shot at any more than Al Parker did. They opened up on us with three or four 50-caliber machine guns. Now I had my excuse to respond.

I called DASC and requested a couple of flights of air; I was taking fire from North Vietnam. They neglected to ask just who fired first and I may have forgotten to tell them. Soon I had a pair of Gunfighters from the 366th Tactical Fighter Wing in Da Nang. The two F-4Ds had ten Mk-82s apiece, and 20 mm.

By now the NVA were madder than hornets. I knew they were going to do everything they could to shoot down the F-4s, so I tricked them. I had one aircraft running in from the west and one running in from the east. I had one plane make his pass but told him not to drop. When he buzzed the hornets and they tried to sting, the other plane could see where the fire was coming from. Naturally we had no idea of how much damage we did that day but a few days later there was a line of new graves with twenty recent burials.

On a regular basis I would check out an M-60 machine gun or an M-79 grenade launcher and take a bunch of ammo on a flight. Due to the heat, we always flew with the side windows open. I'd fly the airplane with my knees and go over a tempting-looking area. When I saw trails come together or what looked like good cover, I'd blast the area with the M-60 or pop a few M-79 40 mm grenades into the trees. If there were any NVA in the neighborhood, they would figure I had seen them so they would shoot back. That was a giant mistake. We couldn't see them, but at close ranges we could hear them firing their AK-47s. They only needed to do it once. I considered it "trolling."

Soon after I got to VMO-6 and had checked out as a fully qualified TACA (Tactical Air Controller Airborne) pilot, Santa came to visit once again. I already had been assigned as chief maintenance test pilot. That meant any time an aircraft had had work done on it that required a test flight, I got to fly it. There was no regulation that forbade carrying a full load of smoke rockets and smoke grenades. So I was already being handed the keys to the Corvette. And I got to do all the training. Basically I was simply more qualified than any of the other pilots, including the senior Bird Dog pilots, because I had so much time in tail wheel equipped aircraft.

Life got even better. Major Drayer made me the scheduling officer for the O-1s on the basis that I knew the plane and the pilots better than anyone else.

Every Marine and Navy officer has a primary occupation. Mine was to be a pilot. But he will also be assigned some collateral job in his squadron. If you were the junior officer in the squadron, you automatically became the SLJO or Shitty Little Jobs Officer and got handed every piece-of-shit job imaginable. We had guys who wanted maintenance experience and we had pilots who felt they needed to understand personnel work and people who wanted the goodies that came with becoming a supply officer. Me? My very most important goal in life was to become the scheduling officer.

If you were the scheduling officer, you didn't have to whine and cringe for better missions. All you had to do was figure out the best hops and spell your name correctly next to them. At the time I think we had about eight pilots and maybe ten planes. Some pilots wanted a lot of combat, one or two wanted only their four hours a month to collect flight pay. I made it crystal clear to all the other Bird Dog pilots to not even bother trying to whine their way into the good missions, for they were mine and I wasn't about to share. I was the past master at cringing and whining to get my way so they couldn't fool me.

As a result of Santa coming early, in December I outflew all the other pilots in the squadron. That was unheard of for a fixed wing pilot in either Bird Dogs or Broncos, to have more time than the pilots of the two seat Hueys. It just wasn't done. Quietly I just went out and flew my ass off. I ended up with 136 hours for the month, or over four hours a day, every day. I even flew two hops on Christmas Day but they were really boring due to the ceasefire in effect for the day.

Just to round out my career as the Bird Dog SLJO, they made me the assistant awards officer. I don't remember who the awards officer was but I do remember he couldn't write for shit. He would assemble the facts of each recommendation and I would make it both readable and exciting.

I did get to look through all the past recommendations for ideas of what to say and what not to say. I remembered that Steve Pless, the OIC of the Marine Detachment at Pensacola, had won the Medal of Honor for a flight he made with VMO-6 just over a year before. I got the file out to read. It proved pretty interesting.

We hear a lot of times that there is a thin line between being brave and being foolhardy. In his case it was perfectly true. Actually Steve Pless came closer to having a court martial than being awarded the Medal of Honor.

When the MOH mission took place, VMO-6 had been operating out of Key Ha, just north of Chu Lai, providing support to Army and Marine units.

On August 19,1967 Steve was PIC (Pilot in Command) of a VMO-6 UH-1e gunship assigned to escort a Marine medevac aircraft when he heard a panicked Army pilot calling for help on the emergency channel. "I still have four men on the ground. The VC are trying to take them prisoner or kill them all; God, can somebody help them?"

We often hear of the "fog of war." This mission demonstrates it clearly. An Army CH-47 transporting wounded soldiers to Chu Lai had made an emergency landing on the beach after receiving small arms fire.

The pilot sent out three men for security while the crew chief climbed on the top of the aircraft to inspect for battle damage. The VC stormed across the beach with small arms fire and explosive charges and the Army pilot immediately took off, leaving the four soldiers to their fate.

The site of the pitched battle lay only a few miles from major Marine and Army facilities at Chu Lai, but the situation rapidly turned into a grade A clusterfuck. Army CH-47s circled overhead, each carrying two 50-caliber heavy machine guns. Army UH-1h transport helicopters were in range, each with two 7.62 internal machine guns, and the entire aerial power of eight Marine Corps fighter and attack bomber squadrons were based just a few miles away at Chi Lai. However, adult leadership had flown out the window when the pilot of the CH-47 abandoned his crew, inadvertently leaving their fate to a known glory hunter. The four soldiers were surrounded and the VC were attacking them with small arms and mortars, wounding all and killing two. This is what's known as a "shit sandwich."

Steve Pless swooped in, and with the assistance of his entire crew, landed on the beach, fought off the VC with rockets, machine gun fire and even pistol fire, loaded the four men on his aircraft and flew the severely overloaded plane out to sea to gain enough air speed to control the plane. His aircraft settled into the tops of the waves four times before getting safely airborne.

I remembered the promise Steve Pless made to me and the other fools in the battalion boxing team back in August of 1965, when he said he was going to go to Vietnam and earn the Medal of Honor.

The Defense Department and the Marine Corps recognized the bravery of the other crewmen of Steve's flight. All three were awarded the Navy Cross, the nation's second highest medal for bravery. I think Steve should have gotten his court martial and the other three crew should have each been given the Medal of Honor. The four-man crew was the most honored aviation crew during the Vietnam War.

For those who think I am being disrespectful of a Medal of Honor winner, I need to tell you about another promise Steve made when in his cups. He said that if ever he was on his motorcycle going out to Pensacola Beach and they started to raise the drawbridge, he was going to go for it and jump the open span. After happy hour on a Saturday night, July 20, 1969, Steve and a friend got on Steve's cycle and drove to the beach. As they crossed the bridge over Pensacola Bay, the drawbridge began to open. Steve went for it. He almost made it.

It's ok by me when fools determined to add a little chlorine to the gene pool accomplish their task. We are never going to have any shortage of fools. But Steve also killed his passenger, and that is unforgivable.

Anyone still convinced of the heroism of Steve Pless should probably check with his wife left without a husband or with his children left without their dad.

We had an unusual mission assigned from above Wing in December. Richard Nixon had been elected President in the 1968 election. He wouldn't take office until January 20, 1969 but wanted to begin serious peace talks with the NVA in Paris as soon as he was sworn into office. He told President Johnson that he wanted the Marines to capture an NVA soldier in uniform in South Vietnam so they could take him to Paris to show the world that North Vietnam really did have uniformed soldiers in the south.

That proved to be a lot harder to do than it sounds. Marine recon teams were good at killing the NVA but weren't worth a damn at capturing them. We didn't fight the kinds of battles that resulted in either Marines being captured by the NVA or the NVA being captured by the Marines.

The biggest number of NVA were in the area of operation of the 3rd Marine Division, so the order went out to the recon teams run by the recon units attached to each battalion, and to the force recon units attached to each regiment, to go capture an NVA. For the next two months every recon unit that could be put in the field was in the field, ordered to capture at least one NVA soldier.

The purpose of recon units is to sneak and peek. If they do their job well and cover up their trail and trash behind them, the enemy never knows they were even in the neighborhood.

When a recon team was put into the field, we would have a CH-46 helicopter carrying the team and their supplies, usually escorted by at least one Huey gunship. The six-man teams would have at least a corporal as the senior man, but in the field the guy in charge was always the guy who had been out on the most missions. Recon teams were the ultimate democracy; they didn't give a shit about rank or seniority, they wanted the most qualified guy running the operation.

A team out in the field took everything they needed with them, except water. The Vietnam jungle had no shortage of water. A full combat load with ammo, a claymore mine or two, chow and perhaps a spare battery weighed 75 pounds or more. Recon teams were almost all true warriors. If a man lacked intestinal fortitude, they wouldn't take him. One stupid move in the field could result in hundreds of NVA chasing them until they killed them all. The NVA hated recon teams.

While the team had selected a primary drop zone to be used, it was a sensible policy for the CH-46 to make a number of dummy runs on other potential landing zones both before and after the drop. When the team did depart the aircraft at their primary zone, they formed a circle right around the zone and sat silently for at least five minutes to listen for the sound of humans around. Naturally if they heard sounds, it meant they were right in the middle of the enemy. In that case they would call for an emergency extraction and di-di out of the area as fast as the airplane could load them up and leave. Di-di was a term the Vietnamese used meaning "get the hell out of Dodge at once."

You could take the story of one day's activities of inserting a single recon team into a zone and make a movie out of it. You had the team itself, with all the internal conflicts that come up when anyone goes into battle. You have the CH-46 with four or five crewmen and pilots and what they go through. How would you like to land on five to ten hilltops out in Indian country with nothing but a shield made of Plexiglas in front of you? The pilots not only wore ceramic bullet bouncers that were supposed to stop a 50-caliber bullet, they also sat on flak jackets to protect the important parts. And you had the Huey gunship pilots who were called on when bullets started flying. So a Huey crew could have an hour or two of screaming boredom which turned into a shit sandwich in a heartbeat.

The Bird Dogs had the very best mission of all. The only time we ever got called was when things had totally turned to hell and they needed someone to unfuck the mission. Most often the team had landed in bad-guy land and pissed off the natives. They would call for an extraction and spend the next four to five hours trying to lose the NVA. It was a race for their lives.

I don't think I ever heard of a recon team member who didn't get at least one Purple Heart. Many recon guys had handfuls of them and they deserved far more other awards than they got. Every mission that resulted in contact with the enemy resulted in actions above and beyond the call of duty. Of all the people we ever worked with, the recon units needed the Bird Dog pilots more than anyone. Literally, we were the difference between life and death to them.

While the effort to capture an NVA was in force, the Bird Dogs found themselves used as radio relays for the active teams. And since there were a lot of teams out in the field, we did a lot of flying. That's why I got so much time in flight during December of 1968 and January of 1969.

We ran into one shit sandwich after another trying to get a team to capture an NVA. The mission was exactly the opposite of what they were good at. A good team knew how to hide and avoid the enemy. When you start trying to get close enough to the enemy to capture one, it really pisses them off and they know you are there. The NVA weren't about to surrender to our guys. As far as they were concerned they owned the jungle and we were the invaders. So on mission after mission we would have a six-man team in contact that needed close air support *right fucking now*.

There were a few times where they captured someone, but the only reason they were able to get him was that he had been injured in combat with the team and he would die before they could get an extraction.

In the military, you never want to come to the attention of the White House or any of the clowns associated with the White House. In most cases, they have not even a single clue as to what the military can or cannot do. In this case Kissinger obviously felt that since the military, meaning the Marines, reported so many NVA in the DMZ and below the DMZ, that to capture just one would be no more difficult than going down to the local 7-11 for a quart of milk.

The White House was on top of the Marine Corps and the Marine Corps was on top of the 3rd Marine Division and Division was on top of the recon units. The poor snuffies out in the field were being poorly served all the way down the chain of command. Everyone was demanding the extraordinary of them, with no thanks for them putting their lives on the line day after day.

Finally in late January of 1969, after many fits and starts, a recon team spotted a handful of NVA carrying an 82 mm mortar tube and base plate down a quiet trail. There must have been half a dozen of them carrying the tube and the rounds for the mortar. The recon team sat in an ambush in place on the trail. Everyone knew exactly what he needed to do. The lucky NVA team member was the guy carrying the base plate for the tube. It weighed the most, and the leader of the recon team figured he would be the most tired and easiest to capture.

When the NVA were exactly where the Marines wanted them, the team opened up with every weapon they had, and in a few seconds had killed all of the mortar team members except the lucky soul carrying the base plate. As the smoke cleared, he stood there in shock wondering why he hadn't been killed.

The recon team grabbed him and headed for the nearest extraction point. They dropped their packs, claymore, radio batteries, water, everything that would slow them down on their 440-yard dash. I remember the radio operator calling for an emergency extraction while panting like he had just climbed Mount Everest without oxygen. They had their man, he was still kicking and the team wanted to get picked up to go home *right now*.

We had gunships standing by, and a CH-46. The extraction went just as we wanted it to and we had the poor NVA sod back to Quang Tri before his buddies started wondering where their mortar team went.

As was carefully planned by Nixon and Kissinger well in advance, the US flew the NVA soldier to Paris, still wearing his sweat stained and filthy NVA uniform, to prove to the world that the nasty North Vietnamese really did have troops in South Vietnam, contrary to their denials.

But they didn't carefully plan everything. Even on military aircraft, all the personnel aboard have to show a passport or travel document to the immigration authorities when they come aboard. The French Immigration officials climbed into the US transport and asked to see the identity documents of all the people on board. Naturally when they came to the tired and bewildered NVA soldier who had no clue at all about what was going on, they asked for his papers. The State Department officials attempted to tell the French officials the saga of how they wanted to expose the North Vietnamese as being the scallywags we knew they were. The NVA soldier didn't have any papers on him because he hadn't been planning a trip to Paris.

Lots of French officials still spoke Vietnamese, or perhaps the soldier understood and spoke some French, but in any case the story soon came out that he was a North Vietnamese soldier claiming to have been kidnapped. And I suppose if you look at it that way, we did kidnap him.

The French officials took the prisoner off the plane and into their own custody. The US State Department officials were told that if they wanted to make an international incident of the affair, they could, but as far as France was concerned, the NVA soldier had been kidnapped by the US. They turned the man over to the North Vietnamese negotiators for the peace agreement, who sent him back to Hanoi after a short but well-deserved R&R in Paris for the young chap.

For me, life settled down into an interesting routine. The senior O-1 pilots finished their 13-month tour and were sent back to the US. I was one of the senior guys there after about a month. I did my two or three flights a day with an odd maintenance test flight when required. After twenty or thirty missions as an FAC it became something ordinary.

Dying on the operating table in 1967 proved a valuable experience. Once you die, you no longer fear death. I feared getting shot down. I feared being wounded. I feared being captured and I feared being a coward, but I didn't fear death. I had been there, done that.

I learned something interesting. Perhaps we should be paying attention to it today. When people don't fear death they will do things that otherwise rational people won't consider. As I write, terrorists have just made a major attack on Paris. Everyone in Europe is in shock that people would do such a thing and then blow themselves up.

That's pretty fucking dumb of us, all of us, including the French. We have turned the entire Middle East into a shithole where anyone with any sense is either picking up a weapon and attacking the invaders or getting out of Dodge.

The US and Israel and Turkey and Saudi Arabia and France and Britain and Canada created this clusterfuck. It all began with the Yinon Plan in 1983 calling for Israel to bust all of its neighbors into tiny slivers so Israel could become the sole remaining power in the Middle East. No doubt anything I say critical of Israel will immediately bring all the whiners out, pouting "anti-Semitism", but the Yinon Plan is a fact, not an opinion. You and I can have opinions about whether Israel actually implemented the plan, but it is a fact that it exists.

In 1996, the dual-national neocons presented Israeli Prime Minister Netanyahu with a position paper they entitled *"A Clean Break: A New Strategy for Securing the Realm."* It read as if it had been written by a gaggle of fools. They were led by Richard Perle, Douglas Feith, David and Meyrav Wurmser, all dual nationals, suggesting that,

> *"While there are those who will counsel continuity, Israel has the opportunity to make a clean break; it can forge a peace process and strategy based on an entirely new intellectual foundation, one that restores strategic initiative and provided the nation the room to engage every possible energy on rebuilding Zionism, the starting point of which must be economic reform.*
>
> *"Rather than pursuing a "comprehensive peace" with the entire Arab world, Israel should work jointly with Jordan and Turkey to "contain, destabilize, roll-back" those entities that are threats to all three."*

Of course this pattern of "destabilizing" the Middle East has destroyed Iraq, Sudan, Somalia, Libya and Syria.

If a person is a dual national citizen of Israel and the US, to whom does he owe his primary allegiance? Many of the dual nationals behind the "Clean Break" went on to high office within the Bush administration and lied the US into a war with Iraq, where we stood to gain nothing and stood to bankrupt our country.

If that wasn't explosive enough, an overlapping group calling itself the Project for the New American Century, led by dual nationals William Kristol and Robert Kagan, advised the United States to adopt a "more elevated vision of America's international role," and suggested that the United States should adopt a stance of "benevolent global hegemony."

In June of 1997 PNAC released a telling "Statement of Principles" that said the nation faced a challenge to "shape a new century favorable to American principles and interest." In order to achieve this goal, the statement's signers called for significant increases in defense spending, and for the promotion of "political and economic freedom abroad." It said the United States should strengthen ties with its democratic allies, "challenge regimes hostile to our interests and values," and preserve and extend "an international order friendly to our security, our prosperity, and our principles."

Shortly after the September 11, 2001 attacks, the PNAC sent a letter to President George W. Bush, advocating "a determined effort to remove Saddam Hussein from power in Iraq", or regime change. The letter suggested that "any strategy aiming at the eradication of terrorism and its sponsors must include a determined effort to remove Saddam Hussein from power in Iraq," even if no evidence surfaced linking Iraq to the September 11 attacks. The letter warned that allowing Hussein to remain in power would be "an early and perhaps decisive surrender in the war on international terrorism." From 2001 through the invasion of Iraq, the PNAC and many of its members voiced active support for military action against Iraq, and asserted that leaving Saddam Hussein in power would be "surrender to terrorism" (taken from Wikipedia).

Regime change happens to be illegal under international law.

General Wesley Clark visited friends at the Pentagon shortly after 9/11. They told him that plans were being laid to invade and destroy seven countries in five years: Iraq, then Syria, Lebanon, Libya, Somalia and Sudan, finishing off with Iran.

I can understand how dual nationals who owe their primary allegiance to Israel might well see those countries as potential enemies of Israel. But unless Israel is planning on unleashing nuclear Armageddon on its neighbors, there simply isn't much Israel could do about it. After all, Israel is a nation of only eight million people.

To me it seems pretty obvious that Israel hijacked the American political system to further its own aims. Israel receives the largest share of the US military aid distributed today, with over 53 per cent of the total handed out around the world. Given that they need not spend their treasure on weapons if the US is stupid enough to provide them for free, Israel recycles the money into political campaigns for the US Congress and Senate. Our legislatures have simply been bought off.

When Prime Minister Netanyahu spoke in front of Congress in early March of 2015, his forty-minute speech was interrupted thirty-nine times for applause by a Congress pretending to be barking penguins, including twenty-three standing ovations. No speaker is that interesting.

Wars cost money as well as the blood of the young. While it's been nice of the Chinese to finance the stupidity of the United States in its role as Israel's attack dog over the last fifteen years, if China put in a market order to sell its stash of T-bills and T-bonds, the US dollar would turn to toast in a minute.

I studied economics. I understand that the United States is functionally bankrupt as a result of the Forever Wars fought in the years after 9/11. Gradually, as the standard of living decreases and the middle class finds that its future and the futures of its children and grandchildren were hocked so the United States could fight wars where we had nothing to gain and everything to lose, others will wake up and realize what they have done.

Back in VMO-6, in December we picked up another two Bird Dog pilots. This time they came from MAG 12 where they had been flying the A-4 Skyhawk. I trained both First Lieutenant Bob Stamper and First Lieutenant Greg Nelson. They would prove to be two of the bravest and most talented O-1 pilots ever to wear Marine green.

Soon after I got to VMO-6 we held an awards ceremony. Every pilot coming to the squadron would be awarded his first Strike/Flight air medal in front of the rest of the squadron. In addition, if there were other awards to be handed out, this is when we had pinned them on. I had been through exactly the same exercise while stationed in Da Nang with VMFA-542. All of the people being given awards were gathered in a group and the rest of the squadron stood at Parade Rest watching respectfully.

It didn't mean squat to me. I already had my first through tenth Air Medals; this was going to be just one more number on the ribbon. The squadron CO, Lieutenant Colonel Zander, handed out the awards.

"First Lieutenant Robert Moriarty, first Strike/Flight award. Front and center," the operations officer called out.

I marched up and stood at attention while Colonel Zander said the usual form of words. "Congratulations, Lieutenant Moriarty. We are pleased to have you with VMO-6."

I saluted and returned to the formation of award recipients. Then much to my surprise, a few minutes later I heard the operations officer call me out again. "First Lieutenant Robert Moriarty, his first Purple Heart. Front and center," he cried out.

I stood there looking like a fool. I hadn't won a Purple Heart. You get those for bleeding. I always thought the purpose of the whole exercise was to make the NVA bleed. After a few moments of utter silence I heard it again, in a voice slightly more shrill this time around.

"Lieutenant Robert Moriarty, first Purple Heart. Front and center. Now if you don't mind, Lieutenant."

I marched up in front of Colonel Zander again. "Congratulations, Lieutenant Moriarty."

"Skipper, I didn't get shot. At least not yet. I can't get a Purple Heart. This isn't mine. It's some sort of mistake," I said quietly, so only he could hear.

Colonel Zander looked down at the certificate and said, "Yes you did. This says you were wounded requiring medical treatment on November 20, 1968. Don't argue with Marine Corps paperwork. If it says you got wounded on November 20, you were wounded."

I wasn't about to accept a Purple Heart in error. That had to have terrible karma attached to it. "Skipper, I didn't check in until November 20. My only visit to medical on the twentieth was when I turned in my medical jacket. Remember, that was the day Tim Moriarty took the round through the canopy."

We both looked around to see if Tim was standing in the formation. Colonel Zander and I both realized what had happened. Lieutenant Moriarty was wounded and earned the Purple Heart as a result of his treatment. But Lieutenant Moriarty was also checking into the squadron on the same day and his medical jacket was out on the counter. Moriarty, Tim was confused with Moriarty, Robert.

I gladly returned the Purple Heart and certificate so it could be given to its owner.

After the aborted effort to capture a living NVA soldier in South Vietnam, the Marine Corps came up with something far more productive. One of the most dangerous areas we ever worked in in Northern I Corps was the A Shau valley. We had Special Forces units in the A Shau as late as 1965 but the NVA took umbrage at their presence and booted them out. It was a natural line of communication from the Ho Chi Minh trail in Laos leading down from North Vietnam. The A

Shau branched off to the east and any supplies destined for use by NVA troops wanting to attack either Da Nang or Hue would pass through the valley.

A new 3rd Marine Division commander took over in mid-1968. General Ray Davis was one of the last of the true warrior Marines. He had a Navy Cross from service in WW II, a Medal of Honor for fighting his unit out of the Frozen Chosin Reservoir, and an additional two Silver Stars for other combat in Korea.

Ray Davis didn't like the concept of having Marine units in I Corps tied down to fixed bases where the NVA could pick and choose their fights. So he ordered the entire 9th Marine Regiment to prepare plans for a two-month attack on NVA base camps and supply depots in the A Shau valley.

The Bird Dogs got some interesting orders in early January of 1969. We were to create landing zones on every suitable hilltop near the A Shau. All the pilots realized something big was just around the corner. It was great. We were called into a briefing with the operations officer. He drew a circle around an area just to the north of the A Shau valley and all the way west to the Laos border.

"Men, we are going to give you three or four flights of air per sortie that you fly. Everyone will be carrying either Mark-84 750-pounders or Mark-85 2,000-pound bombs with daisy cutter fuses. You will schedule four Bird Dog flights a day devoted just to building LZs. I want every hilltop in that circle shaved until it's smoother than a baby's ass. Got it?"

"Yes, sir." What else could we say? This was going to be fun.

Bob Stamper, the former ace A-4 pilot, was one of the most unusual people I would ever meet. Most pilots had some sort of nickname. Mine was Mo. His was Fang, for some reason I never learned. Bob was a skinny little thing, he didn't weigh much over 140 soaking wet.

We both came due for R&R in early January and we figured we could get in twice as much trouble if we went together. Our first choice was Hong Kong and you could get into a lot of trouble in Hong Kong. We flew down to Da Nang and boarded a 707, destination Hong Kong.

It's important for readers to understand that in 1969 the dollar was still king. Our stupid war in Vietnam would knock the dollar off its perch but the world had yet to understand how America was exporting both inflation and the cost of the war throughout the world. We paid fifteen cents for a pack of cigarettes. If you wanted a whole carton, that was $1.40. A bottle of gin was ninety cents and wine slightly more expensive at $1 a fifth. Drinks in the club were a quarter, with beer cheaper at fifteen cents.

Pilots who might divert to Thailand because of bad weather were allowed to keep US greenbacks but otherwise you were required to turn your greenbacks in for MPC (Military Payment Certificates). MPCs changed three or four times in the two years I was in Vietnam. You didn't want to get caught out with an old MPC because at some point in time you couldn't change it. Pilots in VMFA-542 could carry green; after all, they might have to divert. Pilots in VMO-6 in Quang Tri didn't have the fuel to make it to Thailand. We weren't diverting anywhere. We normally couldn't carry green. When you went on R&R you were allowed to change MPC into greenbacks but when you returned from R&R you were required to change your greenbacks back into MPC. MPC had no value outside Vietnam. It was sort of a pseudo currency.

The Fang and I were both first lieutenants with over four years' service, so in 1969 we earned $662.70 a month in base pay and another $150 a month in flight skins. We could splurge in Hong Kong. I think a really nice hotel cost $20 a night.

We checked into our hotel. Every floor in the hotel had a mama-san who looked out for that floor. She and her assistants took charge and made sure you had clean linens and whatever else you needed. You could give them your laundry and shoes and they would return them a few hours later all spick and span. Paying them an extra $1 or $2 a day worked wonders.

Bob went down to meet the family taking care of our floor. Soon he announced that instead of going out boozing and whoring with me, he was going to their house for dinner.

I've met two people in my lifetime with the truly remarkable ability to connect with anyone. One I've been married to for the last twenty-five years and I only wish it had been the last fifty years. My wife Barbara can talk to everyone, from a five-year-old child to a 95-year-old, for five minutes, and they will be convinced they have just made a new best friend for life. She has the most developed sense of empathy I have ever seen. Fang had the same thing.

I'm an elitist and I admit it. I had a best friend when I was six. Why the hell would I want to run around making more friends? After all, how many friends do you need?

The Chinese family and mama-san on our floor adopted Fang and he spent most of his time visiting with them. I couldn't have done it. They didn't speak English. He didn't speak Chinese.

But he wasn't above going to a bar with dozens of cute bar girls looking for short-term relationships with rich American pilots. Bob went to a bank and bought a giant bag of Hong Kong silver dollars. As he told me later, he dragged the bag down to the establishment and dumped it on top of the bar. The mama-san looked at him with eyes glittering with avarice.

"How many girls you want? Make fucky-sucky fi' dollar. How many girls?" she asked.

Bob just smiled and said, "I want them all."

"Oh, that be *verry* expensive. I give you *verry* good deal for all of them."

The unshockable mama-san had never run into any pilot with such a giant appetite before. She was going to clean up. But what Bob asked for next did shock her.

"I want you, too," he said in a calm voice as he pushed a pile of Hong Kong silver dollars across the bar to her. By now the entire group of scantily clad lassies had surrounded Bob and the mama-san and were listening to the transaction with bated breath.

"Close the bar. Throw everyone out except you and the girls. We are going to party tonight."

Bob and all the girls and the mama-san spent the night dancing and talking. Bob was married. He wasn't about to mess around but he could have fun and meet new friends. He did. I don't doubt those bar maids still talk about the Fang.

We returned to Vietnam and got down to more serious work. The 9th Marines began to move units into position and the shit hit the fan.

All the Bird Dog pilots had been creating landing zones for weeks. We saw something in the A Shau we had never seen before. Any time we went below 1,500 feet we took automatic weapons fire. Every single time. In the rest of the area we normally flew in, the NVA didn't dream of shooting at a Marine Bird Dog. They knew that if they did, we had their position pinpointed and they were dead.

In VMO-6 we had three classes of pilots. In the UH-1E gunships we had a combination of a few senior captains and majors working with a lot of first tour pilots, mostly lieutenants. And while the first tour pilots were the youngest pilots in the squadron, in many cases they had the most experience. In the fixed wing squadrons the first tour pilots rarely flew an entire 13-month tour. The Wing wienies all wanted the fixed wing flight time so there was a constant demand for billets.

All of the OV-10 pilots were retreads; they were prior chopper drivers who were offered the OV-10 as a condition of staying in the Marine Corps. The Bird Dog pilots on the other hand were all first tour pilots with at least six months of actual combat flying in fixed wing aircraft doing close air support. As such, the Bird Dog pilots knew the limits of fixed wing aircraft and knew what could and couldn't be done with ordnance.

In combat the assertive win. The enemy is always trying to measure the level of skill and bravery of those they fight. If you pussyfoot around, you send a clear and convincing signal to the enemy that you lack confidence. The British slogan of "Fortune favors the brave" comes to mind. It's true. The few Marine Bird Dog pilots in Quang Tri were the most experienced and most aggressive FACs in southeast Asia. It worked in our favor.

The NVA made a major mistake in firing at Marine Bird Dogs, as it told us they had something important to protect. They never shot down a Marine Bird Dog, they just pissed off the pilots and let us know there were a lot of them down there. The military term was a "target-rich environment."

From late 1968 into as late as 1970 the Army had O-1G aircraft flying out of Dong Ha, about six miles northwest of our base at Quang Tri. Their call sign was Catkiller. Their aircraft were painted a slightly different shade of green. I called it babyshit green. The North Vietnamese knew the Catkillers couldn't control fixed wing closer than one kilometer from friendlies, and that covered most of the area we worked in. So being painted in Army green was like giving the NVA gunners a free pass to shoot, knowing the aircraft couldn't respond.

In Northern I Corps the wind was variable, except in the late afternoon when it picked up speed and came out of the due west.

The Quang Tri airfield had a north/south runway made up of perforated steel matting called Marston matting. Dong Ha used a dirt strip that ran east/west. The Bird Dog had real problems with anything greater than a 15-knot crosswind. You couldn't maintain directional control with more than fifteen knots of wind. I didn't use full flaps with the plane as most pilots did. I wanted directional control rather than slow speed. I could plant one wheel down, the into-the-wind wheel, and land in conditions most of the other guys couldn't. But I had a lot more time in tail draggers than they did.

When the wind was too high in Quang Tri, we would go up to Dong Ha, a five-minute flight from Quang Tri. Once there we either sat around until the wind died down or left the plane overnight and got someone from the squadron to pick us up.

Down the road a few months John Stevens would cause a bit of a problem for me when he ground looped an O-1G on landing. Sure enough, he had believed he could press the limits of the crosswinds and the Trim God proved that he couldn't. The wind was higher than the fifteen knots we used as a limit. He should have flown up to Dong Ha and waited out the crosswinds.

He came down the chute with no power and full flaps into an 18-knot direct crosswind. He wasn't even crabbing into the wind. I watched the whole thing in horror. The airplane touched down on both mains at the same time as he pulled the stick back into his lap in a futile effort to stop the beast. The tail swung around and he caught one wheel in the sand on the edge of the runway. Literally it broke the back of the aircraft. When he and his AO exited the airplane both wore faces as white as a sheet. It was one thing to get killed in combat, another to get killed in a ground loop.

I didn't really worry about the state of the aircraft. There were a lot of times we had more airplanes than pilots to fly them. For some strange reason, not many pilots had the balls to fly the O-1. Overall the Bird Dog took more losses in combat than any other aircraft in Vietnam per flight hour.

For any pilot considering making the Corps his home for the next twenty years, breaking an airplane in an accident was pretty close to a game stopper. Since I was the maintenance flunky, I would have to deal with the civil servant coming up from Phu Bai to inspect the damaged airplane. If possible we needed to convince this civilian inspector that it wasn't pilot stupidity that broke the plane, it was combat and the nasty NVA shooting at it that did the damage.

Gunny Lockwood told me not to worry, he would sort it out so no one could figure it out. I went to inspect the plane before the inspector showed up. Gunny Lockwood ran the O-1 maintenance shop. He had taken a .45 Colt and fired one round up through the horizontal stabilizer of the tail. And then he took a big blade screwdriver and punched another hole under the reservoir for the brake fluid. With great pride he showed me how he took a pair of pliers and waggled the brake line back and forth until it broke and spilled out all the fluid. So when Captain Stevens landed after a harrowing three hours in combat, his steed lacked brakes and that must have caused the crash.

I was impressed with the Gunny and his thinking. But would it fool the inspector? Captain Stevens' career might depend on the answer.

The civilian showed up and carefully walked around the airplane humming and hawing. "Hmmm," he said several times to himself. "Well, I see combat damage so I think we can write this plane off as a combat loss." The Gunny and I smiled at each other for a job well done.

But before the inspector left he sidled up to me and spoke under his breath. "I know what you fuckers did."

I looked at him with unfeigned horror. "Really. What do you mean?" I asked with the most innocent face I could conjure.

"Well, someone took a screwdriver and punched a hole through the tail. I think one of your maintenance guys thought two holes were a lot better than just one," he said, before continuing under his breath, "The hole under the brake reservoir is clearly a bullet hole. I know a bullet hole when I see one. That's what made the brakes fail. So I'll ignore your little effort at sandbagging me and write it off as a combat loss."

I wanted to say, "No, no. You have it exactly reversed. The hole in the tail is a bullet hole for real. We did it with a forty-five. The hole under the brake reservoir is the one we did with the screwdriver." Then I thought about perhaps keeping my mouth shut at least for the moment.

"Well, I guess you figured it out just right. Combat loss, oh well." I had to give him credit for at least figuring out part of it.

Gunny Lockwood and I shared many a laugh and a few beers over the story. It didn't make any difference to the number of airplanes we had available. John Stevens had broken the back of this O-1G but we had another with a bent wing. The Gunny and his guys took the good wing and the good fuselage and paired them together.

Since the aircraft didn't officially exist, when VMO-6 left the country in September of 1969 as part of the Nixon reduction of US forces, they faced the quandary of what to do with an airplane that had no paperwork. So they took a big bulldozer, dug a deep pit and buried it. One day two hundred years from now a farmer will be tilling his fields for a new crop of rice and discover the O-1G that didn't exist.

If John Stevens didn't cause enough work for me with his ground loop, one day he came back from a flight with damage to his wing. According to his story, he was flying dead low and an NVA fired a rocket-propelled grenade at him. The range was so close the RPG didn't arm but it did put a good-sized dent in the leading edge of the wing when it hit.

The problem that Gunny Lockwood and I had was that while the wing was damaged, the wing support that ran from the wing to the fuselage was not. If you can imagine the airplane being inverted and striking the tops of trees, that's what it looked like. The top was damaged but the bottom just under it wasn't damaged. Gunny Lockwood and I lowered many a beer pondering just how John did that damage to the wing but not to the support. I figured he was lying but I couldn't determine how and what.

The Catkillers were used to getting shot at all the time. We flew in exactly the same area doing pretty much the same mission except that we could control ordnance a lot closer to friendlies. We didn't get shot at. They did.

That changed during Operation Dewey Canyon. Every flight took fire. You could hear it even when wearing your helmet. We were both shocked and thrilled at the same time. At first we plotted everywhere we took fire until we realized we took fire everywhere we flew in Dewey Canyon.

We learned as much of what we needed to know to survive combat and also accomplish the mission while in the O-Club sipping a Chivas and water as we did in a cockpit. One of the things we spent a lot of time talking about was bombing friendlies. It seemed to happen to everyone eventually. Those of us who had never bombed friendlies worried on every flight that we might.

If you flew during Dewey Canyon, you had targets on every flight. After all, before we began the operation, they were moving so many trucks through the A Shau it may as well have been a highway. Finally my day of reckoning came. I had a flight of two A-4s from MAG 12. Normally the A-4s were the best bomb droppers we used. But on this day, this pair was terrible. Even though they had enough fuel to give me fifteen minutes and still make it all the way to Saigon if they wanted, these guys wanted one pass, haul ass.

I gave them their instructions and cleared the lead in hot. He managed to drop 1,200 meters long. I told his Dash-2 to ignore where the lead's bombs went and to put his ordnance on my smoke. I cleared him in hot and he dropped 500 meters further from the target than his flight lead had. I gave them zero over zero for BDA and sent them home.

A few minutes later I got the call no FAC ever wanted to hear. The second aircraft had dropped its bombs near a Marine unit out on a patrol and several Marines had been injured.

When you control air strikes or artillery or even naval gunfire, it's vital that you know where all the friendlies are within five miles. The one thing you never do is to have friendlies under the flight path of aircraft or in the bombsight line. If you don't fly over friendlies or fire over them, you can't hit them. I should have been notified of where this patrol was. And when they had planes drop bombs nearby and then fly overhead their position, they should have been screaming on the radio for us not to drop.

I was heartbroken. Our operations got a call from the Division and they wanted a full report. I was cleared of any wrongdoing but still, it was a flight controlled by me and I felt rotten.

Steve Palmason had the most sensible words of wisdom. "Mo, there are two kinds of FACs. There are the FACs that have bombed friendlies and there are the FACs that are going to bomb friendlies. Now you know which you are."

Dewey Canyon was the first and only real Marine regiment-sized operation in Vietnam. It was a classical operation, with two battalions up and one in reserve. Colonel Robert Barrow commanded the 9th Marine Regiment. He moved small grunt units into place onto the LZs we had created and behind them he brought in the artillery units that would support the grunts. Once the artillery units were in place, Barrow started moving the grunt companies out in reconnaissance.

The A Shau was fifty kilometers from LZ Vandergrift. We were operating so far out of our normal area of operation that there were no artillery units capable of firing and supporting the Marines in combat. Since we were over thirty miles inland, no Navy ships could give us naval gunfire support.

We knew before the operation that as many as 1,000 trucks a day were passing down the Ho Chi Minh trail into the A Shau valley. It was more than a simple and small trail or even set of trails.

The NVA plan was first to move supplies into position, and when ready for an attack move their ground units into place. The supplies were separate from the troops who would use them. So you didn't need to kill a lot of the enemy to disrupt their plans; all you had to do was locate their supplies and destroy them.

Operation Dewey Canyon lasted almost 60 days. The 9th Marines saw a lot of heavy combat. Unfortunately it was the time of the winter monsoon and the weather was claggy much of the time. There were times when the supply choppers were sitting on the ramp at LZ Vandergrift filled with food and ammo for the grunts and they couldn't move.

I knew several of the ground FACs from VMFA-542 and from Cherry Point. They were running out of smokes and that was far more serious to them than running out of food. One of the FACs promised me the gun sight off a 122 mm NVA cannon if I would bring him a carton of cigarettes. I don't know if he really intends to pay or not. I just know he hasn't paid up yet.

The Marines inflicted a lot of damage, with confirmed kills of over 1,600 NVA at the cost of 130 Marines killed and 932 wounded. The operation did succeed in disrupting the supply lines of the NVA and the destruction of the largest supply cache to date in the Vietnam War. Colonel Robert Barrow went on to become the 27th Commandant of the Marine Corps before retiring with forty-two years' service.

As the 9th Marine Regiment pulled back to their positions at LZ Vandergrift and Dong Ha, things returned to normal for VMO-6. The recon teams kept stirring up hornets' nests on a real regular basis. The other Marine regiments continued their search and destroy missions throughout Northern I Corps.

In late March or early April of 1969 we got a replacement pilot for the O-1s. Norman Billipp had been flying the A-4 out of Chu Lai for the first half of his tour. I gave him the normal checkout in the Bird Dog and he was soon on his way to becoming one of the qualified FACs. But Billipp had a giant attitude and a chip on his shoulder. He hadn't done anything special during his tour in the A-4 but when he got into the Bird Dog, all of a sudden he knew everything there was to know about forward air control.

We were a tiny group; there were never much more than half a dozen Bird Dog pilots at one time. We were just like little old ladies and gossiped about everything and everyone. It was part of the learning process. Many of the pilots were above 500 missions by then and we weren't impressed with some FNG telling us how to do our job. I was the senior pilot by now and I took Billipp aside and talked to him about his know-it-all attitude. I remember telling him that if he kept up his attitude, it would kill him in less than a month. It went in one ear and out the other. And I was wrong; he lasted five weeks before dying.

There is nothing in combat that kills quite as fast as arrogance. The arrogant always get their asses kicked. It happened with the US when we invaded Iraq. It happens to Israel every time they try to squash Gaza. If you are arrogant, you are going to lose.

On May 7, 1969 Norm Billipp left on an ordinary recon mission to the Khe Sanh area. We had rotten weather and when he and his AO John Hagan failed to return, we wrote it off to a pilot flying into conditions he couldn't handle. It took another twenty-five years to learn that Billipp had flown past Khe Sanh and into Laos. He flew right into the heart of the Ho Chi Minh trail, near Tchepone in Laos. That was the most dangerous area to fly in in aviation history. The NVA operating the 37 mm and 57 mm guns had shot down hundreds of aircraft attacking the series of trails coming together at Tchepone. It was no problem for them to shoot down an O-1 and they did.

We didn't have a single experienced O-1 pilot who would have even dreamed of flying over the trail in a Bird Dog. It was suicide.

I didn't miss Billipp nearly as much as I did John Hagan. You see,

John Hagan was color blind. He had applied for flight training but didn't get accepted because he couldn't pass the medical due to his color blindness.

John and I were out flying one day in Western I Corps, just looking around. I suppose we were at about 2,500 feet. High enough to be cool and low enough to look around. He tells me to look over at an area just north of a small river and I will see some trucks parked under a tree. Since this was Indian country, any trucks there belonged to the NVA. I looked down and didn't see anything at all. So I went down to 1,500 feet to give it a good close look. I still didn't see anything. So I went lower. By now I was convinced I was flying with one of those guys who sees people walking down a trail from three miles away, smoking cigarettes held in their left hands. In other words, guys who make shit up.

I still didn't see anything so I went down to 500 feet and flew right overhead his mythical trucks. I never saw any trucks but I could hear the sound of a bunch of AK-47s being fired at us. I pulled out. We marked the area and called in fixed wing. When we dropped we got a lot of secondary explosions, which means we hit something. Still, I never saw anything except the smoke from the secondaries.

Back at Quang Tri I insisted Hagan tell me just how he knew there were trucks under the trees. I didn't see anything from 500 feet while he claimed to have seen them from 2,500 feet. He explained to me that people who are colorblind can see through camouflage. People with normal vision don't see what is covered but people who see only in shades of brown can see right through camouflage. I asked around and it seemed a lot of people were aware of it. We should have been recruiting people to be AOs based on their color vision. It's a remarkable ability.

I miss John Hagan a lot; he was a hell of a nice guy. Too nice to die because of someone else's arrogance. Billipp tried to do something not a single other pilot in the squadron would have dreamed of trying.

The remains of the two-man crew were recovered in 1995 after records were located in the files of the North Vietnamese about how and when the North Vietnamese shot down aircraft in Laos. We never thought of looking in Laos for the airplane, as no one in his right mind would have flown a Bird Dog over that area.

During May or perhaps June of 1969 I got to preside over the last

UH-34 to get shot down in Vietnam. I was providing radio relays for a small grunt unit near the southern edge of the DMZ. They were out on an ordinary recon patrol looking for signs of the NVA. Someone tripped a land mine and suddenly they had three wounded. The wounds weren't life threatening but for the platoon to continue on the patrol, we needed to pick up the injured Marines.

A lot of activity was going on in I Corps and there weren't any chopper gunships or OV-10s to provide cover. Although I had rarely worked with any of the UH-34 squadrons based at Phu Bai, about fifty miles southeast of us, there was one UH-34 available for a medevac flight. Naturally the pilot wasn't thrilled with the idea of trying to land in what might be a hot zone without gunship support.

There was no sign at all of any enemy activity on the ground other than the booby trap. That may have been set up six months before or twenty minutes before, there was no way of knowing. For all we knew, there may have been three NVA with locked and loaded AK-47s waiting to ambush any medevac foolish enough to land without support.

Candidly I told the UH-34 driver that he would have to figure out for himself what the risk was. While the troops had tripped a booby trap, there was no sign of other activity, but there also was no gunship or OV-10 support and there wouldn't be for hours. The decision to land and pick up the wounded had to be made by the aircraft crew. Bravely, they opted to make the landing.

Just as they touched down, three NVA right in the middle of the LZ popped out of their spider holes and sprayed the UH-34 with AK rounds in an ambush. I always hated it when that happened. The UH-34 lurched out of the zone, trailing smoke and flames behind it. They continued on for about three miles to the west, to crash land at Con Thien. It was the last UH-34 shot down in the war.

A few years back I managed to get in touch with one of the door gunners, who naturally remembered every minute of the flight. The NVA soldiers had managed to fire ninety rounds of 7.62 mm ball ammo at the plane and they hit the plane with every round. It literally was at point blank range. He had removed his bullet bouncer and placed it under him for the mission. He could feel the rounds hitting the ceramic plate and bouncing off. The plane was a write off but not a single one of the crew shed even a drop of blood. The airplane would never fly again but the crew would.

Later in May of 1969 the squadron came up with the strangest order we had to date. Poring through the logbooks of the Bird Dog pilots, someone realized that none of us ever made any night flights. Since Marine Corps regulations required at least ten hours of nighttime every six months, all of the Bird Dog pilots were told to get some.

However, the Bird Dog wasn't a night-qualified aircraft and wasn't equipped for instrument approaches. We were a day-VFR airplane.

Don't ever bother arguing with anyone in the Marines about Marine Corps regulations. As far as the brass was concerned, the regulations came down the mountain with some guy named Moses. And were far more important than those silly Commandments.

In our ignorance we asked the brass just how we were supposed to get out nighttime. As far as I was concerned, some lance corporal in operations should have sharpened his #4 pencil and got to work filling out some timesheets for us.

Here's where it gets really funny. We were the most qualified and valuable group of FACs in Vietnam, in one of the densest combat areas of the country. I was flying two or three missions a day, clocking up to 130 combat hours a month, and the brass wanted me flying at night. For practice. So I could collect flight pay. Were they insane?

When the other O-1 pilots asked just how they were supposed to get ten hours of nighttime, they were told to take off at legal twilight and circle the field for three hours. If you did that four nights in a row, you would have your required night flight time.

To give you an idea of what we had to put up with, you need to understand that everyone drank. Everyone. Except we had one pilot who didn't. We all thought he was crazy. The rest of us drank to the point of being senseless almost every night. Most of us, perhaps eighty per cent, also smoked. No one was concerned about becoming an alcoholic or dying of lung cancer. Hell's bells, we were getting shot at every day as we hurled ourselves at the ground. Who had time to worry about dying of cancer? We had more immediate concerns.

About the same time, the heavies started worrying about how we did our flying. I would schedule all the missions that came down in the evening fragmentation order from Wing. We would launch, and sometimes had a specific mission such as bombing hilltops to make

LZs, or we would do whatever we were assigned by the DASC to fill their needs. That might be troops in contact or a recon insertion or extraction or a simple radio relay. In short, we found that doing what made sense worked perfectly well for us.

But as a war winds down, the guys at the top start getting bored and start coming up with brilliant ideas. If you are a lieutenant colonel with a desire to make Bird, you start thinking of how you can order people around. So each of the pilots was assigned an area of his own. When we had completed our assigned mission we were to go out to our own territory just to look around and see if we could see anything.

I thought it was a pretty stupid idea. We worked best when we solved the biggest problem that existed at any given time. The idea of playing tourist didn't make much sense to me. However, as scheduling officer I got to pick the territory for each pilot. Naturally I took the most interesting for myself: the mouth of the Ben Hai River, the border between North and South Vietnam. I had spent a lot of time up there watching the sand dunes between the Ben Hai River and the Cua Viet River. This area was just north of the sand dunes known as the Street Without Joy, so named by the French and used as the title of a book by Bernard Fall.

The French, Bernard Fall, and Lieutenant Robert Moriarty all understood the sand dunes belonged to the bad guys. What the NVA didn't realize was that when they crossed the DMZ into South Vietnam they were leaving footprints in the sand.

One of the AOs I had done a lot of flying with in VMO-6 was a grunt officer named Dick Webb. If my memory still serves me he was a recon Marine, and a handy guy to fly with.

The military had just come out with this wonderful device called a Starlight scope. It was a telescope that magnified available light and allowed you to look around at night. The NVA couldn't see you but you could see them in this strange and spooky green color.

Dick knew someone who would let us borrow one of the priceless units, but just for the night. It was June 4, 1969. Dick and I were sitting in the O-Club drinking beers. When you have a few beers under your belt it's amazing to see the great ideas you can come up with.

We combined the footprints in the sand with the need for me to get some nighttime and the Starlight scope, and half a dozen beers later we realized that what we really needed to do was to take a Bird Dog up for some nighttime. We would fly offshore from the Ben Hai River so we didn't get in the way of anyone wanting to fire a night fire mission with artillery. And we would use the Starlight scope to figure out just what the crafty little NVA were up to.

I had been blasting the crap out of the whole sand dune area south of the DMZ for a week. I knew they were moving something down at night. There were a lot of footprints in the sand. I checked to see when the tides came in so I could time when they were crossing. I targeted every tree and sand dune and any area where they could be storing supplies. I was on to something because I kept getting secondary explosions. In one mission I could see the rockets that had been blown out of the bunker they had been stored in. They were 140 mm rockets. And that was fairly unusual. The most common NVA rocket was 122 mm. Although the 140 was bigger than the 122 mm, the 122 had a longer range. That told me something. The NVA intended to attack someone from fairly short range.

By ten o'clock Dick and I were half in the bag and we decided to call it a night. He was going to come wake me for our flight at 0300. I was drunk enough that it really didn't matter to me if he showed up or not. It was one of those ideas that didn't work all that well in the light of day but sounded just wonderful in the bar.

Sure enough, Dick came and shook me at 0300. I didn't bother shaving or brushing my teeth, I just let a dirty and smelly flight suit walk over to me so I could don it.

Now I'm not going to tell you I flew a combat mission while still drunk. That would be the wrong message to send out to young people today. But while I wasn't exactly drunk, I wasn't exactly sober either. We found the airplane and managed to take off with no problems. Since we weren't in anyone's H&I fire area (Harassment and Interdiction) the DASC cleared us to fly offshore until we completed our mission.

We got up to the area just off the mouth of the Ben Hai River. North of us was North Vietnam, south was South Vietnam. I looked down and couldn't see anything. If there were people there, they weren't showing any lights. The put up or shut up time came for the Starlight scope. Dick broke it out of its protective case and switched it on. He peered through it for any signs of enemy activity. He saw none.

"Mo, make the plane stop shaking. I can't see a fucking thing I can't focus if it keeps bouncing around."

"Dick, it's a piston engine airplane. They all bounce around. I'll be as smooth as I can." And I really did try.

"Here," he said, "you try it. I can't see shit. You know the area a lot better than I do. Tell me what you can see."

I bought the single tube Starlight scope up to my eyes. Sure enough, it didn't matter what you did, the scope bounced around way too much to see anything.

"Fuck," I said. "This was a dumb fucking idea. All I see is a bunch of green. Screw it. We know they are down there, probably laughing their little asses off at the stupid American pilots flying overhead who can't see shit collecting their nighttime for the quarter. Give me some coordinates just barely south of the DMZ. I'm going to see if I can get a TPQ mission."

We weren't allowed to fire ordnance into the DMZ unless we had taken fire. After all, it was the Demilitarized Zone. At least, it was the Demilitarized Zone for us. It was a great and long supply base camp for the NVA.

I called the DASC and requested a TPQ mission. We had enemy troops in the open carrying supplies and needed to stop them from coming further south. The DASC questioned my coordinates and wanted to make sure we weren't dropping into the DMZ. They also wanted to know just how we spotted the NVA in the open in the middle of the night.

"DASC, this is Fingerprint 42. We have one of those newfangled Starlight scopes so you can see at night," I responded, ignoring the question about just where we were bombing.

The Trim God must have approved my mission because once we got in touch with the TPQ controller, he said that he had a single A-6 coming on station in ten minutes who was carrying 28 of the Mk-82 500-pound bombs. They could give us forty-five minutes on station. The plane could make a dozen runs in that time.

The A-6 showed up. We requested he give us two bombs on the first run and we would correct from there. The TPQ operator made the setup and I could listen as he made the final adjustments to altitude, direction and speed. He instructed the A-6 pilot to drop, and I knew that 20,000 feet above us two Mk-82s had just armed, and 1,000 feet below us some North Vietnamese porters were in for the shock of their lives. The pair of bombs landed about where we told them to drop. We wouldn't figure it out until the next day but actually our first bombs did the most damage. The NVA were moving rockets in for an attack scheduled for early in the morning.

I told the TPQ operator that he must have fed in the wrong winds or something but he had dropped 600 meters south of where I wanted him to drop. "Move your drop 600 meters north and give me six bombs this time," I requested.

I don't know if he realized what we were doing or not, but he did it anyway. We kept moving the bombs around a little section of the DMZ based on nothing more than my seeing footprints in the sand a few days before. We did get some secondary explosions and that is always a good sign of enemy activity.

The flight ended up being 3.1 hours. It would be the first of three missions that day. I would fly 9.3 hours in heavy combat in one day while seriously hung over.

We flew missions every day. We recognized no weekends or holidays except for the official short truces declared on Christmas. The war went on daily and so did we.

We flew back to Quang Tri and I put the airplane to bed. I thanked Dick Webb for the use of the useless Starlight scope and we laughed. I had another flight right away.

"Dick, you need to get to bed and get some rest. You are still way too drunk to sing," I commented. He could hit the sack and get some rest. It was 0630; the sun was barely showing and I had the dawn patrol. I did the paperwork on the aircraft I had just returned and signed out another fueled and armed plane for my next mission.

The schedule called for me to fly up to Dong Ha and pick up an AO for my next hop. I left Quang Tri as the dawn approached and the sun just peeked over the horizon. I called Dong Ha tower and requested permission to land. Just as I touched down, I saw rockets coming just overhead; they were no more than 500 feet above the ground. Everything we do, we do in context. I didn't expect to see rockets flying overhead and so for a moment my brain wouldn't register the rockets I was seeing. I did understand what I saw when they exploded.

"Seaworthy 508E, this is Dong Ha Tower. We are under rocket attack. I highly advise you to take off at once. I repeat, we are under rocket attack. You are cleared for an immediate takeoff."

"Dong Ha Tower, Seaworthy 508E is on the roll. Thanks." I advanced the throttle and off I went. I could see the smoke rising from a dozen or so rockets that had just passed overhead from my right to my left and impacted on the Dong Ha Marine base, home of the 3rd Marine Division. I had been under rocket fire before but had never had them fly right overhead.

So there I was. I had an empty back seat as my assigned AO would be buried deep in a bunker down below on the base waiting for me to show up. However I did have an M-16, a couple of bandoleers of ammo, a box full of smoke grenades and four WP smoke rockets. I thought about it and realized that nothing could stop me from flying a normal combat mission. I had everything I needed except an AO and I could fill him in when I got back to Dong Ha.

I checked in with DASC and reported what I had seen. At the same time I was flying due north to inspect the area where the rockets had been fired from. I could still see the rising dust from where the rockets were fired. As I got closer I saw the site of the rocket launch, and three more sites all aimed at the Dong Ha combat base, but with the rockets still in place.

All at one time I felt dismay, elation and despair; that same feeling you get when your father-in-law goes over a cliff in your brand new Corvette. The rockets were still in place, ready to fire. Any moment now fifty or sixty rockets might shoot off with a billow of smoke and impact on the combat base a few seconds later. This was an emergency.

When the NVA or VC fired rockets at US bases, they used them as an area weapon. The porters carrying the rockets in their tubes would carve a small berm, perhaps three or four feet high and fifty feet long. The firing expert would give them the exact height necessary to get the range they needed and would carefully align the tubes to the right direction. It was just like lining up straws in a long line. Then they would fire off the whole group at some time. There might be as many as twenty rockets in such a line.

I didn't have time to count them; I just knew I needed some firepower pretty damned quick. Normally I would have the AO talking on the artillery net to find out who was ready for a fire mission. But my AO was in a bunker in Dong Ha. So I called up and was assigned an Army 105 battery firing out of Camp Carroll. I loved those guys. They would have a dozen 105 guns in a battery. One gun would fire a WP round and you would give them corrections from where that round landed. In this case it landed pretty close, within a couple of hundred meters of where I wanted the rounds.

So I made my first correction and asked for twelve guns, five rounds and fire for effect. Each 105 tube would fire five rounds as fast as they could reload.

Now a 105 round is only about five inches across. I seem to remember the body itself weighed about 28 pounds. So it was pretty light compared to even a 250-pound Mk-81 bomb. But when an Army battery delivered sixty rounds in less than two minutes, you covered a lot of area. I could see the rounds exploding all over the rocket sites. I fired at one and then the next and eventually the third and final site.

Meanwhile the DASC scared me up some Navy A-4 guys who were really disappointed because all they had left was 20 mm. But 20 mm guns were what I had to use. I had the A-4s lined up in a circular pattern blasting away at the rocket sites. I don't know if I was killing anyone but for certain I was screwing up their ability to fire on the combat base. I can't remember how many artillery batteries I ended up using, it seemed like two or three. I know I had several flights of fixed wing. The best weapon I could have used was 19-shot rocket pods or CBUs but you fight with what you have, not with what you want.

After a full 2.9 hours I landed at Dong Ha to refuel. The winds were still too high to go back to Quang Tri. I could feel my flight suit drenched in sweat and dried salt. I was dehydrated and still more than a little hung over. I hadn't shaved and I looked a mess. I was looking forward to a hot shower, some food and sobering up. It was not to be.

A grunt captain came up to the plane as I shut the power down and asked if I was the Bird Dog pilot who had stopped the rocket attack. I agreed that that was so and added that I needed some rest. He told me that the 3rd Marine Division Commanding General wanted to see me and needed a full report. (General Davis had finished his tour by this time and the division was now under the command of General William Jones. He was another warrior who earned his spurs in battle during

WW II, gaining the Navy Cross and Silver Star for his actions.)

I told the captain that I was in no condition to brief any Marine general; I was unshaven and frankly I stank. The captain reminded me that when Marine generals request the company of first lieutenants, the lieutenants are expected to say, "Yes sir, no sir, three bags full."

I went to brief General Jones. I advised the captain, his aide, to avoid standing downwind of me, as my stench would have killed a goat.

I told the General the whole story about seeing activity in the area for more than a week or two, the abortion of a night flight in an effort to try out the Starlight scope, and my experience when I first landed at Dong Ha with the rockets going overhead.

He wanted to know how I knew something was going on. I responded, "Footprints, General. They left their footprints in the sand when they crossed the mouth of the Ben Hai."

He wanted to launch the reaction force, a company of Marines on fifteen-minute standby, to see what they could find. He requested that I fly another mission to work with the grunts. I grunted in response. First lieutenants do not say "no" to generals unless they want still to be first lieutenants when they die sixty years later.

When I got back to the operations unit at the airstrip all the AOs were out on other flights. The only person there was Bob Stamper. He had flown one observation mission and was waiting for the winds to die down so he could return to Dong Ha.

"Fang, you and I have a mission. I found a bunch of rockets getting ready to fire this morning and the General wants someone to work with the reaction company. I is your new AO. How do you like them apples?" I asked.

Bob Stamper just laughed. He was always laughing.

Fang and I had relieved each other on missions before but there had never been any reason for us to fly together in one plane once I finished training him when he first arrived. I could do everything that someone in the back seat could do, so I was an AO for the day.

Division launched the duty company and they tromped around the area where the rockets had been set up. It seems to me that at the end of the day, we had destroyed an entire enemy battalion. An NVA battalion was about the size of a US company, maybe 240 men. Of those still alive, I suspect they are still wondering just how we found them. It was an accident of flight time requirements.

I think I can remember Jim Lawrence and Greg Nelson flying missions that day in support of the grunt company. My artillery fire, the TPQs from the night before and the morning airstrikes had all contributed to messing up the plans of the NVA commander. As the day ended I had put in 9.3 hours in the air. Of all the combat I saw in Vietnam, this was my longest day.

At the time General Jones was not impressed with Marine aviation at Quang Tri. He refused to fly in a Marine chopper. There were Army units based at Phu Bai and Dong Ha and he would fly only with them. In a way I can understand the issue. The Army would take pilot candidates right out of high school and train them to be helicopter pilots. They were kids and acted like kids. And they were way too stupid to know they could die so they were pretty much fearless. The Army left broken machines strewn on top of almost every hill in South Vietnam but they got the job done. Marine pilots were older; many were married and had children. They knew what they had to lose.

General Jones put me in for a Silver Star and all of the other pilots and AOs in for DFCs. Since the Air Wing wanted to show the grunt general just who had the power, my Silver Star was downgraded to a DFC. During General Jones' entire tour, these were the only awards he recommended for any Marine pilots.

About awards for a minute. During my twenty months in Vietnam, I spent from July until November of 1968 flying the F-4. I earned about ten strike/flight Air Medals that you get for getting airborne and shot at now and again. I transferred to VMO-6 in November and flew there for just over seven months, until July of 1969. I earned another thirty strike/flight Air Medals there. I also got one single mission Air Medal (awarded for heroic achievement) doing something that I can't even remember today.

While I flew from November of 1968 until July of 1969, doing over 700 missions, I was awarded a total of three DFCs between May 25 and June 5, 1969, a twelve-day period. Now the flying I was doing was no more and no less dangerous during that period than before or after it. Frankly, with the kind of flying we were doing, we could have won DFCs every week. The Bird Dog pilots took more fire than any other aircraft in the war. We were the cutting edge of the sword. The NVA feared us the most because they knew the firepower we could deliver.

There is nothing heroic about doing your duty. Guys in the military hate the term "hero" and only use it if they are Remington Raiders. Being heroic means doing something way out of the ordinary. We signed up to become pilots and had to lie, cheat and steal to become Bird Dog pilots. No one called himself a hero we had a lot of very brave men who did their job day after day without complaint.

I think the AO that I enjoyed flying with the most had to have been Dick Webb. Dick had been a senior intelligence NCO with recon before Vietnam. With the expansion of the Marines from about 200,000 in 1964 to 315,000 in 1969, promotions came easy. Staff Sergeant Dick Webb soon became Lieutenant Dick Webb and he began to practice his mission for real.

In 1968 he was on his second tour in Vietnam. He began to fly with VMO-6 as an AO. He was easily one of the most experienced and valuable AOs. I loved flying with him; he carried his weight and offered good advice.

Dick was a Marine's Marine. After one particularly difficult recon team extraction where every member of the team had been wounded but we managed to get them out alive, Dick wanted to fly out to the USS *Repose*, a Navy hospital ship where our wounded Marines got patched up until they could be transferred. Many Marines survived injuries in Vietnam who would have died in earlier wars due to a lack of prompt care.

We caught a ride with a CH-46 taking supplies out to the ship, a few miles off shore.

One of the fellows we went to see had been wounded fourteen times. He was strapped up in a bed with arms and legs going every which way and lines giving support holding up the broken bits until they began to recover. He had holes all over him. He was quite proud of all the wounds. All I could do was think about how, if any one of those wounds had been half an inch one way or the other, momma's little boy would have been going home in a box.

Dick believed that you had to support your men, and part of that support was visiting them when they were wounded. I couldn't take it. This young corporal or PFC was saying, "Thank you, thank you. I owe my life to you guys. If you hadn't done such a great job, I'd be dead.

You guys saved my entire team."

I wanted to cry. This was what it was really all about. We were up safely in our plane while this fellow was getting chased around the jungle by a bunch of pissed off NVA troops who wanted nothing more than to kill him. He was effusive in his thanks but we should have been thanking him. It was an honor to be able to help him.

Few people in the service, including our fellow pilots in the fighter and attack aircraft, gave any respect to the Bird Dog community. The regular grunt units appreciated us but the recon units loved us because they knew we were going to do everything we could to get them home safely.

The most unusual fire missions I ever controlled were with the 16-inch guns off the battleship *New Jersey*, the only WW II battleship made operational during the Vietnam War. The *New Jersey* first supported the 3rd Marine Division in October of 1968, before I got to Quang Tri.

Initially the Marines used a TA-4 (a twin seat version of the A-4) operating from Da Nang to control the ship and its heavy guns. The TA-4 proved impractical because it flew too fast. In addition the NVA would use every trick they could to defeat our propaganda. Since we felt using the *New Jersey* was a victory, the NVA did everything they could to make it a hollow victory. So they shot up the TA-4.

Our powers that be determined that we should use the OV-10 as a spotter, and the NVA did the same thing to the OV-10. They shot it up and made it clear that if any OV-10s showed up to control the *New Jersey*, they were going to get shot down. Finally someone realized that we did have an aircraft in the inventory that was pretty hard to shoot down yet slow enough to see attractive targets. So the Bird Dogs of VMO-6 became the chosen spotters for the *New Jersey*.

Built in 1942 and commissioned in 1943, the *New Jersey* carried nine 16-inch guns firing 2,200-pound shells (manufactured in 1944) a distance of 37,000 meters. In addition, for closer targets the ship carried twenty of the five-inch 38 guns capable of accurate shooting over 14 km.

I loved controlling the *New Jersey*. On the gun-target line, the direct line from the ship to the target, it wasn't very accurate because the ship rolled from side to side. But left or right of the gun-target line it was very accurate. It seemed to me we tended to use the big guns with targets no more than 12-15 miles away. Beyond that distance you were just lobbing the shells, not shooting them.

I don't think that we ever fired closer than 1,000 meters from friendlies. The big gun was not a precision weapon by any means. I think I targeted bunkers or gun positions, maybe trees in the open, I don't remember what exactly but they weren't critical targets.

You used an actual high explosive round as a spotter round, not a WP round. When a 2,200-pound shell goes off, there is no question in anyone's mind where it hit. I liked to ask for three guns and three rounds each. The *New Jersey* would fire off those nine rounds and it was just like the Fourth of July. If you were Charlie the Gook, you had to be wondering just what the fuck was going on. I'm not sure we ever hit anything important but every NVA within five kilometers of one of those shells going off remembers it to this day.

One day I thought that what I needed to do was to photograph the battleship when firing its big guns. I flew off shore to where she was sailing. Naturally I told them of my intentions. They warned me to make sure I stayed out of the gun target line; better yet, I should stay on the seaward side when taking pictures. They got ready to shoot their 16-inch gun; I got ready to snap my 35mm camera. They fired and my plane felt like I had just taken a mortar round. I had no idea that I would be shaken as I was. Wow.

The weapon that bothered me the most in Vietnam had to be the B-52 bomber. When I say it bothered me, I mean that it had to be the biggest terror weapon we used. It had to have terrified the VC and NVA. I have felt the ground shake fifteen miles away from an Arc Light mission. It scared the shit out of me and I wasn't even the target.

B-52s were based in Guam and Thailand. The Air Force needs nice air-conditioned hotels for their pilots, including people to shine your shoes, so they stationed the B-52 jocks at nice bases.

The Arc Light missions basically used three sections of three planes. For a bigger target, they might use multiples of those nine-airplane units. The planes generally carried a mixture of 500 and 750-pound bombs, with a single aircraft capable of carrying as many as 117 bombs at a time on both internal and external stations. When they started dropping their bombs it sounded like the gongs of Hell to any VC or NVA nearby.

The patterns were a mile wide and up to two miles long. Anything caught in the area was either dead or shellshocked. Think carpet-bombing. It must have caused terror on the ground if you were an NVA and saw the pattern of bombs coming your way.

While at Quang Tri I got caught in a couple of rocket attacks. A rocket would hit, then another still closer, and you started to wonder if one of them had your name on it. That was terrifying, and a 122 mm rocket might have an 80-pound explosive head on it. I would not have wanted to be in the flight path of a bunch of B-52s.

The flights I made on June 5, 1969 seemed to have disrupted the beginning of a mini-offensive on the part of the NVA in Northern I Corps. They continued to make major attacks on various firebases for the next two weeks.

Greg Nelson launched on the dawn patrol on the morning of June 17. The NVA had made a major attack on a firebase run by elements of the 3rd Marine Regiment. He caught the NVA inside the wire and called on supporting Huey gunships and flights of fixed wing to destroy the NVA unit. As I recall he took over 45 rounds of AK-47 fire to his plane. That included one round that bounced off his bullet bouncer that he was sitting on.

Greg received the Silver Star for his efforts that day to protect his men. Greg was a true warrior.

I made captain on the June 8, 1969, three months before my twenty-third birthday. I was the youngest captain in the Marines and almost certainly, with the 832 missions I had flown, the fixed wing pilot with the greatest number of missions in Vietnam. Even Steve Pless only flew 780 missions and he was a chopper driver.

In my eight months with VMO-6 I began to realize that we weren't fighting a war to win. We were fighting just to be fighting. The military-industrial complex may have loved it but we were doing nothing more than draining the blood from our young men and draining the gold from our treasury. I participated in operations landing troops on a contested LZ in November and I was doing exactly the same thing for the third or fourth time on the same LZ eight months later. Every time we lost a few helicopters with maybe the crew surviving or perhaps not. The grunts would do patrols around the LZ for a couple of weeks with some getting killed or wounded every day. We did exactly the same thing day after day yet expected different results.

I knew enough to realize that no one wins any war. When talking about war, winning isn't a concept any more than winning a case of herpes. It's always bad. In war all that happens is that one side loses a lot more than the other and eventually figures out it's time to declare a victory and go home. If you walk into a bar and start a fight for no reason and you knock out three teeth of the fool you attacked and lose two of your own teeth, you still lost. You just didn't lose as much as the other guy.

There are no good battles or good wars, only battles you won by never fighting, and peace that is always a victory. Nothing sickens a warrior as much as those who sit on the sidelines waving flags and cheering. War is always a loss. It's true, there is no bad peace or good war.

It was time for me to move on. I put in papers to extend my tour by another six months and requested a transfer to H&MS 17 in Da Nang to have some peace and quiet. On July 2, 1969 I made my last flight with VMO-6.

Chapter 2 (Part 2)
THE DEADLIEST CRIME (CONTINUED)

I wanna go home, I wanna go home
Oh, how I wanna go home.

Last night I went to sleep in Detroit City
And I dreamed about those cotton fields and home
I dreamed about my mother dear, old papa, sister and brother
I dreamed about that girl who's been waiting for so long
I wanna go home, I wanna go home, oh, how I wanna go home.

Homefolks think I'm big in Detroit City
From the letters that I write they think I'm fine
But by day I make the cars, by night I make the bars
If only they could read between the lines.

'Cause you know I rode the freight train north to Detroit City
And after all these years I find I've just been wastin' my time
So I just think I'll take my foolish pride
And put it on a southbound freight and ride.
And go on back to the loved ones, the ones that I left waitin' so far behind.

I wanna go home, I wanna go home,
Oh, how I wanna go home...

Detroit City
Songwriters: Mel Tillis, Danny Dill
Copyright: Cedarwood Publishing 1963

WHILE THAT ETERNITY PASSED as we waited to hear if the recon team survived or not, and perhaps a minute or so passed in the real world, I began to get that sinking feeling in the pit of my stomach. Had I just killed six young American Marines with my foolish actions?

My AO spoke first, "What do we do now? Did we just kill those poor bastards? I'm going to turn in my wings; I can't do this any more. It's bad enough to see these recon guys die day after day but to actually kill them ourselves. I can't do it."

I felt exactly the same way. While we did exactly what the team leader demanded we do, it still wasn't right. Our actions killed the entire team, just as the NVA wanted. This was going to be my last flight for certain. I made one more low pass to see if I could see anything amidst the smoke and wreckage we had caused.

"Motherfucker!" I heard over the FM radio faintly. "Mother*fucker!*"

I couldn't tell what or who was transmitting but he was panting as he continued, "Can you hear me, Seaworthy? I'm as deaf as a doorpost. I can't hear a motherfucking thing. That was a real motherfucker. Can you hear the fucking gooners calling for their mommas? I'll hold the headset up so you can hear. Those motherfuckers got caught in the open. Boy did we fuck those motherfuckers up. Wow. I'm still alive. Let me check on the rest of the team."

"Cloudy Sky. Is that you, Cloudy Sky?" I spoke into my lip mike with a feeling of elation and hope. "What is the status of the rest of your guys, Cloudy Sky? This is Seaworthy Mike, can you give me a status report?"

I got on the UHF radio and called in the 46s that were standing by at LZ Vandergrift. We had two machines on standby and a pair of VMO-6 Huey gunships. We needed to get these guys out before the NVA could recover.

He came back a few minutes later and said, "We have dead and dying gooks all over the place. Everybody on the team has some shrapnel wounds but we are still alive and that's better than it looked like a few minutes ago. Can you get that CH-46 in quick? We want to di-di right fucking now. Seaworthy, you have your shit in one tiny little bag. Thanks, motherfucker. We owe our lives to you."

We had the Hueys blast the shit of the entire area around the pickup zone and the extraction went smoothly. One Marine had died before we came on the scene but in the end the skill and bravery of the team leader saved their lives.

I would never again be called on to make such a dreadful decision.

Chapter 14
WERS-17, DA NANG

Give me a F! (F!)
Give me a U! (U!)
Give me a C! (C!)
Give me a K! (K!)
What's that spell? (FUCK)
What's that spell? (FUCK)

Well, come on all of you, big strong men,
Uncle Sam needs your help again.
He's got himself in a terrible jam
Way down yonder in Vietnam
So put down your books and pick up a gun,
We're gonna have a whole lotta fun.

And it's one, two, three,
What are we fighting for?
Don't ask me, I don't give a damn,
Next stop is Vietnam;
And it's five, six, seven,
Open up the pearly gates,
Well there ain't no time to wonder why,
Whoopee! we're all gonna die.

Feel Like I'm Fixin' To Die Rag
Songwriter: Joe McDonald
Copyright: Joe McDonald 1967

I'VE READ THAT WE DON'T KNOW where elephants go to die. I did learn where they bury Marine Corps Majors who otherwise qualify as shitbirds but somehow got promoted by accident.

My original intention was to extend my tour by six months and to transfer to H&MS 17, where I would fly VIPs around Vietnam and Thailand. At the time, if you extended for six months, the government would give you 30 days' free leave and a round trip ticket anywhere in the world.

I knew the H&MS people desperately needed pilots qualified to be PICs in the S-2F, C-1A and C-117. The Marine Corps almost went along with my plan. I got my transfer to MWSG-17 (Marine Wing Service Group-17) but ended up in the WERS-17 unit (Wing Equipment & Repair Squadron).

MWSG was where the Marines buried majors they couldn't use for anything else because they were pretty useless. MWSG-17 must have had fifteen majors, all doing nothing at all. None of the flying squadrons wanted them, so they transferred them to MWSG-17 to get rid of them.

WERS-17 was even worse. The CO of the unit was the senior major in the Marine Corps. He made his promotion to major during the waning days of the Korean War. I would have been seven at the time. His name was Major Farley and the troops, with great affection, called him Fat Fuck Farley. Since I was the second highest ranking officer in the squadron, normally I would have been the XO of the squadron, but FFF rightly figured that the unit really didn't need an XO, since we only had about 500 troops in total and five officers.

Farley was an 0802, an artillery officer. Now I don't understand much about artillery except how to shoot it. With two Marine Divisions fighting the NVA and VC, I'd think someone would want an artillery officer. But it seemed not. At least, there was one 0802 they didn't want in any artillery unit.

I wasn't the only person in the unit who had no time for the major. His clerks hated him. At the time his office was located in one end of a Quonset hut with a divider in the middle. There were three or four clerks who occupied desks cluttered together at the other end of the hut. A pair of swing doors were the only barrier between the major and the clerks. When they heard him coming through the doors, one of the clerks would discreetly dial his phone number. As he started mumbling some silly order or another to one of the clerks, his phone would ring.

Farley was quite impressed with himself. Actually he was the only really fat officer I ever met in the Marines. Since he had made major, he was guaranteed to be allowed to stay for a 20-year career and retirement but no one seemed to think much of him. But who knows? He was probably thinking that it was Nixon on the line wanting to know what Farley thought about the war. So he would quickly waddle back into the safety of his office and pick up the phone, only to find no one on the other end. But if someone had called him, he probably should wait a few minutes to see if they would call back.

I thought it was a hoot. His people ended up conditioning him to not leave his office. He would try to shout orders over the swinging doors and the clerks just ignored him.

He assigned me two sections of the squadron. One was the refueling area and the personnel that refueled the Marine C-130s that made trips all over the country, moving troops around. The other was the Short Airfield Tactical Section. The SATS setup was a set of arresting cables that you could rig on an airfield made of Marston matting to recover the tactical aircraft such as the A-4 and F-4. This unit had been used at Chu Lai until a permanent concrete runway was constructed.

I had no idea of what either unit did and I didn't care to learn. I was there to sneak rides in the C-117 and S-2 as often as possible. Each section had an E-6 staff sergeant in charge. I called them in and briefed them at the same time.

"Guys," I began. "you know what you are doing and I don't. You don't need me to tell you what to do or when to do it. I am in charge of taking care of you and your people. I want to know every problem we have with the troops before it goes up the line. We sort our problems out here, we don't let the major get involved. I am in charge of R&R for guys when they can get it, and promotions, and any other sticky little issues. Do your job and I'll take care of you. Your job is to take care of your men and to hand it to me if you can't. Do we have an understanding?" I queried.

They looked at each other and realized they were on to a good deal. For the next nine months it worked out well. I had a jeep assigned to me as a result of my position, and I was making over $900 a month in salary and flight pay so I was living high on the hog.

I went over to the H&MS squadron and made myself available to fly the shitty missions. My deal with them was that I would fly one shitty mission if they matched it with a good mission. No one wanted to fly the flare drops at 0300 in the C-117 but everyone wanted to fly to Thailand and spend the night. The squadron checked me out and promptly made me a PIC of everything they had in the unit. I was the only first tour plane commander in the entire Marine Corps for the C-117 or S-2F or C-1A.

The flying was sweet. I used to go to Saigon about once a week. On one of my first trips to the capital, the fragmentation order we got the night before called for me to pick up a load of elephants. Elephants? In my airplane? I think not. When I went over to operations to brief my copilot I asked about the elephants and the ops office laughed. He said I would see when I got to Saigon.

Saigon was actually a more dangerous place than either Quang Tri or Da Nang. While Quang Tri and Da Nang got mortared and rocketed on a fairly regular basis, I never knew anyone actually injured. It was as if the NVA wanted us to know they were still there for us. But in Saigon you had better carry a weapon and wear a flak jacket. All of the hotels and quarters for US servicemen had chicken wire over the windows to keep the VC from tossing in hand grenades.

As PIC, I always flew from the left seat. Wing wienies who needed to make their required four hours a month to collect their flight pay would occupy the right seat. You could fly and land any of the airplanes we were flying out of either seat position. All the copilots I flew with were senior to me. I had a lot of majors and up to bird colonels. No one had any problem flying with a 22-year-old captain. Many of them weren't even interested in flying their legs. I would offer to fly one and let them fly one but many really weren't qualified. As long as they could show the four hours a month in their logbooks they were happy.

We flew the 350-mile two-hour trips to Saigon in peace. With the C-117 flights we carried two crewmen in addition to the two pilots, a crew chief and an assistant. They loved flying with me because I didn't play the "I'm an officer and you are enlisted" crap with them. In most cases they were older than I was. I wasn't planning on sticking around for a career. So as long as they showed up on time and did their job, we got along fine.

When we got to Saigon, a Marine captain showed up with a cargo truck with my elephants. They were ceramic elephants standing about two feet tall. My crew chief had been on many a BUFE flight (Big Ugly

Fucking Elephant). We had twenty-two seats in the C-117 and we filled them. The crew chief carefully strapped a Buffie into each seat. Evidently military wives back in the world of the senior officers had heard of the Buffies and everyone wanted a pair. I think a set of two cost maybe $15, not an inconsiderable sum when you think that gold was only $35 an ounce.

Over time I would haul hundreds of the stupid creatures from Saigon to Da Nang. I became the official elephant man because the other pilots broke them regularly. I thought they were the ugliest things I had ever seen but the guy in Saigon so much appreciated my careful handling of the creatures that he gave me a special gold-trimmed pair before I left Vietnam.

Of all the flights I made with H&MS 17, the most unusual was when I hauled a house cat to Saigon for a Navy nurse who was having an affair with one of the bird colonels at Wing. It was a cat. A perfectly ordinary house cat of uncertain lineage, but the nurse loved her cat. At the time Pan Am regulations and the rules of Vietnam said that to ship a cat out of the country, it needed to have a distemper shot and have a vet sign off that it was healthy a month later.

Vietnamese didn't have pets. If you were a cat and wanted a home, you had to feed yourself and earn your keep making sure rats and mice didn't eat the rice. There were no free rides for pets. If you were a dog, you had better understand the difference between a VC and a US soldier, depending on which was the enemy of that particular village. There were no cute cuddly lap dogs in Vietnam. None. As a matter of fact, lots of dogs were eaten. They not only had to earn their food, they became food.

So there was one vet in the entire country, in Saigon. One day I was fragged to take a Marine corporal and his prisoner to Saigon. The prisoner was the stupid cat. A house cat of uncertain lineage that had his own guard armed with a Colt .45 automatic pistol. I shrugged when they told me what I was carrying. Nothing could be goofier than carrying Buffies. I thought.

I had a Marine bird colonel as a copilot. Bird colonels don't chat with mere captains so I had a long boring day in front of me. I thought.

We made our normal takeoff from Da Nang. Once we got to altitude, I set the autopilot. The corporal guarding the cat came up to the cockpit to tell me the cat was unhappy at being trapped in his cage

"Sir, do you mind if I let the cat out of the cage? He'll probably be a lot happier." The corporal asked nicely.

"Sure, there isn't any place for him to go but keep an eye on him. If he gets loose and we don't return him tonight, we are both going to be privates tomorrow," I replied. That was a really bad idea.

Now if you have ever had a mommy cat that had kittens, you know that she will first find the quietest and most hidden place she can, to make sure her kittens are protected as they are born. Well, this cat had exactly the same idea. Once the corporal opened the door to the cage, the now pissed off cat shot out like a lightning bolt.

It seems the most secluded place on the airplane was behind and underneath the copilot's instrument panel. The cat made a mad dash and jumped under the panel. I saw it coming and grabbed it by the tail. That pissed off the feline furball even more and the little prick bastard bit me right on the web of skin between my thumb and forefinger. Somehow the cat knew the most painful place to bite a Marine captain. I'm yanking on the cat's tail, trying to keep it from getting any further under the instrument panel while screaming for the corporal to get his ass up to the cockpit to grab the cat and begging the colonel for help.

Marine captains don't demand anything from Marine colonels. They may request politely but they don't demand or even ask with a firm tone of voice. Marine colonels are used to being worshipped and any deviation from the norm is quickly noticed.

"Colonel, sir. Colonel, can you give me a hand catching this fucking cat? He's got his teeth into my hand and if I let go he's going to get fried under the panel. Colonel? Colonel? Sir, a little help please?"

The colonel put his nose outside his side of the airplane and watched the rice paddies slowly pass by below. He clearly didn't give a shit about either the house cat or my hand. There is a reason that, given the choice between a copilot and a wet soggy sandwich, I always opt for the wet soggy sandwich. If you are in grievous pain from a house cat biting the shit out of your hand, the soggy sandwich might care. The copilot, not.

Eventually the corporal and I got our hands on the cat and hauled him out from beneath the panel. I told the corporal to shove the cat back in the cage and to ignore its wailing and moaning until we were back on the ground at Da Nang.

We got some wheels in Saigon and took the stupid cat to the vet. While I was sitting in the reception room waiting for it to get the needed spike, I saw an Army guy with a big cage containing two strange looking cats. They were the size of house cats but had markings like a tiger. They looked like tiny tigers. I asked the soldier what he was doing with them.

"Well, sir. These are Vietnamese ocelots. They are related to tigers but they stay small. I have a matched pair, a female and a male. But I have to sell them. My unit is leaving next week and if they get their shots today, I can't take them out of the country for thirty days. Would you like to buy them?" he asked in a plaintive voice.

Oh, I wanted those ocelots. At the time you could pretty much bring anything into the US. If I had a breeding pair of tiny ocelots, I could start an entire new industry.

"How much do you want for them?" I asked.

"I need $100 for the pair," he responded sadly.

"How about $50 for the female? I don't have any more than that with me," I said, even more sadly.

"Sorry sir, but I can't split them up. I'd love to help you but they have to stay together and I need $100 for them."

If you have noticed lately, there is no industry selling tiny tiger-marked Vietnamese ocelots in the US today. That's because I didn't have $100 with me that day.

Easily the most enjoyable flight I ever made in Vietnam was when I picked up twenty Red Cross donut dollies at Tan Son Nhat airport in Saigon. The Red Cross sponsored several hundred young female college graduates to hand out coffee and donuts to the troops. One day I got a call telling me to leave at 0800 the next day with one of our C-117s to pick up a batch of the young women and take them wherever their orders called for.

The women all turned out to be twenty-two or twenty-three years old and had eyes as big as saucers as they looked around in wonder. They all looked as if they were expecting an attack at any moment. At the time we had about 500,000 soldiers and Marines in-country and no more than 500 round-eye women. Even the plain looking Red Cross workers had men drooling after them. The donut dollies wore pinstripe blue uniforms that looked a lot like nurses' uniforms. They would be attached to a command and get chopper rides to some of the most desolate places in the entire country. I have to give them credit, they were troopers all.

I met the girls at their plane when they landed. It reminded me a lot of trying to herd cats. I told them that they needed to list how many people were being dropped off at each spot and to give me the list so I could prepare a flight plan. It took two hours just to get their entire luggage under control. By now my crew chief was in stitches. He thought it was very funny. I wondered if he really wanted to ever fly with me again. When I asked him he responded, "Yes, sir. Sorry, sir." But he did giggle now and again.

We made our list, we filed our flight plan and we left. Since Saigon is pretty much as far south as you can get in the country, we plodded north, dropping off two or three of the women at each landing field. Some of the girls were really hot and I didn't mind my role as the cool Marine aviator with everything under control.

Eventually we made our way back to Da Nang, where the last few maidens were to be stationed. One dark-haired beauty caught my eye. We made plans for me to come over to the Red Cross house and take her out for dinner. The relationship grew for months and eventually we became engaged.

Woodie Patton told me years before never to have a relationship with a woman more fucked up than I was. I should have listened. The donut dolly was a real beauty but not dealing with a full deck.

September of 1969 approached. I put in for my extension leave. I wanted to see every spot I could on my round trip ticket. So I looked at a globe and determined that Helsinki in Finland was about as far from Vietnam as I could possibly travel. At the time we were issued paper tickets and could make an unlimited number of stops. I went to Boulder, Fort Lauderdale, London, Paris, Helsinki, Geneva, and Florence.

Under my arm I had a well-thumbed copy of Frommer's *Europe on $5 a Day*. You could travel, eat and sleep on $5 a day in 1969. While not all my accommodations were first class – in Switzerland I slept in a tiny room underneath the stairs – I had a wonderful vacation.

I spent all of September and October on leave. I arrived back in Vietnam on October 31, 1969 as the war was dying down.

The 3rd Marine Division left Vietnam for Okinawa in November of 1969. VMO-6 had left already for Okinawa the month before. I never found out where the O-1G aircraft ended up; I think the Marines turned them over to the Army. By late 1969 we only had three O-1Cs still in-country. They sat on the apron at H&MS 17 for many months before being turned over to the ROK Marines (Republic of Korea) operating just south of Da Nang.

Sometime in December of 1969 I got a call asking if I was available to cover a convoy of jeeps going from Chu Lai to Da Nang. When MAG 12 and MAG 13 left Chu Lai in the fall of 1969 it seems they left over 150 jeeps. While these jeeps had official-looking numbers and papers, it seems the Marine Corps had never entered them onto their inventory. Of course they were all stolen, mostly from the Air Force and Army. That was considered good clean fun. For most of the time, the Army, Navy and Air Force were viewed as just as much the enemy as the VC and NVA.

I overflew the convoy all the way from Chu Lai to Da Nang. It was nothing short of amazing to see this long line of jeeps, each maintaining twenty meters of separation from the one in front so a mine might take out one vehicle but not more. Of course there was no danger of VC attack at all. The VC were spending way too much time laughing at how the 1st Marine Air Wing was going to explain how they had 150 more jeeps than existed on the inventory. The VC knew that eventually they were going to end up driving the jeeps because the Marines weren't about to tell the Air Force and Army where they could pick up their jeeps.

Before his election Nixon had promised he had a secret plan to end the war. In reality all he had to do was listen to the junior officers and snuffies fighting it on his behalf. We all knew the solution was to simply declare a victory and send everyone home. That's pretty much what they did. Tricky Dick had no secret plan, it was just another lie by a politician to get elected.

During the fall of 1969 and into the early months of 1970 I made a couple of trips up to Quang Tri. The Dong Ha combat base was pretty much a desert. The local Vietnamese had ripped our hooches apart. They stole every piece of wire and light fitting they could get their hands on. The 101st Airborne had moved onto the base from where they had been stationed at Phu Bai but they didn't make any improvements. They didn't even cook their own chow. The Army cooked it in Phu Bai and sent it up in trucks. It was pretty obvious the war was winding down.

There was little enemy action. The NVA and VC knew that all they had to do was outlast the stupid Americans. When our last troops had marched onto ships and on the freedom flights leaving Vietnam, they would have their day.

Sometime during that period Major Farley called me into his office. Silently he slid a couple of documents across the desk to me. I began to read. They were my second and third DFCs.

"That makes three for you now, doesn't it?" he asked casually. "They must be handing them out like candy bars up there in Quang Tri."

Normally when they hand out medals someone makes a big deal of it. I've never been a big fan of ceremony, but this was about as casual and meaningless as it could be. And this buffoon who had never seen a day of combat in his life had likened my DFCs to Snickers bars. I just picked up the documents and left. What can you say to a fool?

All the signs of the war winding down began to appear. I was seeing small units being marched around Da Nang in formation. That I had never seen in eighteen months in-country.

In January absolute proof that the war was over was presented to me. Remember, my deal with operations was that I take the crap flights if I got dibs on the good flights to Saigon and Thailand.

One day my name showed up on the schedule for a night flare hop. We would load a C-117 with half a dozen guys and maybe 100 flares. They were about six feet long and had a cord attached to them. You hung the cord on a cable inside the plane and tossed a flare out when you needed one. The troops who never saw combat loved the night flare runs because it made the war seem real to them. I would be the backup for the primary flare ship.

Sometime in the fall of 1969 VMO-2, our sister squadron that had been stationed in Marble Mountain, moved their entire OV-10 unit to the southeast corner of the Da Nang airbase. They occupied the same hangers that we were in when I was flying with VMFA-542.

The Marine Corps had devised a way that you could hang flares on an OV-10 and they wanted to test how it worked. Since they were going to do some night practice bombing in preparation for Tet 1970, some bright spark determined we should combine the two missions. The OV-10 would control the flights of fixed wing and drop flares for them at the same time. In the C-117, I would be a backup for them.

One of the things I had never done as an F-4 pilot and never heard of being done during the time I flew Bird Dogs was to run a night close air support mission. Bombing was a daylight affair unless you were doing a TPQ.

Not only were they going to do a practice night bombing, it was make believe. They weren't actually hitting a target, this was pure practice. To make it even more insane, the fixed wing aircraft were going to do a 10-degree dive dropping snakes and napes. This seemed like a recipe for disaster from my point of view. But nobody asked me.

I'm in a high orbit at 10,000 feet, safely to the side so I don't get in anyone's way. The OV-10 doing the controlling is flown by Lieutenant Colonel Moriarty, who was CO of VMO-2 at the time. He's down around 4,000 feet. He brings in a pair of A-4s from MAG 12 and they do just fine. They are dropping their soft ordnance down a valley about fifteen miles south of Da Nang, where no one cares what they do. The OV-10 seems to function just fine as a flare ship. I have absolutely nothing to do.

After the A-4s leave, a pair of F-4Js from MAG 13 checks in with the same ordnance load, snake and napes for a shallow delivery. In the mountains. At night. For practice.

The lead aircraft rolls in and drops his napes pretty much where the OV-10 told him to drop. Dash-2 rolls in, is cleared hot, and all of a sudden we see what looks like a giant napalm go off and something spinning in air before a really big explosion goes off when it hits the ground. I realize at once what just happened. Everyone else is stunned into stupidity.

The flight lead starts calling on the radio, "Dash-2, have you pulled off target?" and "Dash-2, what's your pos?" and "Dash-2, where are you?" He becomes more shrill with every call. He knows what just happened and he doesn't want to admit it. Dash-2 of the flight just hit the ground doing nighttime soft ordnance delivery for practice in the mountains. What could you possibly expect to go wrong?

I came up on the radio. "This is Seaworthy Mike in the C-117.

Dash-2 just hit the ground. That big fire down there is the remains of his plane. Lead, you may as well head back to Chu Lai, there is nothing you can do here."

The OV-10 took charge of the emergency. He asked, "Anyone got any idea of how you can tell if the ejection seats have been fired on an F-4?"

I responded, "Sure. I used to be an F-4 jock. The seats are on a long rail that extends up and back after an ejection. They look like pipes. If they managed to eject, you will see two parallel pipes sticking out of the cockpit."

The OV-10 called back to his unit and requested a Cobra gunship be launched. When the Cobra came out, the OV-10 requested he go down and inspect the smoldering wreckage of the F-4 to see if the rails were extended or not. To everyone's great surprise, they were extended, and both crew had ejected.

The OV-10 ran short of fuel and had another VMO-2 aircraft come out and spell him. Many years afterwards I learned that Fred Smith, later founder of FedEx, flew that second OV-10 on the scene.

I continued to fly circles overhead in the hope of being able to do something. The Cobra was flying at about 1,500 feet. He soon heard on the emergency channel, 243.0, a call from the pilot. Then the RIO came up and said that he was ok. The Cobra managed to talk the two crew into a clearing where at least they were together. Now we needed to get them out of there. No doubt every VC within twenty miles was moving post haste to get to the scene.

Since I had HF radio on my plane, I called Air Force headquarters in Saigon to request the Jolly Greens, the giant CH-53 helicopters used for rescues, launch and pick up our airmen. Typical of the Air Force, they said the Jolly Greens made rescues only during daylight hours. No kidding. You can get shot down 24 hours a day but we will only pick you up if the sun is shining.

We called the chopper group and asked them to send a CH-46. They did, the crew was picked up safely and everyone went home. I realized that when you start losing airplanes because you are doing practice bombing at night, the war is pretty much over.

Due to the increased racial tension, largely due to the murder of Martin Luther King and the simmering discontent from blacks in the

US, problems began to appear amongst the troops in Vietnam. No one wanted to fight the war, especially for "whitey." I think there were more Americans killed and injured in 1970 in Vietnam from blue-on-blue shootings, fragging and self-inflicted wounds than from enemy action.

Since October of 1969, the sole remaining O-1C aircraft in the Marine inventory had been sitting on the ramp at H&MS-17. In early March of 1970 someone asked me if I would provide some training for the ROK Marines. Our Marine Corps was donating the three airplanes to them. I agreed in a moment. So on March 8, 1970 I made the last two flights of the O-1 for the Marine Corps. We took off from Da Nang, flew to their area of operations and fired off a couple of 2.75 WP rockets. Frankly if you can fly the fixed pitch prop version of the Bird Dog known as the O-1G, you can fly the variable pitch prop model of the aircraft known as the O-1C.

It was not only the last combat flight of a Marine O-1; it was also the end of a 58-year era of Marines flying piston engine aircraft in combat. Since the first flight by a Marine in 1912, Marine aircraft had been piston engine. The O-1 was the last of a breed. Sure, we still had some gasoline burners in our hands but none were combat aircraft.

On March 19, 1970 I made my very last flight in the Marine Corps and in Vietnam. I had my orders to report to MCAS El Toro, California. It was a good time to be leaving. As I learned a few years ago, a couple of days after I left the Marine Corps pulled something I had never heard of before.

There was an HML squadron based in Phu Bai flying UH-1E gunships. Often they were tasked to escort Army choppers dropping Special Operations Group teams in Laos. The SOG teams were CIA-controlled recon teams operating across the border in Laos. Members came from Army Special Forces or were specially trained soldiers similar to our force recon units. They did exactly the same thing in Laos that our guys did in Northern I Corps.

The CIA always took security to an absurd degree. When SOG teams went into Laos, or even North Vietnam for that matter, they went "sterile" – they carried nothing that identified who they were or where they came from. A lot of times they would carry a Swedish-K 9 mm submachine gun or whatever their preferred weapon was, including a lot of AK-47s, and wear any uniform except American.

The teams were looking for evidence of movement down the Ho Chi Minh trail. That was dumb, for we could hear them driving down the trail every night. There was no secret about it. But when the SOG teams were discovered by the NVA, somehow the NVA were supposed to be unable to guess where they came from.

So some guy gets shot in combat and is captured by the NVA while wearing Israeli utilities and carrying a Swedish-K submachine gun. Were the NVA supposed to be so dumb they wouldn't realize they were being spied on by Americans?

In March of 1970 a pair of UH-1E gunships from the HML squadron at Phu Bai was escorting some Army slick Hueys carrying an SOG team into Laos. Hueys came in two basic variations, the gunships carrying offensive weapons and slicks designed only for carrying troops. In this mission, the Marines supplied the gunships, the Army supplied the slicks.

Now from a pilot's point of view, Laos and South Vietnam looked exactly the same. There may have been a line drawn carefully on maps but you can't see those lines from the air. Laos was bad-guy territory. We got shot at every time we flew over Laos by some very accurate and dedicated AAA gunners. The airplane flying the SOG team got shot out of the LZ and barely made it back to South Vietnam and safety. One of the UH-1E gunships got shot down and landed in a ball of flames near the border.

Pilots do their very best to help other pilots. One of the other HML pilots was convinced there might have been survivors of the crash. He flew over the crash site a few days later just to see if anyone might have survived. A tall white guy wearing nothing but green skivvies came running out of the bush waving his arms in the air. Someone had survived the crash or the NVA had set up a very convincing ambush.

The chopper driver sped back to Phu Bai and reported what he had found. The rest of the squadron pilots were overjoyed at the opportunity to rescue one of their own. But when the squadron CO reported the incident to Saigon the CIA made an upper level decision to leave the crewman in Laos since we weren't supposed to be there in the first place.

One tradition of the Marines which is hammered home, starting in boot camp, is that Marines never leave their dead behind. Marines believe that if they are killed in combat, nothing would stop the Marine Corps from recovering their remains and sending them home.

War corrupts everyone who participates. They start gloriously, with bands playing and young women cheering. They end with the government lying and cheating and young women in tears. By 1970 the Marine Corps had forgotten its traditions and its honor. In March of 1970 they not only left their dead behind, they left their living behind. The CIA made the decision to abandon the crewman in Laos because legally we weren't there.

That pissed off a lot of the HML pilots. After all, if the Marines could leave someone behind after his plane was shot down, why wouldn't they do the same thing when it was your turn in the barrel?

They pissed off two more of the HML pilots than was safe for management. One crew assigned to the next combat mission went out to their fully armed aircraft. They did an air taxi to the end of the runway where the arming crew removed the safely pins from their ordnance and they took off for what might well be their last mission in a Marine aircraft.

The pilots got the aircraft up to speed and flew directly over the squadron operations buildings at rooftop level before entering a high perch position. Shortly thereafter the squadron CO got on the radio in a fury and demanded the pilots land for their court martial for flat hatting the squadron. The pilots replied that if they were going to get court martialed, it would be for firing rockets into the command bunker before shooting up the entire squadron area and all of the aircraft. Either the CO agreed immediately to the launch of a rescue mission to retrieve the missing crewman or he would find his fleet of planes smoldering in the wind.

I would love to have been a fly on the wall of that CO's office when he heard that transmission. He had a mutiny on his hands and he could either do as the pilots demanded or lose all of his planes.

They did launch a rescue mission at once; they did recover a living pilot who had survived the crash a week earlier in Laos. Then they covered it up. You won't find any reports of that particular mission in any USMC history book.

Myself, if someone asked me if I really cared if the Marines left my dead body behind if I got shot down, I'd reply that it really wouldn't make any difference to me. I did participate in dozens of missions where men died during the recovery of dead bodies from earlier action. But if I was alive after getting shot down and I realized my guys had left me behind, I'd be triple pissed.

Chapter 15
3rd MARINE AIR WING,
EL TORO, CALIFORNIA

When you're weary, feeling small,
When tears are in your eyes, I will dry them all;
I'm on your side. When times get rough
And friends just can't be found,
Like a bridge over troubled water
I will lay me down.
Like a bridge over troubled water
I will lay me down.

When you're down and out,
When you're on the street,
When evening falls so hard
I will comfort you.
I'll take your part.
When darkness comes
And pain is all around,
Like a bridge over troubled water
I will lay me down.
Like a bridge over troubled water
I will lay me down.

Bridge Over Troubled Water
Songwriter: Paul Simon
Copyright: Paul Simon Music 1970

I ARRIVED BACK in the US in late March. For all the stories of how US troops were being cursed and spat on, I never saw it. The American public had turned against the war but that didn't necessarily mean they turned against American servicemen. I would be released on May 1, 1970 so the base attached me to the CG's headquarters for the six weeks

I needed to serve before being released.

All my unmarried buddies from Vietnam and Cherry Point were staying on the beach. I moved in with a bunch of them for the short time I would be there. The first night after I arrived back proved interesting. I was given a fold-out couch to sleep on. I unfolded it and out dropped a plastic bag of what looked to be oregano. I held it up to the light to determine just what it was. "Why, this looks just like marijuana," I reported brightly.

I looked around the room. Everyone was staring at the ceiling and whistling out of tune. Someone dared ask, "Do you want to try some?"

"Well, I guess so. What does it do for you?"

"Not much other than you will get a bad case of the nibblies," came the response.

One of the guys broke out some rolling papers and started to roll a joint. For a guy who had never done it before, he sure looked like he knew exactly what he was doing. He took a toke and passed the joint to me. I took my first puff and almost choked. "Take another puff and hold it in," he suggested. So I did.

I didn't feel anything. I didn't see dragons or strange lights, my head stayed on my shoulders. Could it be that the effects of marijuana had been exaggerated by the powers that be? The guys sat me in front of their stereo and had me put on a nice headset. It was a really great headset; I could hear everything more clearly than I ever had before.

"You guys got any cookies?" I asked. I didn't feel anything at all unusual.

For the next six weeks, until I got out, I was assigned to the headquarters of the Wing. The base adjutant asked me to write a report on the future of general aviation in southern California and how it might affect MCAS El Toro. Every day I would check out a vehicle and drive to Los Angeles to study documents at the Federal Aviation Authority in connection with my report.

On one day as I exited the base commander's offices, I saw a lieutenant colonel approaching. As we passed, I saluted. He didn't return the salute so I couldn't drop my arm.

"You. Marine. What the fuck is wrong with you?" he demanded, sounding a lot like a DI.

I was pretty dumbfounded. I had no idea what his problem was. I dropped my salute and said, "I don't know what you are getting at, sir."

"You are a fucking disgrace to your uniform. Have you bothered looking at yourself in a mirror lately?" he snarled, with his face right in mine.

"Sir, what seems to be the problem? I looked in the mirror this morning while I was shaving and it looked fine to me," I answered. I was starting to get pissed. I hadn't been treated like this since boot camp.

"Captain, your hair is a fucking mess. It looks like you haven't had a haircut in a month. Get your ass over to the PX and get a haircut right now. Do you hear me, Marine?" He was nearly shouting now.

"Sir, yes sir." That's all I could say. I turned and went back into my office to call the motor pool to cancel my vehicle. You either had to pick up your vehicle by 0900 or notify them if you were going to be late. For certain I was going to be late. The colonel followed me into the office.

I picked up the headset and dialed the number for the motor pool and began to cancel the vehicle. The colonel came over and pushed the disconnect button down when I was halfway through my call.

"Captain, I gave you a direct order. Go to the PX *now* and get a real Marine haircut," he demanded with a shrill tone.

For a minute I sat and simmered. At increasing volume I responded, "Colonel, when I was in boot camp my DI told me that if I was ever given an illegal or unreasonable order, I had an absolute right to demand that the person giving the order put it in writing. So sit your ass down and put that fucking order in writing." I was madder than a wet cat.

My boss, the base adjutant, a full bird colonel, walked into the room as if he hadn't heard the screaming going on.

"Gentlemen, what seems to be the problem here?" he asked calmly.

The lieutenant colonel pipes up, "I gave this Marine a direct order to get a haircut immediately and he came back in here to make a phone call, sir."

The full colonel looked at me. "Did he order you to get a haircut?"

"Yes sir, he did." That's all I could say.

"Well, son, I suggest you go get a haircut while I have a little chat with the colonel here."

I walked the two blocks to the PX and went into the barbershop; it was just opening. I sat in the first chair as I was the only person needing a haircut that early in the morning. Typically at the time, staff NCOs gave the haircuts to earn a little spare cash. One of them put on his white outfit and came over to look at me.

"What do you want?" he asked, and eventually got around to adding, "sir." As if to make sure I understood the relationship between company grade officers and staff NCOs.

"I want a haircut," I spat out.

"What for? You don't really need it." Now he was telling me something I already knew.

"Just trim it so I know it's been cut," I suggested. He did, and I was out of the chair in five minutes.

I got back to the base commander's office to hear an interesting conversation coming from the CG's office. Actually it sounded a lot more like an ass-chewing.

"Colonel, I don't know who the fuck you think you are but I see that young man in my office every day. If I thought for a moment that he really needed a haircut, I might mention it to him. I haven't because he hasn't needed one. We do not need you to tell us when our men need haircuts. Do you understand me, colonel?" Wow, that sounded just like the base commander speaking.

The voice continued, "I doubt you bothered looking at his decorations while you were so busy studying every hair on his head, but that 23-year-old captain is one of the most decorated pilots in the war, with about 800 missions trying to protect your sorry ass. He is exactly the sort of officer we are trying to keep in the Corps and assholes like you are driving them out. Get out of my goddamned office and don't let me ever see you chewing out on of my people again." Wow, that really did sound like the CG.

The lieutenant colonel shot out of the building like his pants were on fire. He didn't even inspect my haircut as he went by.

I thought to myself: I entered the pre-Vietnam Marine Corps in 1964; I made it through the Vietnam Marine Corps; welcome to the post-Vietnam Marine Corps.

If I had had any intention of staying in the Marines for a career, that light colonel made my mind up for me. I didn't need fifteen more years of chickenshit from him or people like him.

Chapter 16
THOUGHTS ON PEACE

Why do birds suddenly appear, ev'ry time you are near?
Just like me, they long to be close to you.
Why do stars fall down from the sky, ev'ry time you walk by?
Just like me, they long to be close to you.

On the day that you were born the angels got together.
And decided to create a dream come true.
So, they sprinkled moon dust in your hair of gold,
And starlight in your eyes of blue.
That is why all the girls in town follow you all around.
Just like me, they long to be close to you...

On the day that you were born the angels got together.
And decided to create a dream come true.
So, they sprinkled moon dust in your hair of gold,
And starlight in your eyes of blue.
That is why all the girls in town follow you all around.
Just like me, they long to be close to you...
Just like me, they long to be close to you...

(They Long To Be) Close To You
Songwriters: Hal David, Burt F. Bacharach, Chun Yat Lei
Copyright: Casa David LP, New Hidden Valley Music Co 1970

VARIOUS GROUPS OF PEOPLE offer their opinions on war. Many
times it's like blind people trying to describe an elephant by only
touching one part. Even for the people who went through a war, there
are so many different things happening that it's hard to get a valid
objective perspective. And there are those who want to offer
disinformation for one reason or another.

I got to see the war in Vietnam for about twenty months. I flew nine different aircraft. I flew every military mission you can fly in a plane except for dropping nuclear weapons. I worked very closely with the grunts. Naturally I didn't see every single aspect, but does anyone?

There has been a lot of simply bad information released about Vietnam. We did lose the war from a tactical and practical point of view. All the while China and North Vietnam were calling the US a paper tiger, they were perfectly accurate.

We had no strategy other than just to fight the war. No one ever even tried to define victory. Our enemies, however, knew exactly what victory meant to them. They wanted to control their own destiny. They wanted to run their own country and had been fighting for independence since 1930.

Ho Chi Minh and Vietnam were not enemies of the United States in 1945, they weren't enemies of the United States in 1964 in the Tonkin Gulf, and they aren't enemies of the United States today. But Ho Chi Minh would take support from any source in his battle for independence from the French. The USSR and China supported Ho Chi Minh, so in the eyes of the US State Department, he must be an enemy.

That fundamental mistake led to the deaths of 58,209 American boys, a cost of over $700 billion in 1970 dollars, the deaths of over two million Vietnamese, and in what we now call collateral damage, the deaths of almost 300,000 civilians in Cambodia.

The entire legal, and I use the term "legal" in the loosest way, the legal basis for the war from the US position was the Gulf of Tonkin Resolution passed in August of 1964. According to President Johnson, fully supported by the military, two US destroyers were sailing along peacefully in international waters, more than twelve miles from the North Vietnamese coast. With no warning and without cause, the nasty North Vietnamese Navy sent its PT boats out into international waters to attack the destroyers.

The Pentagon Papers would reveal that far from sailing along innocently through international waters, the destroyers were actually escorting South Vietnamese PT boats making commando raids on North Vietnamese bases. This was called OPLAN 34-A. In short, the North Vietnamese were defending their bases in their country from aggressive force from a foreign power.

I've heard from a number of sources and from a lot of guys who did fight in the war that we didn't really lose it from a military point of view, we were stabbed in the back by the news media and the government wouldn't allow us to win. If the military had been allowed to use all its power, we could have won the war.

The argument is nonsense on its face. If you have ever felt 1.5 million pounds of bombs go off fifteen miles away when 27 B-52s dropped 108 of the 500-pound bombs apiece in a massive Arc Light mission, you would realize that we did use every weapon we could, except for nuclear weapons. The NVA and VC were armed with AK-47s and light infantry weapons. We attacked them with the most powerful weapons used by the most powerful military in the world.

The US government *did* cut the military off at the knees. We lost a lot of American pilots and crew due to government stupidity. For example, whenever we were going to mount a major bombing attack, we notified the North Vietnamese a day in advance so they could get civilians out of the area. That's insane. Who would advise their enemy in advance of an attack?

The news media at least did their job fifty years ago. Not all of them. Not all of the time. But a few honest reporters did have the courage to tell the truth. It's an axiom, but an accurate axiom, that truth is the first casualty of war. The military loves to lie and loves to cover up their mistakes. But if the US taxpayers are going to fund a war, and they will in one form or another, they have a right to know what is going on. And if the military screws up, it should not be covered up.

When we were bombing Laos and Cambodia, the North Vietnamese knew, the Laotians knew, the Cambodians knew, the South Vietnamese knew, our pilots knew. The only people who didn't know were the American public in whose name the war was being fought.

We lost the war for two reasons.

(1) The North Vietnamese were fighting for independence. They held the moral high ground from the gitgo.

(2) They beat us from a military point of view. They were more willing to take casualties than we were.

The participation of American forces in the Vietnam War was a mistake based on a fundamental misunderstanding of the issues.

At some point, and it might have been as early as the Spanish American war or as late as WW II, the US economy began to turn into a warfare state; an economy whose primary purpose is to conduct aggressive warfare on other countries. Certainly it flowered between the end of WW II and the farewell address in 1961 of Dwight Eisenhower, our greatest general in history.

While Eisenhower supported the concept of a permanent arms industry, he also warned us:

> *"In the councils of government, we must guard against the acquisition of unwarranted influence, whether sought or unsought, by the military-industrial complex. The potential for the disastrous rise of misplaced power exists and will persist. We must never let the weight of this combination endanger our liberties or democratic processes. We should take nothing for granted. Only an alert and knowledgeable citizenry can compel the proper meshing of the huge industrial and military machinery of defense with our peaceful methods and goals, so that security and liberty may prosper together."*

The Vietnam war was not fought for the freedom of the Vietnamese people or the safety of the American people. We fought the war for the military-industrial complex. Those running the arms industry finally understood that all they had to do to prosper was to recycle excess profits right back into the reelection campaigns of Congress and the Senate.

Over the next forty years the military-industrial complex would become far more powerful and far more dangerous to the health, wealth, and safety of the American people.

During my war, I believed all the lies coming from the US government. It never occurred to me or to any of the guys I flew with that everything we had been told was fiction. We thought we were fighting to protect Americans and the right of the Vietnamese to self-determination. We believed North Vietnam was the aggressor. It never occurred to us to question just how it was the Viet Cong were somehow a threat to Hawaii and could invade at any time.

Times have changed, and today we have the internet. Soon after the military held an awards ceremony honoring Pat Tillman with a Silver Star for his bravery against the Taliban in 2004, the world discovered

262

that in fact he was shot and killed by his own men in a "friendly fire" event. And while Americans were still glowing in pride at the thought of Jessica Lynch becoming a one-woman fighting brigade, we learned that in fact she had been knocked unconscious in an ambush, never fired a round in defense and had not been a POW. The "raid" to recover her from a hospital bed was a waste of time and manpower. The administration at the hospital had called the US military to come get her.

You can believe that a daring Seal Team 6 raid took place to kill or capture Osama Bin Laden in May of 2011. You have a choice of five different and conflicting versions of events handed out by the government. No one in the Obama administration bothered mentioning that Osama Bin Laden actually died at Tora Bora in mid-December of 2001, his death reported in newspapers all over the world.

While the United States has been engaged in a series of almost constant tiny wars since independence in the 18th century, the pace moved into higher gear with the appointment of Allen Dulles as the first civilian director of the CIA in 1952. The CIA morphed from an intelligence agency into a secret, off-the-books government accountable to no one. Dulles sponsored coups in Iran in 1953, Guatemala in 1954, assassination plots by the dozen against Fidel Castro and finally the failed Bay of Pigs invasion in 1961. After that fiasco President Kennedy fired Dulles, but the die had been cast. The CIA became a shadow government with both an air force and military units of its own. And its own agenda.

In Vietnam the CIA set up the Phoenix Program. It was called an anti-terrorist program but in fact the US became a state sponsor of terrorism. Between 1965 and 1972, when it was spun down, the Phoenix Program resulted in the murders of over 26,000 people, mostly civilians. The South Vietnamese used the program to get even with their enemies. In no case did I ever see or use any intelligence derived from the torture of up to 81,000 civilians. The CIA ran its own parallel war at the same time as we ran an actual war. While we supported them, they did not support us.

This shadow government in the US gained more and more power as it sponsored more and more state terrorism as time went by. During the Vietnam War there was a vibrant and active anti-war program including many anti-war songs expressing the displeasure of Americans at fighting a war no one saw any reason to fight.

No one spoke up against the Phoenix Program because no one even knew it existed. There was debate against the war in general but no debate about the Phoenix Program. You can't debate what you don't know exists. I know that as a warrior fighting in Vietnam, we gained no advantage at all from the program. It simply was a shadow war of terrorism against the people of Vietnam.

By 1990 the US had progressed to simply making up wars. In July of 1990 the US ambassador to Iraq, April Glaspie, had a meeting with Saddam Hussein. Hussein was concerned with what he believed to be a plot against Iraq by Kuwait and Iran. Kuwait had been slant drilling into the Rumaila oil field, costing Iraq some $1 billion a year in revenue.

Glaspie told Hussein, "We have no opinion on the Arab-Arab conflicts, like your border disagreement with Kuwait. . ." Hussein took the statement as a green light on the part of the US for him to invade Kuwait. The US promptly created a coalition of 39 countries to fight Iraq and then invented an Iraqi army poised on the border with Saudi Arabia, ready to invade. It was all fiction. Hussein actually agreed to withdraw from Kuwait, but as would be the case with the second Gulf War, the US wanted war.

Desert Storm was an entirely one-sided war. The US lost 148 soldiers, Iraq had between 20,000 and 35,000 killed and an additional 75,000 wounded. Iraq lost 3,700 tanks, 2,140 artillery pieces, and had 240 aircraft destroyed and 19 ships sunk. It was an overwhelming victory on the part of the US.

Perhaps the best quotation to come from the war came from the Secretary of Defense, Dick Cheney, a year after the war ended. In 1992 he was quoted as saying, "The question in my mind is how many additional American casualties is Saddam worth? And the answer is: not that damned many."

The US continued its containment program against Iraq with no-fly zones and an embargo that resulted in the deaths of at least 500,000 children by the time of the *60 Minutes* interview in 1996. But Israel was determined to have more. Even though we knew Iraq had no program of weapons of mass destruction (WMD) and was no threat to anyone, the US used the 9/11 attack as a smokescreen to prepare for a second and more deadly war in Iraq. It would lead to the biggest military fiasco

264

in world history as Israel managed to bankrupt the US and the US managed to bankrupt the world.

By this time Dick Cheney was Vice President and had surrounded himself with an entourage of mostly dual national neocons howling for the blood of Saddam Hussein on behalf of Israel, which saw every surrounding country as a potential enemy that had to be destroyed. Armed with a bushel load of options on Halliburton stock, Cheney thought that young Americans dying for democracy in Iraq was a simply spiffing idea. Americans would do well to ask themselves, if a person holds an Israeli passport and a US passport, just whom do they owe their allegiance to? I think the answer is obvious.

The war began in 2003 and seems doomed to last forever. It was the first of a series of Forever Wars fought not for freedom and democracy but by and for the shadow state government. Neither peace nor victory was ever a goal.

Wars benefit the few and cost the many. Since 2001 the US has fought in Iraq, in a shadow war in Iran, and in further wars in Afghanistan, Syria, Somalia, Sudan, Libya and Pakistan. We have CIA armed forces in dozens of other countries. None of these wars benefits America or Americans.

Some, such as the second Iraq war, were simply made up out of whole cloth. While Hussein was a jerk, he was our jerk and no threat to anyone. We went in, destroyed his army and economy and started a religious war that seems without end. Between Iraq and Afghanistan, we have destroyed the financial structure of the world and the consequences will be more obvious with each passing day.

While peace is a desirable alternative any time at all, the absence of war is always a good idea. The world is closer to a nuclear WW III now than at any time in my lifespan. The US, Israel, Turkey and Saudi Arabia all believe they can run Syria better than the Syrians. If a free election were held tomorrow, Assad would remain as president. He's as big a thug as anyone else in a neighborhood of countries run by thugs. Democracy is one of those terms US politicians love to bandy about when running for election but become uncomfortable with when Gaza or Syria votes for opponents of Israel.

Russia has interests in Syria. Russia has always hankered for warm water ports, which is why Crimea is so important to them. The USSR and later Russia have maintained access to the port of Tartus in Syria since 1971. The US, Great Britain and France of course have no strategic or political interests in Syria. It's a testament to the power of the Zionist lobby that those countries have chosen to support and arm terrorists in order to over throw the government of Assad.

There is no civil war in Syria. There are bands of terrorists supported by a variety of outside interests fighting over the corpse of the country in the same way that the western powers destroyed Libya. If Russia were to allow a similar debacle in Syria the result would be the same.

Israel has always been a giant fan of disorder in the Middle East, believing that it gains power if all of its neighbors descend into chaos. But the law of unintended consequences says that breaking things always makes things worse. Some 43 per cent of all Syrians have been displaced by the conflict. Refugees from the fighting in Iraq and Syria are pouring into Europe and threaten to destroy the entire concept of a European Union.

Between the chaos in the Middle East and the continuing slow motion train wreck of the world's financial system, our world is undergoing the greatest change since the Peace of Westphalia signed in 1648 that ended the 30 Years' War. The Treaty of Westphalia essentially created the concept of a "nation state" with sovereignty over its own territory and domestic affairs.

With the advent of the internet, we no longer need big and powerful nations. The USSR became the first goliath to collapse but I believe it was not the last. Instant communication means that governments can no longer control the narrative. When Assad's Syrian government was accused of staging a chemical weapons attack on its own people, it took mere hours for that false flag operation to be exposed. When Israel mounts another massacre on the world's biggest open-air prison in Gaza, the world takes notice and everyone can decide for themselves who the victims are and who is the aggressor.

The banking system is collapsing. I don't mean to say it's going to collapse, it's collapsing as I write. Only few recognize it today but when the system grinds to a halt after the banks steal all the deposits of their customers, the world will get it. We may well have our first worldwide revolution as a result. We have already seen just how thrilled the populations were when the banks closed in Argentina, Greece, Italy and Spain. The popularity of Trump and Sanders is a monument to just how pissed Americans are at their government, with recent polls showing 81 per cent of those polled were unhappy with the Federal government. When the banks close, the 99 per cent are going to be some kind of pissed.

The United States began the process of living beyond its means by printing money after the Bretton Woods agreement in 1944. It sounded like a great idea to Europe as a way of funding their cradle-to-grave social programs. Now the world is awash in a sea of debt that can never be paid back.

All debts get settled. Either the borrower pays them or the lender pays them. The world had its last opportunity to settle the books in 2008 in the GFC, and failed. Now the debt level is so high it will take a great collapse to return to sanity.

The good news is that we have far more government than we can reasonably afford. All governments have been buying votes by making promises they could not possibly afford. It's not an issue of taxes; no government could afford to tax their voters enough to pay for the promises they have made. We will have less government in the future simply because we can't afford them; and, with any luck at all, fewer wars. The world has gone full cycle since the Peace of Westphalia.

Peace is never popular. No politicians ever won election on a plank of peace. It's ingrained in humans to want wars for a variety of reasons. But we will have peace because we can no longer afford constant war. The cost is too high.

71124252R00168

Made in the USA
Columbia, SC
21 May 2017